# AFRICA

PRENTICE HALL
Needham, Massachusetts
Upper Saddle River, New Jersey

# Program Authors

## Heidi Hayes Jacobs

Heidi Hayes Jacobs has served as an educational consultant to more than 500 schools across the nation. Dr. Jacobs is an adjunct professor in the Department of Curriculum on Teaching at Teachers College, Columbia. She completed her undergraduate studies at the University of Utah in her hometown of Salt Lake City. She received an M.A. from the University of Massachusetts, Amherst, and completed her doctoral work at Columbia University's Teachers College in 1981.

The backbone of Dr. Jacobs's experience comes from her years as a teacher of high school, middle school, and elementary school students. As an educational consultant, she works with K–12 schools and districts on curriculum reform and strategic planning.

## Brenda Randolph

Brenda Randolph is the former Director of the Outreach Resource Center at the African Studies Program at Howard University, Washington, D.C. She is the Founder and Director of Africa Access, a bibliographic service on Africa for schools. She received her B.A. in history with high honors from North Carolina Central University, Durham, and her M.A. in African studies with honors from Howard University. She completed further graduate studies at the University of Maryland, College Park, where she was awarded a Graduate Fellowship.

Brenda Randolph has published numerous articles in professional journals and bulletins. She currently serves as library media specialist in Montgomery County Public Schools, Maryland.

## Michal L. LeVasseur

Michal LeVasseur is an educational consultant in the field of geography. She is an adjunct professor of geography at the University of Alabama, Birmingham, and serves with the Alabama Geographic Alliance. Her undergraduate and graduate work are in the fields of anthropology (B.A.), geography (M.A.), and science education (Ph.D.).

Dr. LeVasseur's specialization has moved increasingly into the area of geography education. In 1996, she served as Director of the National Geographic Society's Summer Geography Workshop. As an educational consultant, she has worked with the National Geographic Society as well as with schools to develop programs and curriculum for geography.

## Special Program Consultant
**Yvonne S. Gentzler, Ph.D.**
School of Education
University of Idaho
Moscow, Idaho

## Content Consultant on Africa
**Barbara Brown**
Africa Studies Center
Boston University
Boston, Massachusetts

## Content Consultant on North Africa
**Laurence Michalak**
Center for Middle East Studies
University of California
Berkeley, California

PRENTICE HALL
Simon & Schuster Education Group
A VIACOM COMPANY

Upper Saddle River, New Jersey
Needham, Massachusetts

ISBN 0-13-433685-2

1 2 3 4 5 6 7 8 9 10   01 00 99 98 97

**On the Cover**

❶ West African batik fabric

❷ West African ebony statue of a hunter

❸ Cowrie shell belt

❹ African mask

❺ Brass model of a traditional African dwelling

❻ Wood carving of a giraffe

# Content Consultants for the World Explorer Program

**Ancient World**

**Maud Gleason**
Department of Classics
Stanford University
Stanford, California

**East Asia**

**Leslie Swartz**
Harvard University
East Asian Outreach
Program at the
Children's Museum
of Boston
Boston, Massachusetts

**Latin America**

**Daniel Mugan**
Center for Latin American
Studies
University of Florida
Gainesville, Florida

**Middle East**

**Elizabeth Barlow**
Center for Middle
Eastern and North
African Studies
University of Michigan
Ann Arbor, Michigan

**Religion**

**Michael Sells**
Department of Religion
Haverford College
Haverford, Pennsylvania

**Russia, Eastern Europe,
Central Asia**

**Janet Valliant**
Center for Russian,
Eastern European, and
Central Asian Studies
Harvard University
Cambridge,
Massachusetts

**South Asia**

**Robert Young**
South Asia Regional
Studies
University of
Pennsylvania
Philadelphia,
Pennsylvania

**Western Europe**

**Ruth Mitchell-Pitts**
Center for West European
Studies
University of North
Carolina
Chapel Hill, North
Carolina

# Teacher Advisory Board

**Jerome Balin**
Lincoln Junior High
School
Naperville, Illinois

**Linda Boaen**
Baird School
Fresno, California

**Nikki L. Born**
Harllee Middle School
Bradenton, Florida

**Carla Bridges**
Concord Middle School
Concord, North Carolina

**Bruce L. Campbell**
Walled Lake Middle
School
Walled Lake, Michigan

**Barbara Coats
Grabowski**
Russell Middle School
Omaha, Nebraska

**David Herman**
North Carroll Middle
School
Hampstead, Maryland

**Fred Hitz**
Wilson Middle School
Muncie, Indiana

**William B. Johnson**
La Mesa Junior High
School
Canyon Country,
California

**Kristi Karis**
West Ottawa Middle
School
Holland, Michigan

**Kristen Koch**
Discovery Middle School
Orlando, Florida

**Peggy McCarthy**
Beulah School
Beulah, Colorado

**Deborah J. Miller**
Whitney Young Middle
School
Detroit, Michigan

**Lawrence Peglow**
Greenway Middle School
Pittsburgh, Pennsylvania

**Lyn Shiver**
Northwestern Middle
School
Alpharetta, Georgia

# The World Explorer Team

*The editors, designers, marketer, market researcher, manager, and manufacturing buyer who made up
the World Explorer team are listed below.*

Jackie Bedoya, Bruce Bond, Ellen Brown, David Lippman, Catherine Martin-Hetmansky,
Nancy Rogier, Olena Serbyn, Carol Signorino, John Springer, Susan Swan

# TABLE OF CONTENTS

# OF SPECIAL INTEREST

**A hands-on, active approach to practicing and applying key social studies skills**

**Engaging, step-by-step activities for exploring important topics in Africa**

**High-interest selections written by African authors that highlight values**

**HEROES**

## MAPS

## CHARTS, GRAPHS, AND TABLES

# READ ACTIVELY

**H**ow can I get the most out of my social studies book?

How does my reading relate to my world? Answering questions like these means that you are an active reader, an involved reader. As an active reader, you are in charge of the reading situation!

The following strategies tell how to think and read as an active reader. You don't need to use all of these strategies all the time. Feel free to choose the ones that work best in each reading situation. You might use several at a time, or you might go back and forth among them. They can be used in any order.

## BEFORE YOU READ

### Give yourself a purpose

The sections in this book begin with a list called "Questions to Explore." These questions focus on key ideas presented in the section. They give you a purpose for reading. You can create your own purpose by asking questions like these: How does the topic relate to your life? How might you use what you learn at school or at home?

## Preview

To preview a reading selection, first read its title. Then look at the pictures and read the captions. Also read any headings in the selection. Then ask yourself: What is the reading selection about? What do the pictures and headings tell about the selection?

## Reach into your background

What do you already know about the topic of the selection? How can you use what you know to help you understand what you are going to read?

# WHILE YOU READ

## Ask questions

Suppose you are reading about the continent of South America. Some questions you might ask are: Where is South America? What countries are found there? Why are some of the countries large and others small? Asking questions like these can help you gather evidence and gain knowledge.

## Predict

As you read, make a prediction about what will happen and why. Or predict how one fact might affect another fact. Suppose you are reading about South America's climate. You might make a prediction about how the climate affects where people live. You can change your mind as you gain new information.

## Connect

Connect your reading to your own life. Are the people discussed in the selection like you or someone you know? What would you do in similar situations? Connect your reading to something you have already read. Suppose you have already read about the ancient Greeks. Now you are reading about the ancient Romans. How are they alike? How are they different?

## Visualize

What would places, people, and events look like in a movie or a picture? As you read about India, you could visualize the country's heavy rains. What do they look like? How do they sound? As you read about geography, you could visualize a volcanic eruption.

# AFTER YOU READ

## Respond

Talk about what you have read. What did you think? Share your ideas with your classmates.

## Assess yourself

What did you find out? Were your predictions on target? Did you find answers to your questions?

## Follow up

Show what you know. Use what you have learned to do a project. When you do projects, you continue to learn.

# AFRICA

**T**he name Africa probably came from the Latin word *aprica,* meaning "sunny." In much of Africa, the sun does shine brightly. It warms cocoa plantations, bakes the deserts, bounces off skyscrapers, and melts the snow on mountaintops. Each morning, the African sunrise awakens one eighth of the world's population in fifty countries. In the chapters that follow, you'll spend the day with some of them.

## Guiding Questions

The readings and activities in this book will help you discover answers to these Guiding Questions.

- What are the main physical features of Africa?

- What factors have shaped Africa's cultures?

- Why have many Africans been moving to cities in recent years?

- What connections do African nations have with the United States and the world?

- What factors influence the ways in which Africans make a living?

## Project Preview

You can also discover answers to the Guiding Questions by working on projects. Preview the following projects and choose one that you might like to do. For more details, see page 176.

**Africa on Stage** Create a play about growing up in an African country. Pick out characters, plan a plot, write the script, and present your play for an audience.

**Africa in Art** Prepare a mini-museum of traditional African mask-making. Research different kinds of masks, how they are made, and what they mean.

**Africa 2000** What will life in Africa be like in the twenty-first century? Hold a conference with speakers, ethnic refreshments, and press coverage.

Left, South African children at school. Above left, a desert-dwelling Tuareg mother and child. Right, twins at a ceremony in Ghana.

**EXPLORER's JOURNAL**

A journal can be your personal book of discovery. As you explore Africa, you can use your journal to keep track of the things you learn and do. You can also record thoughts about your journey. For your first entry, write your thoughts on where in Africa you would like to go and what you would want to see there.

*Learning about Africa means being an explorer and a geographer. No explorer would start out without first checking some facts. Begin by exploring the maps of Africa on the following pages.*

## Relative Location

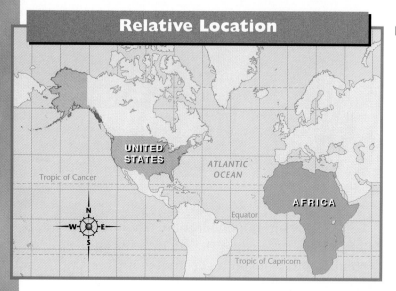

## LOCATION

**1. Explore Africa's Location** One of the first questions a geographer asks about a place is "Where is it?" Use the map to describe Africa's location relative to the United States. What ocean lies between Africa and the United States? Note that the Equator extends through Africa. What role might the Equator play in the climates of nearby countries? How do you think climates of the United States might differ from the climates of Africa?

## REGIONS

**2. Explore Africa's Size** How big is Africa compared to the United States? On a separate sheet of paper, trace the map of the United States and cut it out. How many times can you fit it inside the map of Africa?

## Relative Size

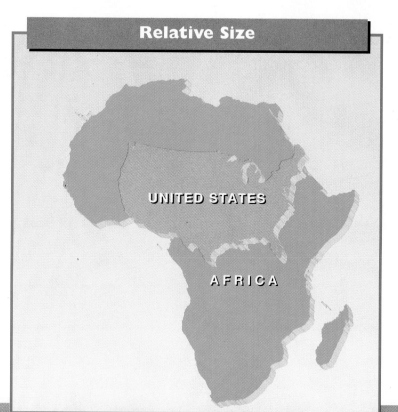

**3. Find Africa's Lakes** There are several large lakes in Africa. Name four of them. What countries do they border? In what part of the continent do you find the most lakes?

**4. Predict How Location Affects Economic Wealth** Fifteen African nations are landlocked. That is, they do not border any ocean. Find them on the map. Landlocked nations are often poor. How do you think a landlocked location might affect a nation's economy?

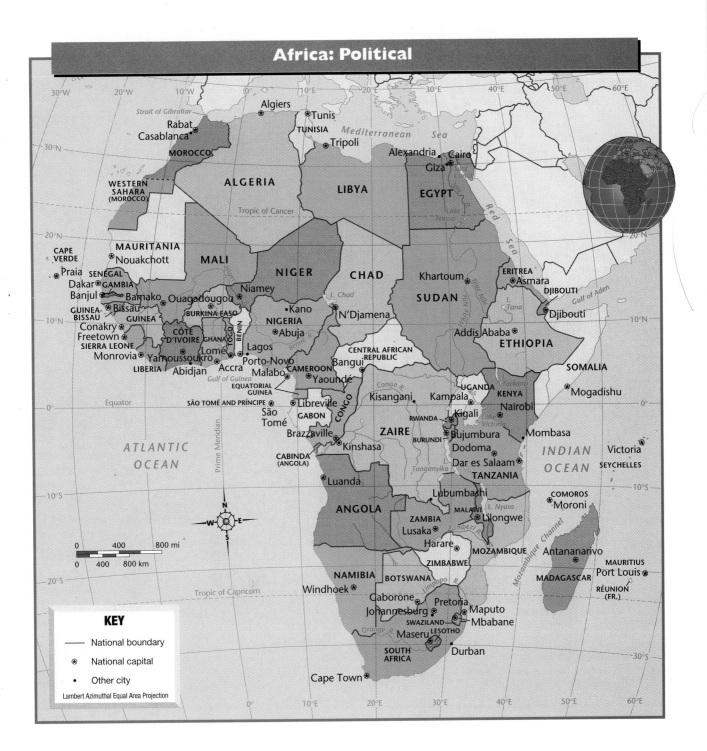

## Africa: Political

**KEY**

— National boundary

⊛ National capital

• Other city

Lambert Azimuthal Equal Area Projection

## 5. Investigate Africa's Physical Features

Parts of Africa's coasts have very narrow strips of flat plains. Cliffs rise steeply from these plains. The interior is high and somewhat flat, forming a huge plateau. Find Southern Africa on the map below. It extends south of 10°S. The cliffs arise where the dark green areas meet the light green areas. Trace these cliffs with your finger. Note that in some places they extend nearly along the coast. Is Africa's plateau higher in the western part of the continent or the southeastern part?

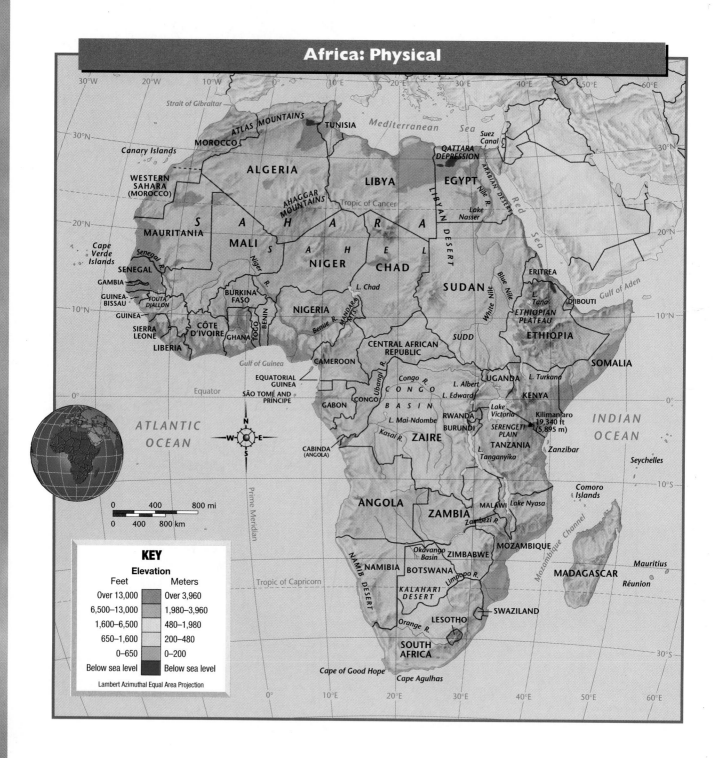

**Africa: Physical**

**KEY**

**Elevation**

| Feet | Meters |
|---|---|
| Over 13,000 | Over 3,960 |
| 6,500–13,000 | 1,980–3,960 |
| 1,600–6,500 | 480–1,980 |
| 650–1,600 | 200–480 |
| 0–650 | 0–200 |
| Below sea level | Below sea level |

Lambert Azimuthal Equal Area Projection

## REGIONS

**6. Find Geo Cleo** Geo Cleo has gone off on one of her flying trips. This time she's gone to Africa, but she hasn't told anyone exactly where in Africa she's traveling. Read the messages Geo Cleo radioed from her plane. Then use the map below and the maps on the two previous pages to locate the city described in each message.

**A.** *I'm in a region of tall grasses and few trees, or a savanna. I've landed in a city in Ethiopia near 10°N and 40°E.*

**B.** *Not too many places in Africa have Mediterranean vegetation. And I'm not even anywhere near the Mediterranean Sea! I am flying over a city on a very narrow coastal plain. The cliffs here are really steep.*

**C.** *Today, I flew above tropical rain forests growing right along the Equator. Going north, I saw these magnificent forests change into open grasslands, or savanna. I've just landed in a city in the savanna region north of where the Benue River meets the Niger River.*

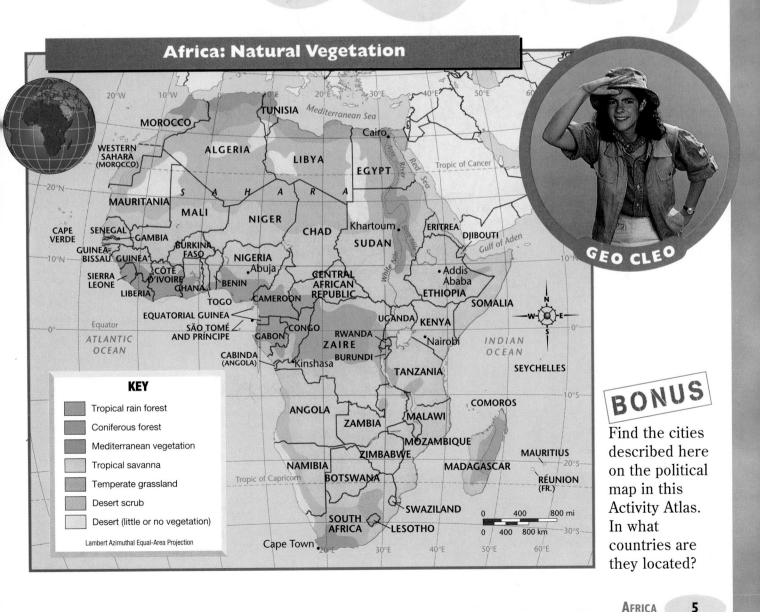

### Africa: Natural Vegetation

**GEO CLEO**

**KEY**

- Tropical rain forest
- Coniferous forest
- Mediterranean vegetation
- Tropical savanna
- Temperate grassland
- Desert scrub
- Desert (little or no vegetation)

Lambert Azimuthal Equal-Area Projection

**BONUS**

Find the cities described here on the political map in this Activity Atlas. In what countries are they located?

## INTERACTION

### 7. Estimate the Impact of Desertification

Desertification means a loss of vegetation. In African lands bordering the Sahara, desertification is turning grasslands into deserts. A long period of little or no rainfall may cause desertification. People may cause it, too, by allowing livestock to overgraze the savanna and by cutting trees for firewood. The map on this page shows the spread of desertification in Africa from 1970 to the present. Which countries were affected most by the desertification? How would the loss of all vegetation, including farm crops, affect the people in these countries?

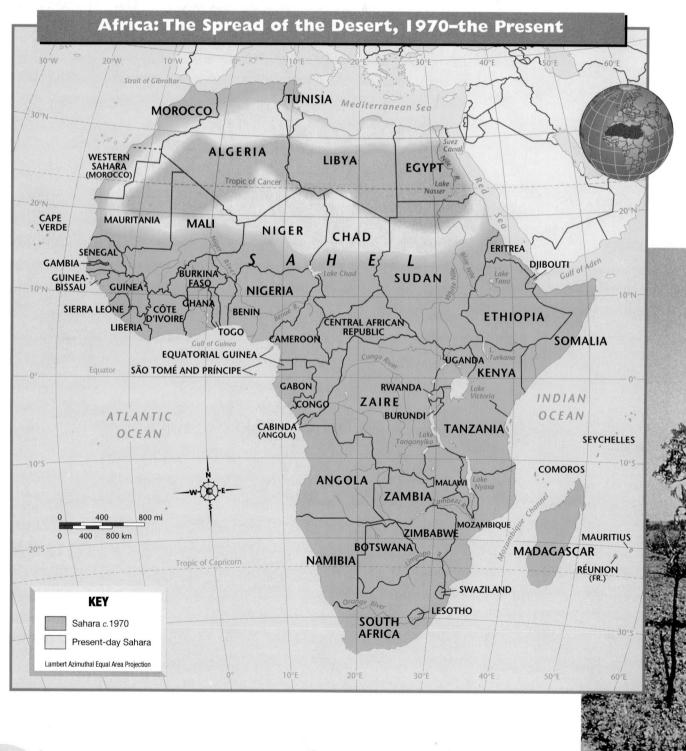

**Africa: The Spread of the Desert, 1970–the Present**

KEY

Sahara c. 1970

Present-day Sahara

Lambert Azimuthal Equal Area Projection

**8. Analyze Rainfall in the Sahel** The Sahel is a region in Africa just south of the Sahara. The Sahel has been especially affected by desertification. The graph below shows rainfall in Niger, a country partly in the Sahel. What general trend do you see in Niger's rainfall?

In which year did the heaviest rainfall occur? Which year has had the least rainfall? What effect do you think the amount of rainfall has had on desertification?

▼ Very little rain falls in the Sahel.

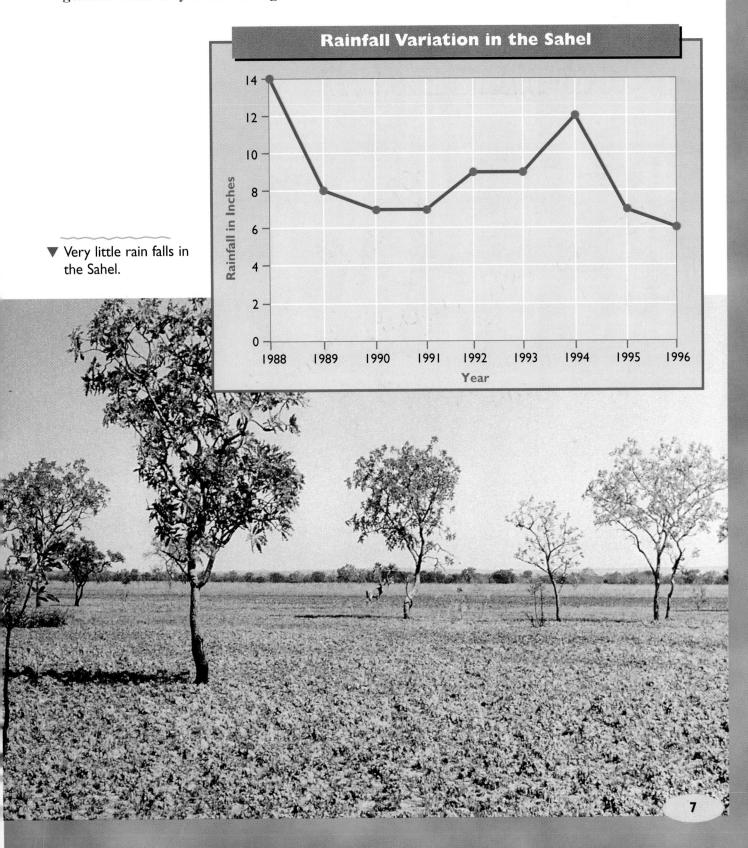

**Rainfall Variation in the Sahel**

Rainfall in Inches

Year

# CHAPTER 1

## AFRICA

# Physical Geography

### SECTION 1
**Land and Water**

### SECTION 2
**Climate and Vegetation**

### SECTION 3
**Natural Resources**

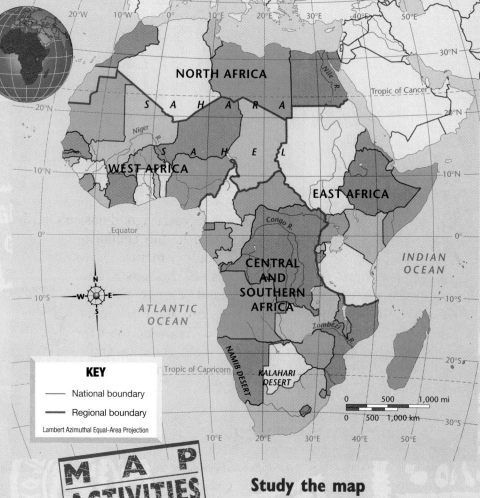

**KEY**

— National boundary

— Regional boundary

Lambert Azimuthal Equal-Area Projection

# MAP ACTIVITIES

*This map shows four regions of Africa. Each region contains many different landforms and climates. Start exploring the geography of Africa by doing the following activities:*

### Study the map
What region of Africa is the largest? Which is the smallest? Through what regions do the major rivers flow?

### Consider the geography
Notice that some African nations are much larger than others. As you read this chapter, think about how landforms and climate might have affected the political boundaries of Africa.

# Land and Water

**Reach Into Your Background**

Think about the state in which you live. What different landforms are in your state? Are there any mountains or valleys? How do these landforms affect your daily life?

**Questions to Explore**

1. Where is Africa located?
2. What are Africa's most important landforms?

**Key Terms**

plateau
elevation
escarpment
rift

cataract
silt
fertile
tributary

**Key Places**

Sahara
Great Rift Valley
Nile River
Congo River
Niger River
Zambezi River

▼ Scientists found the bones of this type of dinosaur on more than one continent. This clue made them suspect the continents were once connected.

Scientists believe that over 200 million years ago, dinosaurs easily walked from the continent of Africa to the continent of South America. That's because Africa and South America were connected. Find Africa on the world map in the atlas at the back of this book. As you can see, it would be pretty hard to walk from Africa to South America today. How did Africa and South America become separated? About 190 million years ago, forces within the Earth caused South America and Africa to move apart, forming the southern part of the Atlantic Ocean.

## The Four Regions of Africa

Africa can be divided into four regions: (1) North, (2) West, (3) East, and (4) Central and Southern. Each of these regions contains many different climates and landforms.

North Africa is marked by rocky mountains and seemingly endless stretches of the world's largest desert, the Sahara. Find the Sahara, which is almost the size of the United States, on the physical map in the Activity Atlas. What countries include part of the Sahara?

West Africa, the continent's most populated region, consists mostly of grasslands. The soil in the grasslands is good for farming. Find West Africa on the map at the beginning of the chapter. What geographic features border this region to the north and south?

East Africa contains many mountains, and **plateaus,** large raised areas of mostly level land. The east also has areas of grasslands and hills. Find East Africa on the map at the beginning of this chapter. What East African countries have sea coasts?

Much of Central and Southern Africa is flat or rolling grassland. The region also contains thick rain forests, mountains, and swamps. The Namib (NAHM eeb) Desert of the country of Namibia and the Kalahari (kal uh HAHR ee) Desert of Botswana are in this region.

## Africa's Major Landforms

Africa can be described as an upside-down pie. If you were to slice Africa in half from east to west, you would see that much of the continent is a plateau that drops off sharply near the sea.

**The Plateau Continent**   Africa is often called the "plateau continent." That is because the elevation of much of the land area is high. **Elevation** is the height of land above sea level.

▼ In the Atlas Mountains of Morocco (below), some people adapt to steep slopes by building houses along the sides of the mountains. Some people living in the lush rain forests of Zaire (inset, upper left) take advantage of the tropical vegetation by gathering honey from bees' nests in the trees.

Most of Africa is plateaus and mountains. Africa's few plains lie mostly along its coasts, like this one at Cape Coast, Ghana. In fact, except for two basins in the Sahara, all of Africa's lowland areas lie within 500 miles (805 km) of the coast. **Critical Thinking** Based on this photograph, how do you think people living on Africa's coastal plains might make a living?

Each of Africa's four regions has mountains. The highest are in East Africa. Mount Kilimanjaro is Africa's tallest mountain. It rises to a height of 19,341 feet (5,895 m).

**Coastal Plains Edge the Continent** Along much of Africa's coast is a strip of coastal plain. This strip of land is dry and sandy at some points. It is marshy and moist at other places. Look at the political map in the Activity Atlas. Find the city of Accra, in the West African country of Ghana (GAHN uh). Here, the coastal strip is only 16 miles (25 km) wide. It ends at a long **escarpment,** or steep cliff, that is about as high as a 100-story skyscraper.

**The Great Rift Valley** Mount Kilimanjaro is located on the edge of the Great Rift Valley in East Africa. The Great Rift Valley was formed millions of years ago, when the continents pulled apart. A **rift** is a deep trench. The rift that cuts through East Africa is 4,000 miles (6,400 km) long. Most of Africa's major lakes are located in or near the Great Rift Valley.

**READ ACTIVELY**

**Connect** What part of the United States contains a deep trench?

## Africa's Rivers

Four large rivers carry water from the mountains of Africa's plateaus to the sea. They are the Nile, the Congo, the Zambezi, and the Niger (NI jur). The rivers are useful for traveling. But they are broken in places by **cataracts,** or rock-filled rapids. Cataracts make it impossible for ships to sail from Africa's interior to the sea.

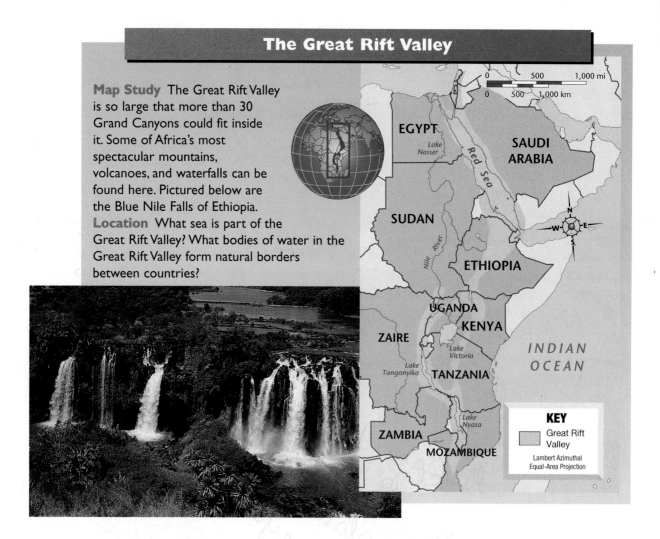

## The Great Rift Valley

**Map Study** The Great Rift Valley is so large that more than 30 Grand Canyons could fit inside it. Some of Africa's most spectacular mountains, volcanoes, and waterfalls can be found here. Pictured below are the Blue Nile Falls of Ethiopia.
**Location** What sea is part of the Great Rift Valley? What bodies of water in the Great Rift Valley form natural borders between countries?

**KEY**

Great Rift Valley

Lambert Azimuthal Equal-Area Projection

**The Nile River** The Nile is the longest river in the world. Its length, more than 4,000 miles (6,400 km), is almost twice the width of the United States. The sources of the Nile are the White Nile in the country of Sudan and the Blue Nile in the highlands of Ethiopia. From these two sources, the river flows north and spills into the Mediterranean Sea.

People have farmed the land surrounding the Nile for thousands of years. At one time, the Nile flooded its banks regularly. Farmers planted their crops to match the flood cycle of the river. The floods provided water for the crops and left behind a layer of **silt,** which is the tiny bits of rock and dirt that build up on the bottoms of rivers and lakes. Silt helps make soil **fertile,** or able to grow a lot of plants.

About 30 years ago, Egypt's government built the Aswan High Dam to control the flooding of the Nile. As the water backed up behind the dam, it created Lake Nasser. Lake waters are channeled to water crops that grow in the desert. Water rushing through the dam makes electricity.

**The Congo River** The Congo River flows through the rain forest of the country of Zaire (zy IHR) in Central Africa. Look at the map at the beginning of the chapter. What ocean does the Congo River flow into? At 2,900 miles (4,667 km), the Congo is Africa's second-longest

### LINKS ACROSS THE WORLD

**The Mississippi River** Like the Nile in Africa, the Mississippi River in North America occasionally overflows its banks. It also leaves behind silt, which fertilizes the farmland along the river's banks.

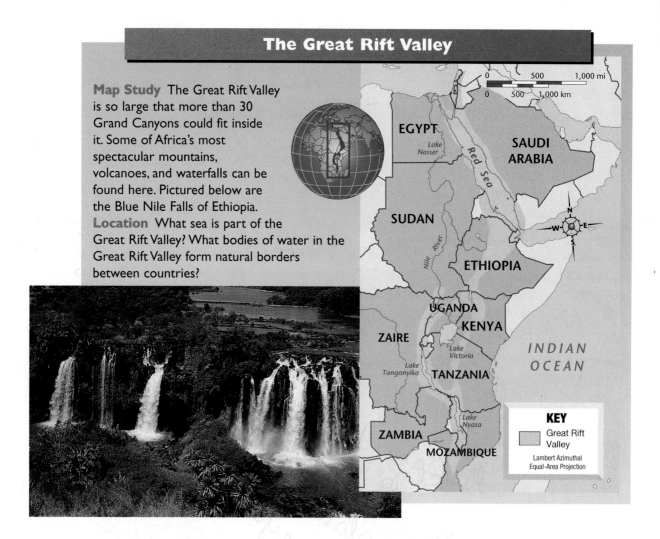

river. It is fed by hundreds of **tributaries,** or small rivers and streams that flow into the larger river. People in this region grow grains and cassava to make into porridge. Cassava is a starchy plant a little like a potato. They also catch fish in the Congo with basket traps.

**The Niger River**   Africa's third-longest river, the Niger, begins its journey in the West African country of Guinea (GIN ee). The river flows north and then bends south for 2,600 miles (4,180 km). The Niger provides water for farms in the river valley. People make a living catching fish in the river.

**The Zambezi River**   The fourth-longest of Africa's rivers, the Zambezi, is in southern Africa. It runs through or forms the borders of six countries: Angola, Zambia, Namibia, Botswana, Zimbabwe (zim BAHB way), and Mozambique (moh zam BEEK). The Zambezi is 2,200 miles (3,541 km) long. Boats can travel the river's upper section.

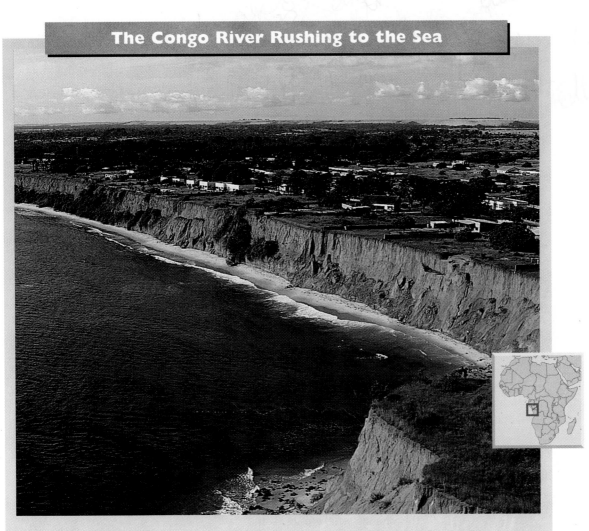

**The Congo River Rushing to the Sea**

The Congo River flows very fast—every second, the equivalent of more than 100 swimming pools full of water flows past its mouth.

The African name for Victoria Falls means "The Smoke That Thunders." Victoria Falls lies on the Zambezi River, which crosses 2,200 miles (3,540 km) and six countries. It is broken by many waterfalls. **Critical Thinking** Based on this photo, why do you think the Zambezi River is not used as a major trade route?

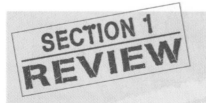

People have used the Zambezi's strong current to make electricity. About halfway to its outlet in the Indian Ocean, the Zambezi plunges into a canyon, creating Victoria Falls. People can sometimes see the mist and spray of the falls from up to 40 miles (65 km) away.

## SECTION 1 REVIEW

1. **Define** (a) plateau, (b) elevation, (c) escarpment, (d) rift, (e) cataract, (f) silt, (g) fertile, (h) tributary.

2. **Identify** (a) Sahara, (b) Great Rift Valley, (c) Nile River, (d) Congo River, (e) Niger River, (f) Zambezi River.

3. Why is Africa called the "plateau continent"?

4. (a) How do people use the rivers of Africa? (b) What makes them difficult to use?

**Critical Thinking**

5. **Drawing Conclusions** Most of the people in North Africa live north of the Sahara near the Mediterranean Sea. If the Sahara were a grassland with rivers and forests, would this change where people in North African countries live? Why?

**Activity**

6. **Writing to Learn** List several landforms in Africa you would like to visit. Explain why you would like to go there and what you would do on your trip.

# Climate and Vegetation

## Reach Into Your Background

Think about the climate where you live. What kind of weather do you have in the summer? What kind of weather do you have in the winter? What are the months when you have summer? What are the months when you have winter?

## Questions to Explore

1. What types of climates and vegetation are found in Africa?
2. How do climate and vegetation affect how Africans make a living?

## Key Terms

irrigate
oasis
savanna
nomad

## Key Places

Sahel
Namib Desert
Kalahari Desert

A trip to Africa sounds like a great adventure. But packing for the trip might prove harder than you think. What would you pack for a two-week journey to Africa? As you read about Africa's climates and vegetation, see if you would add any items to your list.

## What Influences Climate?

Look at the climate map on the following page. Find the Tropic of Cancer and the Tropic of Capricorn. As you can see, much of Africa lies between these two lines of latitude. This means that most of Africa is in a tropical climate region. Notice that the Equator runs through this midsection of the continent. These regions are usually hot.

Many parts of Africa are indeed hot. But much of Africa is not. That is because location near the Equator is not the only influence on climate. The climate of a place may depend on how close it is to large bodies of water. Major landforms also affect climate. So does the elevation of a place.

▼ If you visit Botswana during the rainy season, be prepared to get wet. Floods like this one, on the Okavango River Delta, are common.

# Africa: Climate Regions

**KEY**

- Tropical wet
- Tropical wet and dry
- Semiarid
- Arid
- Mediterranean
- Humid subtropical
- Marine west coast
- Highlands

Lambert Azimuthal Equal-Area Projection

**Map Study** In some of Africa's deserts, children as old as six or seven are amazed when it rains. It rains so seldom in these regions that children may never have seen rain before. In tropical wet regions, it rains almost all the time. But most other regions of Africa have two seasons—rainy and dry. **Location** What climate is most common in Africa along the Equator? What climate is most common near the tropics of Cancer and Capricorn?

**Distance From the Equator** Africa's location near the Equator means that most of the continent is warm. A place's location in relation to the Equator influences the seasons. North of the Equator, winter and summer occur at the same time as they do in the United States. South of the Equator, the seasons are reversed. For example, July in South Africa is the middle of winter.

**Higher, Cooler: The Role of Elevation** Elevation, or height above sea level, also affects climate. The higher the elevation, the cooler a place tends to be. Mount Kilimanjaro, Africa's highest peak, is located very close to the Equator. Yet ice and snow blanket the peak of Kilimanjaro year round.

The countries of Ethiopia and Somalia provide another example. They are about the same distance from the Equator, yet they have different climates. Ethiopia is on a very high plateau. Much of Ethiopia has mild temperatures and much rain. Farmers there grow a wide range of crops—including bananas, coffee, dates, and oats. Because Ethiopia usually gets plenty of rain, many farmers there do not **irrigate,** or artificially water, their crops.

Somalia is at a much lower elevation than Ethiopia. Its climate is hot and dry. Farming is possible only in or near an oasis, where crops can be irrigated. An **oasis** is a place where springs and fresh underground water make it possible to support life in a region that gets little rain.

**Unpredictable Rainfall** Rainfall varies greatly from one region of Africa to another. Along parts of the west coast, winds carry moisture from the warm ocean over the land. Rainfall averages more than 100 inches (250 cm) per year. Compare that to your own height in inches. Forty inches (100 cm) of rain might fall during June alone. But in parts of the Sahara in the north and Namib Desert in the south, it may not rain at all for several years in a row.

Farmers who live in dry regions can never be sure whether there will be enough rain for their crops. Some farmers

**READ ACTIVELY**

**Predict** How do you think elevation affects the climate regions in Africa?

▼ What clue in this picture shows that it is Mount Kilimanjaro's high elevation that keeps its snow from melting?

**Kimberley, South Africa**

**Makanza, Zaire**

**Curved lines** show temperatures in Fahrenheit degrees. **Bars** show rainfall in inches.

**Chart Study** The vegetation of Kimberley, South Africa, is mostly desert scrub. Makanza, Zaire, lies in a tropical rain forest. **Critical Thinking** What differences do the climate charts show that would explain why Kimberley is in a hot, dry region while Makanza is in a tropical rain forest?

choose to plant a variety of crops, each needing different amounts of rainfall. These farmers hope they will have at least one successful crop. The charts on this page show rainfall in two cities that have very different climates. Which city do you think would have the best climate for farming?

# Vegetation

Look at the vegetation map in the Activity Atlas. Near the Equator are rain forests. Farther from the Equator lies a region of tall grasses, called the **savanna.**

**Tropical Rain Forests** Tropical rain forests are regions where it rains nearly all the time. The moisture supports a rich environment of trees, plants, and animals. Find the tropical rain forest region on the vegetation map. The tropical rain forest region used to be much larger. It covered much of Central Africa. Through the years, people cut trees from the forest to use the wood or to clear land for farming. Rain forest lands, however, do not make good farmland. Once the trees are cut down, heavy rains wash away the nutrients that make soil fertile.

**Visualize** Visualize the rain forest in the country of Cameroon. What might it look like and sound like?

**Tropical Savannas** Much of Africa north and south of the rain forest is tropical savanna. Tall grasses, thorny bushes, and scattered trees grow in the savanna region. Some grasses grow as high as a person's head.

The climate of the tropical savanna is tropical wet and dry. This means that the savanna has two seasons: dry and wet. During the dry season, farming is impossible. Trees lose their leaves and rivers run dry. People use the season to trade, build houses, and visit friends. In the wet season, the land turns green, and farmers plant their crops.

▲ The acacia tree produces a substance that is used in candy, glue, and ink. It grows in tropical savanna regions.

**Deserts in Africa** Beyond the savanna lie the deserts. The immense Sahara extends across most of North Africa. This desert covers almost as much land as the entire United States.

The southern edge of the Sahara meets the savanna in a region called the Sahel (SAH hil), which is the Arab word for shore or border. The Sahel is very hot and dry. It receives only 4 to 8 inches (10 to 20 cm) of rain per year. Small shrubs, grass, and some trees grow there.

The Namib and Kalahari deserts extend over much of Namibia and Botswana in Southern Africa. These deserts, like the Sahara, feature landscapes of bare rock, towering rock formations, sand dunes, and a few areas of small bushes and grass.

A journalist traveling in the Namib Desert described the region:

> "There was sand everywhere, an impossible amount of sand covering thousands of square miles and heaping into dunes as high as 1,200 feet. The ultimate sandpile. It was uniformly fine and found its way into everything. I blinked sand from my eyes, blew it from my nose, spit it from my mouth and throat."

Nomads make their living in the Sahara. **Nomads** are people who move around to various places to make a living. Some nomads are traders, and others hunt game and gather food. Most nomads are herders, however. They travel to places where they know they can get water and food for their herds of goats, camels, or sheep.

Some nomadic herders live mainly in the mountainous areas. In spring, they leave their winter grazing grounds in the foothills and head

▶ These Berber nomads are traveling across the country of Morocco, through the Sahara.

up into the mountains. Other nomads live mainly in the flat desert areas. During the dry season, they set up tents near oases. When the rainy season comes, they move their goats and camels to better pastures.

## Building Good Health

The climate people live in can affect their health. Throughout Africa there are regions that present health risks to livestock and humans. In rain forest regions, the moist environment is home to many disease-carrying insects. Even in the drier grasslands, disease and illness take their toll.

Nearly one fifth of Africa is home to the tsetse (TSET see) fly, a pest that makes raising cattle almost impossible. The bite of the fly kills cattle and brings a disease called sleeping sickness to humans. African researchers, together with cattle herders, have worked to find ways to control the spread of the tsetse fly. Cattle herders in Kenya are setting traps for flies. Herders in the country of Uganda use netting sewn into a tent that contains poison to catch flies.

**READ ACTIVELY**

**Connect** Do you know of any diseases that are spread by insects in the United States? If so, how do people keep the disease from spreading?

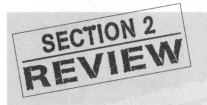

## SECTION 2 REVIEW

1. **Define** (a) irrigate, (b) oasis, (c) savanna, (d) nomad.

2. **Identify** (a) Sahel, (b) Namib Desert, (c) Kalahari Desert.

3. What three factors affect the climate of Africa?

4. What most affects farming in Africa, rainfall or temperature? Explain.

**Critical Thinking**

5. **Recognizing Cause and Effect** If Mount Kilimanjaro were located in Canada instead of Kenya, would the climate at its peak be much different? Why or why not?

**Activity**

6. **Writing to Learn** Now that you know more about the climate and vegetation in Africa, make your new packing list for a two-week trip to Africa. Explain why you are bringing each item. (Hint: you may want to decide exactly which regions of Africa you will be visiting before you make the list.)

# Natural Resources

**BEFORE YOU READ**

**Reach Into Your Background**

Have you ever heard the saying, "Don't put all your eggs in one basket?" What do you think this saying means?

**Questions to Explore**

1. What are Africa's major natural resources?
2. How are Africans developing these resources?

**Key Terms**

subsistence farming
cash crop
economy
diversify

"**Tete Quarshie:** I have a humble request to make of you, my noble friend. I hope you will not turn deaf ears to my cries. Here, in this load, I bear the seeds of a wonderful tree which, if cultivated in this land, will bless its sons everlastingly with wealth, and people far and near with health. These are the seeds of the cacao tree which I have brought with me from across the sea. . . . Would you, therefore, be kind enough to grant me a mere acre of land in this neighborhood to try my luck, and yours, and that of this country as a whole?"

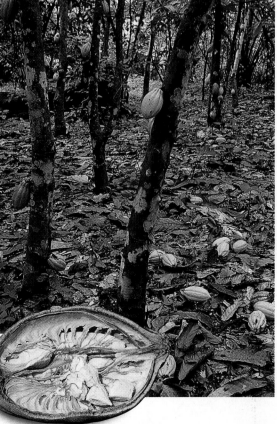

▼ To make milk chocolate from cacao beans, shown below, chocolate makers grind the beans, and then mix them with lots of milk and sugar.

**T**hese words come from a short play, *Cocoa Comes to Mampong.* The play tells the story of cocoa in the West African country of Ghana. Cacao trees, from which cocoa and chocolate are made, used to grow only in Central and South America. As people in the Americas, Europe, and Africa began to trade with one another, they found that cacao trees could be grown in West Africa. In the play, the people granted the land to Tete Quarshie, who raised the first successful crop of cacao in Ghana.

**LINKS**

**ACROSS THE WORLD**

**Farming Equipment**
Corn and wheat farmers in the United States often use heavy machines to work the land. Most African farmers could not use such machines. They would destroy the thin layer of topsoil on most African farms.

# Agricultural Resources

Some Africans are farmers living in areas with fertile soil and much rain. But most Africans have land that is hard or impossible to farm because of poor soil or too little rain.

**Farming to Live**   The map on the next page shows how much of Africa's land is used for subsistence farming. Subsistence farmers raise crops to support their families. They sell or trade a few crops for other items they need. In northern African countries such as Morocco, farmers raise barley and wheat. They also irrigate fields to grow fruits and vegetables. Farms at Saharan oases in Egypt produce dates and small crops of barley and wheat.

In countries that contain dry tropical savanna, such as Burkina Faso (bur KEE nuh FAH soh) and Niger, subsistence farmers grow grains. In regions with more rainfall, farmers also grow vegetables, fruits, and

## Families Farming for a Living

Most subsistence farmers in Africa are women. Often, however, the whole family helps out. A family from Chad plows land in preparation for planting (below left). Families usually harvest crops by hand in Ethiopia (below right) and Ghana (right). **Critical Thinking** How do you think farming to provide food for your family is different from farming cash crops?

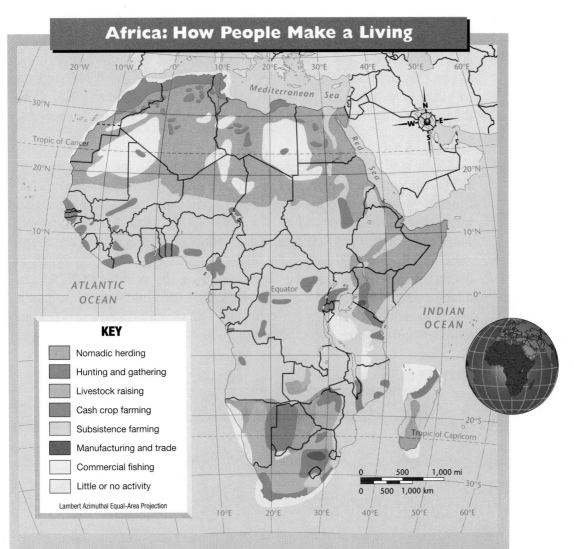

## Africa: How People Make a Living

**KEY**

- Nomadic herding
- Hunting and gathering
- Livestock raising
- Cash crop farming
- Subsistence farming
- Manufacturing and trade
- Commercial fishing
- Little or no activity

Lambert Azimuthal Equal-Area Projection

**Map Study** Most of Africa's workers make a living by farming or herding. **Regions** In what regions of Africa do workers make a living in other ways? How do workers in these areas make a living? **Critical Thinking** Why do you think that some parts of Africa have little or no economic activity?

roots such as yams and cassava. Tapioca, which is used in the United States to make pudding, is made from cassava. In West Africa, corn and rice are important crops. People in many of Africa's cultures fish or raise goats or poultry.

**Crops for Sale** In all regions of Africa, farmers raise crops to sell. These are called **cash crops.** Farmers in Côte d'Ivoire (koht deev WAR), Ghana, and Cameroon grow cash crops of coffee and cacao. Farmers in Kenya, Tanzania, Malawi, Zimbabwe, and Mozambique grow tea as a cash crop.

In recent years, more and more farmers have planted cash crops. As more land is used for cash crops, less land is planted with crops to feed families. In some regions, this practice has led to food shortages when cash crops have failed.

**READ ACTIVELY**

**Ask Questions** What else would you like to know about farming in Africa?

**Harvesting Trees** Hardwood trees grow in all four regions of Africa. People can earn money by cutting down trees and selling them. Thousands of acres of these trees have been cut and the wood shipped to other countries. A number of countries, such as Kenya and Côte d'Ivoire, are planting trees by the thousands in order to save the forests.

# Mineral Resources

Farming is the major part of Africa's economy. An **economy** is all the things people do to make a living in a particular place. Mining is also important to Africa's economy.

Parts of Africa are rich in mineral resources. In North Africa, nations such as Libya and Algeria have large amounts of petroleum, which is used to make oil and gasoline. In West Africa, the country of Nigeria is a major oil producer. Ghana was once called the Gold Coast because it was a leading exporter of African gold. Other mineral resources from Africa include copper, silver, uranium, titanium, and diamonds.

**READ ACTIVELY**

**Predict** How do you think most African countries use their mineral resources?

**Africa: Mineral and Energy Resources**

KEY

- Bauxite
- Coal
- Cobalt
- Copper
- Diamonds
- Gold
- Iron
- Petroleum
- Hydroelectric power

Lambert Azimuthal Equal-Area Projection

**Map Study** Most of Africa's people work in agriculture, yet most of Africa's exports are produced by miners. **Regions** Southern Africa is famous for its diamond industry. What other regions of Africa produce diamonds? **Interaction** Which resource shown on this map can be used without being used up?

# Balancing Crops, Minerals, and Industry

Most of Africa's workers are farmers. That makes the economy sensitive to rainfall and to the price of crops. African countries are now trying to diversify their economies. To **diversify** means to add variety. These countries are working to produce a variety of crops, raw materials, and manufactured goods. A country with a diverse economy will not be hurt as much if a major cash crop fails or if world prices for one of its major mineral exports suddenly drops.

Mining requires many workers and costly equipment. Throughout much of Africa, foreign companies mine African resources and take the profits. This system does little to help African economies. In addition, Africa has few factories to make products from its own raw materials. Therefore, many African countries want to diversify their economies to include manufacturing.

▼ All over Africa, people are moving to cities to apply for jobs in factories like this one. These men work on the assembly line at the Livingstone Car Plant in the country of Zambia.

# SECTION 3 REVIEW

1. **Define** (a) subsistence farming, (b) cash crop, (c) economy, (d) diversify.

2. Why are African governments working to diversify their economies?

3. Compare subsistence farming with farming to raise cash crops. How are they similar? How are they different?

**Critical Thinking**

4. **Identifying Central Issues** What are some important natural resources in Africa?

**Activity**

6. **Writing to Learn** List some of Africa's natural resources that you and your family use. Then, write a paragraph that explains which you would miss most if you did not have it—and why.

# Interpreting Diagrams

Africa is a giant. More than three times bigger than the United States, it covers close to 11,700,000 square miles (more than 30,000,000 sq km). That is about one fifth of all of the land in the world. If you drove across Africa at its widest point going 65 miles (105 km) per hour, without stopping for gas or sleep, it would take you about 72 hours. Traveling north-to-south, the trip would take about 77 hours.

A quick look at a world map will impress upon you Africa's great length and width. But the map will not show you its enormous elevations, or height.

One of the most effective ways to see Africa's elevations is to study a cross-sectional diagram of this gigantic land.

## Get Ready

You already know that a diagram is a figure drawn to explain something. A *cross section* is basically a slice of something viewed from the side. For example, if you were to cut an apple in half, and look at the exposed cut, you would be looking at a cross section of the apple. If you drew a picture of what you saw, you would have a cross-sectional diagram of that apple.

You can get a good idea of a cross-sectional diagram by making one of your own—and having some fun as you do it. You'll need:
- modeling clay
- a butter knife
- pen and paper

## Cross-Sectional Diagram of Africa South of the Sahara

GREAT RIFT VALLEY (western)

GREAT RIFT VALLEY (eastern)

Lake Kivu

VIRUNGA MTS.

SERENGETI PLAIN

KENYA HIGHLANDS

Lualaba River (Congo)

MITUMBA MTS.

Lake Victoria

14,764 ft (4,500 m)

CRYSTAL MOUNTAINS

Congo River

Congo Basin

ATLANTIC OCEAN

INDIAN OCEAN

Sea level 0

6,562 ft (2,000 m)

0    200    400 mi
0    200    400 km

# Try It Out

**A. Create a continent.** Take a fist-sized ball of modeling clay and shape it into an imaginary continent. First, flatten it out. Then mold the continent into any shape you want. Mold mountain ranges, valleys, plateaus, and any other landforms you wish.

**B. Cut the cross section.** When you've finished, put your "clay continent" flat on a table. Use the butter knife to cut it in half at its widest point.

**C. Look at your result.** Pick up one-half of your continent and look at the cut side edgewise. You are looking at a cross section of your imaginary continent.

**D. Sketch what you see.** By sketching a side view of your model, you have made a cross-sectional diagram of your imaginary continent. How does the diagram reflect the vertical shape of the continent? Write the answer on the back of your cross-sectional diagram.

# Apply the Skill

The illustration above is a cross-sectional diagram of Africa. Use it to complete the following steps.

**1** **Understand the diagram.** Just as you cut your clay continent at a certain place, the cross-sectional diagram of Africa shows the continent "cut" at a certain place. Does this cross section show Africa from east to west or from north to south? How is elevation indicated on the diagram? What geographic features are labeled on the diagram?

**2** **Learn from the diagram.** What is the lowest point on the diagram? What is the highest point? How large a range in elevation is this? How far below the surrounding landscape does the Great Rift Valley drop?

# Review and Activities

## Reviewing Main Ideas

1. Why are some parts of Africa cold even though they are near the Equator?

2. List four major physical features of Africa. Choose one and describe what it is like.

3. Explain why there is little or no farming in much of North Africa and parts of Southern Africa.

4. How is subsistence farming in Africa different from farming to raise cash crops?

5. (a) List three cash crops raised in Africa. Where are they grown? (b) Name one mineral resource of Africa. Where is it found?

6. Explain why many African nations are trying to diversify their economies.

## Reviewing Key Terms

Use each key term below in a sentence that shows the meaning of the term.

1. plateau

2. elevation

3. escarpment

4. rift

5. cataract

6. silt

7. fertile

8. tributary

9. irrigate

10. oasis

11. savanna

12. nomad

13. subsistence farming

14. cash crop

15. economy

16. diversify

## Critical Thinking

1. **Identifying Central Issues** Explain the meaning of this statement. Give an example to support it. "People in Africa tend to live in grassland regions."

2. **Recognizing Cause and Effect** How did the yearly flooding of the Nile affect farmers in the Nile Valley? How did the building of the Aswan Dam affect the farmers?

## Graphic Organizer

Copy the chart onto a sheet of paper. Then fill in the empty boxes to complete the chart.

| | Amount of Rainfall | Temperature | Crops Grown |
|---|---|---|---|
| Desert | Little or none | Hot | Dates, barley, wheat in or near oases |
| Tropical Savanna | | | |
| Uplands and Mountain Regions | | | |

# Map Activity

### Africa

For each place listed, write the letter from the map that shows its location.

1. Nile River
2. Congo River
3. Sahara
4. Namib Desert
5. Zambezi River
6. Kalahari Desert
7. Niger River
8. Great Rift Valley

# Writing Activity

**Writing a Short Report**
Describe some problems Africans face that are caused by Africa's landforms or climate. Give some examples of how Africans are solving these problems.

## Internet Activity

Use a search engine to find **AfricaOnline.** Choose **Kids Only** and then choose **Learn About Africa.** Scroll to the bottom and click on the **Land** icon. What are the types of climates in Africa? Learn about the land and climates of Africa and then test your brain power with some fun, on-line quizzes.

# Skills Review

**Turn to the Skills Activity.**

Review the steps for interpreting a diagram. Then complete the following: (a) In your own words, describe what a cross-sectional diagram is. (b) What information can you find on a cross-sectional diagram?

# How Am I Doing?

Answer these questions to check your progress.

1. Can I describe the location of Africa?
2. Do I understand how climate influences farming activity in Africa?
3. Can I identify some mineral resources of Africa?
4. Can I name some large landforms in Africa?
5. What information from this chapter can I use in my book project?

# AFRICA

# Shaped by Its History

ATLANTIC OCEAN

Mediterranean Sea

**AFRICA**

Thebes

Meroë

Tombouctou

Nile R.

Niger River

Congo River

Malindi

Mombasa

Kilwa

INDIAN OCEAN

Zambezi River

Great Zimbabwe

**KEY**

Ancient Egypt
2686 B.C.–1070 B.C.

Nubia
6000 B.C.–A.D. 350

Aksum
900 B.C.–A.D. 600

Ghana
A.D. 300s–A.D. 1200

Mali
A.D. 1240–A.D. 1500

Songhai
A.D. 700s–A.D. 1591

Lambert Azimuthal Equal-Area Projection

0    500    1,000 mi

0  500  1,000 km

# MAP ACTIVITIES

*This map shows some of Africa's great empires, kingdoms, and cities. Note that they did not all exist at the same time. Start exploring the history of Africa by doing the following activities:*

**Study the map**
Compare this map with the political map of Africa in the Activity Atlas. Which countries took their names from early empires and kingdoms?

**Consider locations**
Notice that most of these empires and cities are close to rivers or oceans. How do you think the locations of empires and cities affected their development?

# Africa's First People

**Reach Into Your Background**

What are some of the things you remember from your past? Do you remember your very first day of school? What is the earliest birthday you can remember? All those things are part of your personal history.

**Questions to Explore**

1. What techniques did early Africans use to get food?
2. How did important ideas and discoveries spread throughout Africa?
3. What civilizations arose along the Nile River?

**Key Terms**
hunter-gatherer
domesticate
fertile
surplus
civilization
migrate
ethnic group

**Key People and Places**
Louis Leakey
Egypt
Nubia

Today the dry sands of the Sahara cover most of North Africa. But until about 4,000 years ago, this large area held enough water to support many people and animals. Scientists think that Africa's first farmers lived there. Paintings on cliffs and cave walls tell their story.

But the history of people in Africa is even older. Several million years earlier, the continent's first people lived in East Africa. We know this because of the stones and bones they left behind. These East Africans may have been the very first people to live on the Earth.

## Hunter-Gatherers

The earliest humans probably survived by gathering wild fruits, nuts, and roots. These **hunter-gatherers** also hunted animals for meat and clothing. They made tools out of wood, animal bones, and then stone. The first use of stone tools marks the beginning of a period scientists call the Stone Age.

These stone tools worked very well. The scientist Louis Leakey found some of the first evidence of early people in East Africa. He also taught himself to make and use their tools. Using a two-inch, 25,000-year-old stone knife, Leakey could skin and cut up a gazelle in just 20 minutes.

▼ This painting was found in Algeria. The horns on this woman's helmet show that the Sahara may once have supported animal life.

When hunter-gatherers settled down in one area and began farming, they faced longer, harder work days. Farmers spent many hours tilling the soil, planting seeds by hand, tending fields, harvesting crops, and caring for domesticated animals. They used only tools such as these, which they could make by hand. Farmers used axes (left) to clear the land. After butchering a cow, sheep, or goat, farmers used scrapers (top) to clean the hide, and cleavers (bottom) to cut the meat. **Critical Thinking** Since farming is harder work than hunting and gathering, why would a hunter-gatherer want to become a farmer?

**The Thirst Zone** Africa's first farmers probably lived in Algeria, in North Africa. Thousands of years ago, more rain fell in this region. But today, much of North Africa is known as the "Thirst Zone." People need to drink about 2.5 quarts (2.4 l) of water per day. People also use water for washing and farming. All in all, each person needs at least 21 quarts (20 l) of water per day. In the Thirst Zone, only about five quarts (5 l) of water per person is available.

## Farming and Herding

Between 10,000 and 6,000 years ago, hunter-gatherers began to farm and to herd animals. The first farmers probably planted wild grains such as wheat, barley, sorghum, and millet. At first, gatherers just protected the areas where these grains grew best. Then, they began to save some seed to plant for the next year's crop.

Later, people began to **domesticate** plants, or adapt them for their own use. They threw away seeds from weaker plants and saved seeds from stronger ones. People domesticated animals by breeding certain animals together.

Domesticating plants and animals meant people could plant their own crops. They did not have to travel to places where grains were already growing. As a result, they could settle in one place. Most people settled where the land was **fertile,** or productive. Some communities produced a food **surplus,** or more than they needed. Surpluses allowed some people in the community to do work other than farming.

## Civilizations on the Nile

Over hundreds or thousands of years, some Stone Age farming groups became civilizations. A **civilization** is a society with cities, a government, and social classes. Social classes form when people do a variety of jobs. As a result, some people are rich, some are poor, and others are middle class. Civilizations also have architecture, writing, and art. One civilization arose on the Nile River about 5,000 years ago.

◄ This Egyptian wall painting shows Nubian princes arriving in Egypt. At first, Egypt ruled Nubia, but later, Nubia conquered much of Egypt.

**Egypt** Each summer, the Nile River flooded its banks. It left a layer of fertile silt that was ideal for farming. People began farming along the banks of the Nile by around 4000 B.C. They settled in scattered villages. Over the centuries, these villages grew into the civilization of ancient Egypt.

Ancient Egypt was ruled by kings called pharaohs (FAY rohz). The people believed the pharaohs to be gods as well as kings. When pharaohs died, they were buried in pyramids. People painted murals and picture-writings called hieroglyphics (hy ur oh GLIF iks) on the walls in the pyramids.

Egyptian civilization included more than just the pyramids. The Egyptians were advanced in paper-making, architecture, medicine, and mathematics.

**Nubia** Starting in about 6000 B.C., several civilizations arose south of Egypt. This area was called Nubia. The final and greatest Nubian kingdom arose in the city of Meroë (MER oh ee) during the 500s B.C. It thrived until about the middle of the A.D. 300s. Meroë was probably the first place in Africa where iron was made.

## The Bantu Migrations

By about 500 B.C., West Africans had learned to heat and shape iron. They used it to form parts of tools such as arrowheads, ax heads, and hoe blades. The strong iron tools made farming easier and created food surpluses. As a result, West Africa's population increased.

Around 2,000 years ago, a group of people who spoke Bantu (BAN too) languages began to **migrate,** or move, out of West Africa. They were looking for new land to farm. Over hundreds of years, these

**READ ACTIVELY**

**Visualize** What does a pyramid look like?

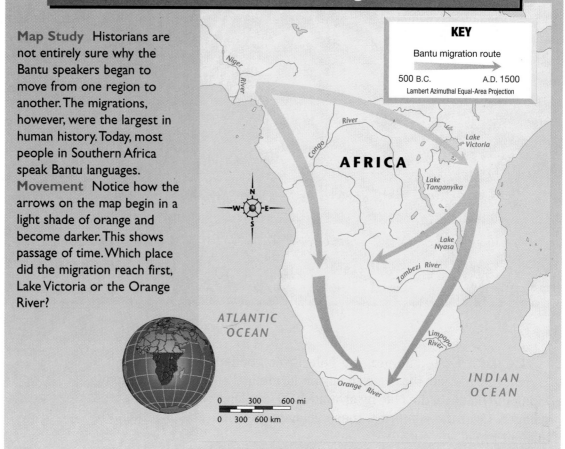

## Routes of the Bantu Migrations

**Map Study** Historians are not entirely sure why the Bantu speakers began to move from one region to another. The migrations, however, were the largest in human history. Today, most people in Southern Africa speak Bantu languages. **Movement** Notice how the arrows on the map begin in a light shade of orange and become darker. This shows passage of time. Which place did the migration reach first, Lake Victoria or the Orange River?

**KEY**

Bantu migration route

500 B.C.          A.D. 1500
Lambert Azimuthal Equal-Area Projection

Niger River

Congo River

River

Lake Victoria

AFRICA

Lake Tanganyika

Lake Nyasa

Zambezi River

Limpopo River

ATLANTIC OCEAN

Orange River

INDIAN OCEAN

0   300   600 mi
0   300   600 km

Bantu-speakers settled in Central and Southern Africa. They introduced farming, herding, and iron tools to these regions. Today, people in this part of Africa belong to hundreds of **ethnic groups,** or groups that share languages, religions, family ties, and customs. But almost all of these ethnic groups speak Bantu languages.

# SECTION 1 REVIEW

**1. Define** (a) hunter-gatherer, (b) domesticate, (c) fertile, (d) surplus, (e) civilization, (f) migrate, (g) ethnic group.

**2. Identify** (a) Louis Leakey, (b) Egypt, (c) Nubia.

**3.** How did iron tools, farming, and herding spread to Southern Africa?

**4.** Name some achievements of ancient Egyptian and Nubian civilizations.

**Critical Thinking**

**5. Drawing Conclusions** How did early Africans adapt to their environment?

**Activity**

**6. Writing to Learn** Make a poster that illustrates, step-by-step, an important idea from this section. For example, you might show how scientists learn about early people or how ideas spread from one part of Africa to another.

# Kingdoms and Empires

## BEFORE YOU READ

### Reach Into Your Background

What things do you own or have at home that were made in other countries? What things were made in the United States? Make a short list and share it with a classmate.

### Questions to Explore

1. How did trade enrich Africa's kingdoms and city-states?
2. How did the religion of Islam spread to different parts of Africa?

### Key Terms
Quran
pilgrimage
Swahili
city-state

### Key People and Places
Mansa Musa        Songhai
Aksum             Tombouctou
Ghana             Kilwa
Mali              Zimbabwe

In the year A.D. 1, a Greek writer made a list of things you could buy in Adulis, East Africa. Adulis was the most important city in Aksum, a bustling trade center along the Red Sea. There, you could buy:

> "Cloth made in Egypt . . . many articles of flint glass . . . and brass, which is used for ornament and cut pieces instead of coin; sheets of soft copper, used for cooking utensils and cut up for bracelets and anklets for the women; iron, which is made into spears used against the elephants and other wild beasts, and in their wars."

▼ These beads are from Zimbabwe, but thanks to the traders of Aksum, they could have journeyed all the way to Europe or India.

## Aksum

Aksum was located in East Africa. If it still existed today, it would be in the countries of Ethiopia and Eritrea. Around 1000 B.C., African and Arab traders began settling along the west coast of the Red Sea. They were the ancestors of the people of Aksum. Over time, Aksum came to control trade in

**Ask Questions** What questions do you have about trade in ancient Africa?

the Red Sea. Aksum came to power after the Nubian kingdom of Meroë fell. By then, Aksum controlled a trade network that stretched from the Mediterranean Sea to India.

Ideas, as well as goods, traveled along trade routes. The Christian religion traveled to Aksum along these routes. In the mid-300s, many people in Aksum became Christian. Aksum became a center of the early Ethiopian Christian Church. But Aksum began to decline in the 600s. Then Arabs took control of much of the region's trade.

## West African Kingdoms and Trade Routes

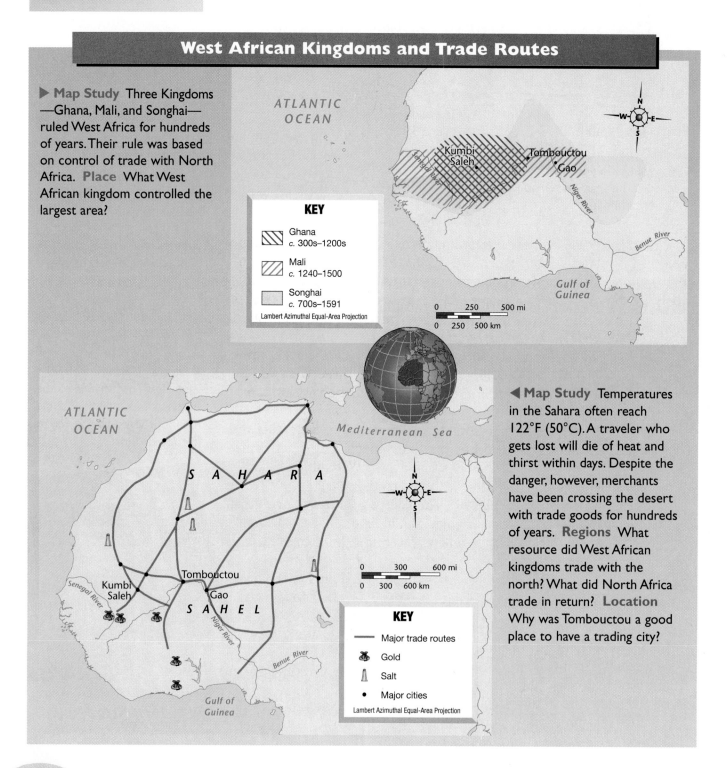

▶ **Map Study** Three Kingdoms —Ghana, Mali, and Songhai— ruled West Africa for hundreds of years. Their rule was based on control of trade with North Africa. **Place** What West African kingdom controlled the largest area?

**KEY**

Ghana
c. 300s–1200s

Mali
c. 1240–1500

Songhai
c. 700s–1591

Lambert Azimuthal Equal-Area Projection

0    250    500 mi
0    250    500 km

◀ **Map Study** Temperatures in the Sahara often reach 122°F (50°C). A traveler who gets lost will die of heat and thirst within days. Despite the danger, however, merchants have been crossing the desert with trade goods for hundreds of years. **Regions** What resource did West African kingdoms trade with the north? What did North Africa trade in return? **Location** Why was Tombouctou a good place to have a trading city?

0    300    600 mi
0    300    600 km

**KEY**

— Major trade routes

🏺 Gold

⛉ Salt

• Major cities

Lambert Azimuthal Equal-Area Projection

▲ Impressed with Mansa Musa's gold, Europeans included a picture of him on their maps of Africa. He appears in the lower right-hand corner of this map.

# West African Kingdoms

As Aksum declined, great kingdoms arose on the other side of the continent, in West Africa. The power of these kingdoms was based on the trade of salt and gold. People need salt to survive, especially in hot areas like West Africa. The people of West Africa had no local sources of salt. However, they had plenty of gold. For the people of North Africa, the opposite was true. They had salt, but no gold.

A brisk trade between North Africa and West Africa quickly grew. Control of this trade brought power and riches to three West African kingdoms—Ghana (GAH nuh), Mali (MAH lee), and Songhai (SAWNG hy).

**Ghana**   Look at the map on the previous page. Note that the kingdom of Ghana was located between the Senegal and Niger rivers. From this location Ghana controlled trade across West Africa. Ghana's kings grew rich from the taxes they charged on the salt, gold, and other goods that flowed through their land. The flow of gold was so great that Arab writers called Ghana "land of gold." But in time, Ghana lost control of the trade routes. It gave way to a new power, the kingdom of Mali.

**Mali and the Spread of Islam**   The kingdom of Mali arose in the mid-1200s in the Upper Niger Valley. The word Mali means "where the king lives." Mali's powerful kings controlled both the gold mines of the south and the salt supplies of the north. In Mali, the king was called Mansa, which means "emperor."

Mali's most famous king, Mansa Musa, gained the throne about 1312. His 25-year reign brought peace and order to the kingdom. An Arab visitor to Mali found "safety throughout the land. The traveler here has no more reason to fear thieves than the man who stays at home."

**READ ACTIVELY**

**Visualize** Visualize the court of the king of Ghana. How would you know you were in the presence of wealth and power?

**ACROSS THE WORLD**

**The Spread of Islam** From Arabia, Islam began to spread west through Southwest Asia and North Africa in the 600s. But Islam also spread east—to central Asia, India, Pakistan, Bangladesh, and Indonesia. The Muslim community in the country of Indonesia is one of the largest in the world.

Mansa Musa based his laws on the **Quran** (koo RAHN), the holy book of the religion of Islam. Over the centuries, Muslim traders had spread their religion into many parts of Africa. Muslims are followers of Islam. Mansa Musa and many of his subjects were Muslims.

In 1324, Mansa Musa made a **pilgrimage**—a religious journey—to the Arabian city of Mecca. Muslims consider Mecca a holy place. Muhammad, the prophet who first preached Islam, was born there. Mansa Musa brought 60,000 people with him on his pilgrimage. Eighty camels each carried 300 pounds (136 kg) of gold. Along the way, Mansa Musa gave people gifts of gold.

Mansa Musa's pilgrimage brought about new trading ties with other Muslim states. It also displayed Mali's wealth. Hearing the reports, Europe's rulers grew interested in African gold.

**Songhai** After Mansa Musa's death around 1332, Mali declined. Mali was finally destroyed by a new empire called Songhai. In time, Songhai became West Africa's most powerful kingdom. Songhai's rulers controlled important trade routes and wealthy trading cities.

The wealthiest trading city, Tombouctou (tohn book TOO), also was a great Muslim learning center. People said of Tombouctou:

> "Salt comes from the north, gold from the south, and silver from the city of white men. But the word of God and the treasures of wisdom are only to be found in Tombouctou."

Invaders from North Africa defeated Songhai in 1591. But Songhai people still live near the Niger River, and Islam remains important in the region.

# East African City-States

As in West Africa, trade helped East African cities to develop. Around the time that Aksum declined, trading cities arose along East Africa's coast. Traders from these cities used seasonal winds to sail northeast to India and China. They carried animal skins, ivory, and gold and other metals. When the winds changed direction, the traders rode them home. They brought many goods, including cotton, silk, and porcelain.

Trade affected the culture of coastal East Africa. Some of the traders who visited the area were Muslims. Many of them settled and introduced Islam to East Africa. In time, a new language developed in the area. Called **Swahili** (swah HEE lee), it

**East African Trade Routes**

**KEY**

→ Trade routes

Lambert Azimuthal Equal-Area Projection

Cairo
To Mediterranean
Mecca
To India
Mogadishu
Malindi
Mombasa
Kilwa
INDIAN OCEAN
To East Asia
Great Zimbabwe
Sofala

0   500   1,000 mi
0   500   1,000 km

**Map Study** Traders visiting East African city-states could buy gold from Africa, cotton from India, and porcelain from China. **Location** How were the East African city-states ideally located to become centers of trade?

## Trade in East Africa

As early as A.D. 1100, traders in East Africa bought and sold goods from many parts of the world. Traders bought animal skins, gold, and ivory, or elephant tusks (above left), from Africa and sold them in India and China.

From India, traders brought back cloth, grain, oil, and sugar. From China, they brought back dishes and vases made of porcelain, a hard substance made by baking clay (above right).

was a Bantu language with some Arab words mixed in. Today, many East Africans still speak Swahili.

Some East African cities grew into powerful city-states. A **city-state** is a city that has its own government and often controls much of the surrounding land. Among the greatest of these city-states were Malindi (muh LIN dee), Mombasa (mahm BAH suh), and Kilwa (KIL wah). Look at the map on the previous page. How do you think the locations of these city-states helped them to become important trade centers?

**Kilwa** Ibn Battuta (IHB uhn bat TOO tah), a Muslim traveler from North Africa, visited Kilwa in 1331. He had seen great cities in China, India, and West Africa. But Battuta wrote that Kilwa was "one of the most beautiful and best-constructed towns in the world." In Kilwa, people lived in three- and four-story houses made of stone and sea coral.

Kilwa and other East African city-states grew rich from trade and taxes. Traders had to pay huge taxes on goods they brought into the city. "Any merchant who wished to enter the city paid for every five hundred pieces of cloth, no matter what the quality, one gold [piece] as entrance duty," reported one visitor. "After this, the king took two thirds of all the merchandise, leaving the trader one third."

In the early 1500s, Kilwa and the other city-states were conquered by the European country of Portugal. The Portuguese wanted to build their own trading empire.

◄The walls of Great Zimbabwe are more than 600 years old. Builders created them without using mortar or cement.

**Zimbabwe** South and inland from the East African city-states lay another great trading civilization. Great Zimbabwe (zim BAH bway) was located near the bend of the Limpopo (lim POH poh) River in Southern Africa. Great Zimbabwe reached its peak about the year 1300. Today only ruins of it remain. But once, more than 200 gigantic stone buildings covered the area. (Great Zimbabwe means "stone dwelling.")

Upon seeing the ruins in the late 1800s, European explorers did not think that Africans had the skill to build them. They were wrong. The builders were the Shona, a group of Bantu speakers who had lived in the region since the 900s.

# SECTION 2 REVIEW

1. **Define** (a) Quran, (b) pilgrimage, (c) Swahili, (d) city-state.

2. **Identify** (a) Mansa Musa, (b) Aksum, (c) Ghana, (d) Mali, (e) Songhai, (f) Tombouctou, (g) Kilwa, (h) Zimbabwe.

3. On what was the wealth and power of the city-states based?

4. How did Islam become a major religion in West and East Africa?

**Critical Thinking**

5. **Drawing Conclusions** How did Ghana, Mali, and Songhai become wealthy from gold and salt even though they did not mine either one?

**Activity**

6. **Writing to Learn** You are a traveler visiting one of the West African kingdoms or city-states. Write a short letter home about some of the things you see.

# The Conquest of Africa

## BEFORE YOU READ

**Reach Into Your Background**

What actions would you take to get something you really wanted? What would you do to hold on to something that was already yours?

**Questions to Explore**

1. Why did European contact with Africa increase?
2. What were the effects of European rule in Africa?

**Key Terms**
colonize

**Key People and Places**
Olaudah Equiano
Gorée
Cape of Good Hope

On the island of Gorée (gaw RAY), off the coast of the West African country of Senegal, stands a museum called the House of Slaves. It honors millions of Africans who were enslaved and shipped across the Atlantic Ocean. Many Africans passed through this building. Their last view of Africa was an opening called "The Door of No Return." Beyond it lay the ocean and the slave ships bound for the Americas.

## Europeans on the Coast

The Atlantic slave trade began in the 1500s and continued through the late 1800s. But contact between Europeans and Africans began long before that. In North Africa, Europeans traded for gold from the empires of Ghana and Mali, and for salt from the Sahara. Why do you think Europeans' first contacts with Africans took place in North Africa?

After 1500, Europe's relationship with Africa changed. It had begun as trade between equals. But it turned into the enslavement and forced migration of millions of Africans. The African slave trade ended in 1860. Then Europeans wanted Africa's natural resources. By 1900, European countries had divided Africa among themselves.

▼ The Door of No Return in Senegal led to a pier, where slave ships were waiting to sail to the Americas.

## ACROSS THE WORLD

**Europeans and the Americas** Christopher Columbus sailed extensively along the coast of western Africa. He traveled several times to the Portuguese trading post in the Gold Coast. On these journeys, he sometimes found pieces of wood floating from the west. These signs helped to convince Columbus that there was land to the west. Such convictions increased his desire to take the journey westward.

▼ In 1482, the Portuguese built this fort, Elmina Castle, in Ghana to protect and supply its trade with West Africa.

In the 1400s, Portuguese explorers began exploring the coast of West Africa. They wanted to trade directly for West African gold and ivory, instead of dealing with North African merchants. They also wanted to trade with Asia.

Many inventions helped the Portuguese explore Africa's coast. The Portuguese used a lateen sail, a triangle-shaped sail designed in North Africa. The lateen sail allowed ships to sail against the wind as well as with it. And better instruments, such as the astrolabe (AS troh layb), helped sailors navigate at sea. With these improvements, Portuguese sailors became the first Europeans to travel south along Africa's coasts.

At first, both Africans and Europeans traded together as equals. Africans traded gold, cotton, ivory, skins, metal objects, and pepper. In return, Europeans traded copper, brass, and clothing. Europeans brought corn, cassava, and yams from the Americas. These plants became food crops in Africa. Some Africans also became Christians.

But soon this balance was upset. In 1497, three Portuguese ships rounded the tip of Southern Africa and sailed north along Africa's east coast. The wealth of the East African city-states amazed the Portuguese. More Portuguese ships followed—not to trade but to seize the riches of the city-states. Portugal controlled trade on East Africa's coast until well into the 1600s.

The Dutch, French, and English soon followed the Portuguese. They set up trading posts along Africa's coasts, where sailors could get supplies. The Dutch built a trading post on the Cape of Good Hope at Africa's southern tip. Soon, settlers arrived. They moved inland, building homes and farms.

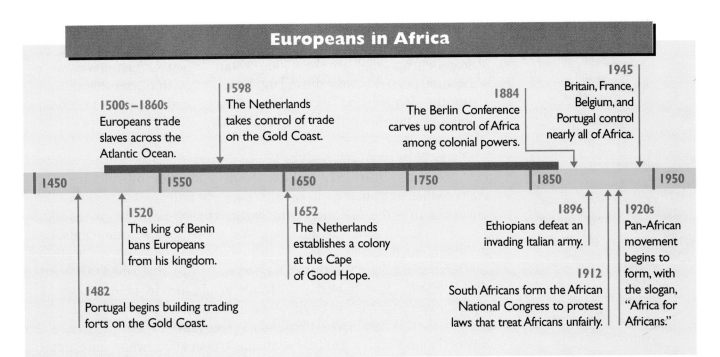

## Europeans in Africa

**1500s–1860s** Europeans trade slaves across the Atlantic Ocean.

**1598** The Netherlands takes control of trade on the Gold Coast.

**1884** The Berlin Conference carves up control of Africa among colonial powers.

**1945** Britain, France, Belgium, and Portugal control nearly all of Africa.

1450     1550     1650     1750     1850     1950

**1520** The king of Benin bans Europeans from his kingdom.

**1652** The Netherlands establishes a colony at the Cape of Good Hope.

**1896** Ethiopians defeat an invading Italian army.

**1920s** Pan-African movement begins to form, with the slogan, "Africa for Africans."

**1482** Portugal begins building trading forts on the Gold Coast.

**1912** South Africans form the African National Congress to protest laws that treat Africans unfairly.

▲ Africans resisted European colonization, but, as this time line shows, Europe slowly took control of more and more of Africa. What year did an African country defeat a European army?

As Europeans spread out, sometimes by force, their relations with Africans worsened. But the growing trade in enslaved Africans poisoned future contacts between Africans and Europeans the most.

## The Atlantic Slave Trade

Before the 1500s, slavery was common in Africa. But slaves usually won their freedom after a few years. Some became important citizens among the people who had enslaved them. Slaves could even be bought out of slavery by their own people.

Then the European powers began to build colonies in North and South America. They practiced a new type of slavery there. The Europeans treated slaves like property, not like people. Freedom in the future was out of the question. The African slave trade did not end until the 1800s. By then, millions of Africans had been taken from their homelands, never to return.

**The Demand for Slaves** Spanish, Portuguese, and Dutch settlers in the Americas needed workers for their plantations and mines. At first they enslaved Native Americans. But many Native Americans became sick and died from diseases or brutal working conditions. Others ran away. To replace them, the Europeans started to import enslaved Africans.

The Europeans thought that Africans would make good slaves. Africa's climate was similar to that of the Americas. Africans were skilled farmers, miners, and metal workers. They also did not know the territory. It would be almost impossible for them to escape.

By the 1600s, Portuguese traders were trading goods for African slaves. Some African groups refused to join the trade. But other groups

Visualize Visualize the inside of a slave ship. What do you think it would have been like to cross the Atlantic in these conditions?

sold slaves captured during battles. In return, the Europeans gave the Africans cheap guns. By the 1700s, about 78,000 African slaves were being transported across the Atlantic each year. But even this did not satisfy the demand for slaves. Some African leaders began to kidnap people from neighboring areas to sell as slaves.

**The Horror of Slavery** Captured Africans were branded with hot irons. In the slave ships, captives lay side by side on filthy shelves stacked from floor to ceiling. They got little food or water on the journey across the Atlantic. As many as 20 percent of the slaves died during each crossing. To make up for these losses, ships' captains packed in more people.

Olaudah Equiano (oh LOW duh ek wee AHN oh), described this horrible experience in a book he wrote about his life. In 1756, at age 11, Equiano was captured and sold at a slave auction. He was sure he was going to die: "When I looked around the ship and saw a large furnace of copper boiling and a multitude of black people of every description chained together . . . I no longer doubted of my fate."

Equiano proved luckier than most African slaves. In time, he was able to buy his freedom. For most slaves, freedom was little more than a distant dream.

## The Cramped Journey Across the Atlantic

▲▼ Enslaved Africans were packed in tightly, with no room to sit up or move about (left). When Olaudah Equiano (below) left Africa, he faced from three to six weeks of lying on a shelf below decks.

**The Effects of Slavery on Africa** Some Africans grew wealthy from the slave trade. But the slave trade was a disaster for Africa. The people who were sold as slaves were the youngest, healthiest, and most capable workers from the region. If a country loses its best people, it is hard for it to grow and become strong.

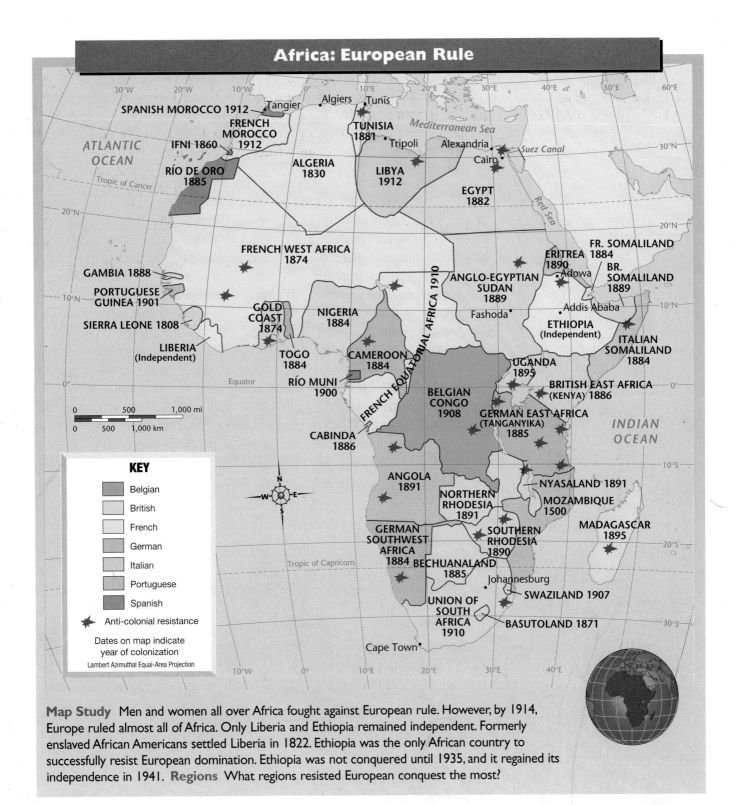

## Africa: European Rule

SPANISH MOROCCO 1912
Tangier
Algiers  Tunis
FRENCH MOROCCO 1912
TUNISIA 1881
Tripoli
Alexandria  Suez Canal
IFNI 1860
ATLANTIC OCEAN
ALGERIA 1830
LIBYA 1912
Cairo
RÍO DE ORO 1885
Tropic of Cancer
EGYPT 1882
Red Sea
FR. SOMALILAND 1884
FRENCH WEST AFRICA 1874
ERITREA 1890
Adowa
BR. SOMALILAND 1889
GAMBIA 1888
ANGLO-EGYPTIAN SUDAN 1889
PORTUGUESE GUINEA 1901
Addis Ababa
SIERRA LEONE 1808
GOLD COAST 1874
NIGERIA 1884
Fashoda
ETHIOPIA (Independent)
ITALIAN SOMALILAND 1884
LIBERIA (Independent)
TOGO 1884
CAMEROON 1884
Equator
RÍO MUNI 1900
FRENCH EQUATORIAL AFRICA 1910
UGANDA 1895
BELGIAN CONGO 1908
BRITISH EAST AFRICA (KENYA) 1886
CABINDA 1886
GERMAN EAST AFRICA (TANGANYIKA) 1885
INDIAN OCEAN
ANGOLA 1891
NYASALAND 1891
NORTHERN RHODESIA 1891
MOZAMBIQUE 1500
GERMAN SOUTHWEST AFRICA 1884
SOUTHERN RHODESIA 1890
MADAGASCAR 1895
BECHUANALAND 1885
Johannesburg
SWAZILAND 1907
UNION OF SOUTH AFRICA 1910
BASUTOLAND 1871
Cape Town

0   500   1,000 mi
0   500  1,000 km

**KEY**
- Belgian
- British
- French
- German
- Italian
- Portuguese
- Spanish
- ⭐ Anti-colonial resistance

Dates on map indicate year of colonization
Lambert Azimuthal Equal-Area Projection

**Map Study** Men and women all over Africa fought against European rule. However, by 1914, Europe ruled almost all of Africa. Only Liberia and Ethiopia remained independent. Formerly enslaved African Americans settled Liberia in 1822. Ethiopia was the only African country to successfully resist European domination. Ethiopia was not conquered until 1935, and it regained its independence in 1941. **Regions** What regions resisted European conquest the most?

# Europeans Carve Up Africa

After the slave trade ended, Europeans then began to raid Africa's interior for resources. They wanted the resources to fuel the new factories that were springing up all across Europe. Europeans also saw Africa as a place to build empires.

Africans fiercely resisted European conquest. But their cheap guns proved no match for Europe's weapons. Europeans carried the Maxim gun, the first automatic machine gun. A British author wrote at the time:

> "Whatever happens we have got
> The Maxim-gun; and they have not."

Europeans competed with each other to gain African territory. But they did not want to go to war with each other over it. In 1884, leaders of several European countries met in the German city of Berlin. They set rules for how European countries could claim African land. By 1900, European nations had colonized many parts of Africa. To **colonize** means to settle an area and take over its government. One newspaper called this rush for territory "the scramble for Africa."

Not all European countries ruled their colonies the same way. The Belgian government directly ran the Belgian Congo (now the country of Zaire). But Nigeria was run by Africans who took orders from British officials. In all cases, the African people had little power in government.

The scramble for Africa caused lasting harm. Europeans had gained power in part by encouraging Africans to fight each other. Europeans also took the best land to farm. In some areas, they forced Africans to labor under terrible conditions. Finally, Europeans drew new political boundaries. These boundaries divided some ethnic groups and forced differing groups together. These boundaries were to cause much conflict in Africa.

**Ask Questions** What questions do you have about the effect of European colonization on the people of Africa?

## SECTION 3 REVIEW

1. **Define** colonize.
2. **Identify** (a) Olaudah Equiano, (b) Gorée, (c) Cape of Good Hope.
3. How did relations between Africa and Europe change over time?
4. In what different ways did the Europeans govern their African colonies?

**Critical Thinking**
5. **Identifying Central Issues** How did the European conquest affect Africa?

**Activity**
6. **Writing to Learn** Write two brief editorials about the European conference in Berlin. Write one editorial from the point of view of an African. Write the other from the point of view of a European who attended the conference.

# Independence and Its Challenges

## BEFORE YOU READ

### Reach Into Your Background

People have different ideas about what independence means. For some, it means having the freedom to make their own decisions. What does independence mean to you?

### Questions to Explore

1. What techniques did African nations use to win independence from European powers?
2. What challenges did new African leaders face after independence?

**Key Terms**
nationalism
Pan-Africanism
boycott
democracy

**Key People**
Robert Mugabe
Léopold Sédar Senghor
Kwame Nkrumah

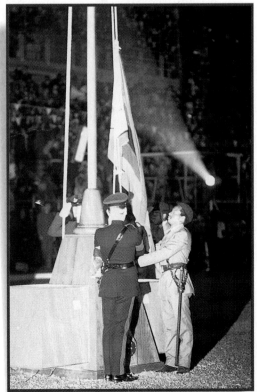

▼ When Zimbabwe's flag went up for the first time, the country became independent of Great Britain.

On April 18, 1980, the people of Rhodesia took to the streets. They had recently elected Robert Mugabe (mu GAHB ee) as Prime Minister. It was the first free election in Rhodesia's history. People waited excitedly through the night. At midnight, the British flag came down for the last time. People cheered loudly. At that moment, the British colony of Rhodesia became the independent country of Zimbabwe.

The fight for independence had been hard and sometimes violent. Now, Prime Minister Mugabe asked all the people to work together. They would have to build a new nation. "The wrongs of the past must now stand forgiven and forgotten," said Mugabe. Zimbabwe was one of the last African countries to win independence. But the movement for freedom in Zimbabwe had begun many years before.

## The Growth of Nationalism

Many Africans dreamed of independence after Europe's scramble for Africa in the late 1800s. In 1897, Mankayi Sontanga (mun KY ee suhn TAHN guh) put this dream to music. His song was called "Bless, O Lord, Our Land of Africa." Sontanga's song expressed the growing nationalism of Africans. **Nationalism** is a feeling of pride in one's homeland.

**Education and Nationalism**   Many African leaders worked to encourage pride in being African. The colonial powers had drawn political borders that brought together many ethnic groups. Some of these groups were old rivals. African leaders saw that to end colonial rule, they would have to build a spirit of togetherness.

Nationalism grew during the early 1900s. In 1912, Africans in South Africa formed a political party. Today this party is the African National Congress (ANC). Party members protested laws that limited the rights of black South Africans. Five years later, African lawyers in British West Africa formed the West African National Congress. This group also worked to gain rights for Africans, including the right to vote.

**Pan-Africanism**   In the 1920s, Africans formed a movement called **Pan-Africanism.** This movement stressed unity and cooperation among all Africans. Pan-African leaders tried to unify all Africans, whether they lived in Africa or not. Their slogan was "Africa for Africans." The movement won many supporters.

One of the greatest leaders of Pan-Africanism was Léopold Sédar Senghor (san GAWR) of Senegal. Senghor was a poet as well as a political leader. He encouraged Africans to look carefully at their traditions. They should be proud of their culture, he said. Senegal became independent in 1960, and Senghor became its first president.

## Pan-Africanism in the U.S.

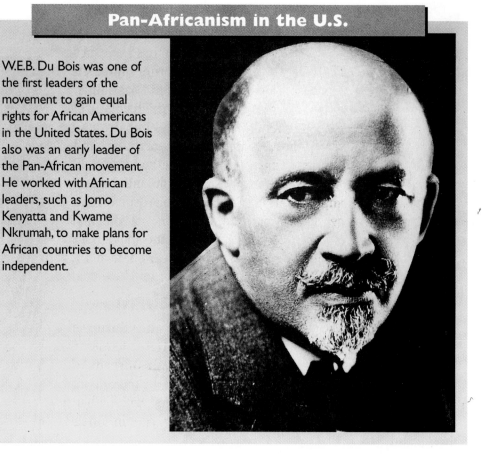

W.E.B. Du Bois was one of the first leaders of the movement to gain equal rights for African Americans in the United States. Du Bois also was an early leader of the Pan-African movement. He worked with African leaders, such as Jomo Kenyatta and Kwame Nkrumah, to make plans for African countries to become independent.

These Ghanaians fought in the British army in 1942. Here, they are on their way to defend North Africa against the armies of Germany and Italy. Fifteen years later, they and other Ghanaians achieved independence for their own country. **Critical Thinking** During World War II, Allied armies fought to preserve democracy around the world. How do you think fighting in the war affected Africans' feelings about democracy and independence?

# World War II

A major boost to African independence came unexpectedly in the 1930s and 1940s, out of a global conflict called World War II. A group called the Allies included Great Britain, France, and the United States. They fought the armies of Germany, Italy, and Japan, who were invading much of the world. German and Italian forces invaded North Africa.

Africa played a huge role in support of the Allies. The colonies supplied metals for guns and other equipment. Allied planes used their airfields to move supplies into Asia. African soldiers fought and died to help free Europe from conquest. About 80,000 soldiers from Tanganyika, alone, served in the British Army.

Africans came home victorious. Now, they wanted their own freedom. One soldier said, "We have been told what we fought for. That is 'freedom.' We want freedom, nothing but freedom."

# Different Paths to Independence

The war not only inspired Africans to win their freedom. It also weakened colonial powers like Great Britain. Many people in Britain felt that they could no longer afford a colonial empire. The United States and the Soviet Union—Britain's allies during the war—began to speak out against colonialism.

**READ ACTIVELY**

**Ask Questions** What else would you like to know about how African nations became independent?

**KEY**

Independent nations by 1945

Gained independence 1945–1959

Gained independence since 1959

Status in dispute

★ Sites of civil wars and ethnic clashes, 1990s

Lambert Azimuthal Equal-Area Projection

**Map Study** Independence was only the first step toward peace in some African countries. Civil wars have torn some countries since independence. **Movement** The West African country of Ghana was one of the first African countries to become independent. Based on the map, how do you think Ghana's independence affected its neighbors?

British leader Harold Macmillan realized that Britain would not be able to keep its African colonies. "The winds of change are blowing across Africa," he said. Soon, European countries began to give up their African colonies.

Some colonial powers let go willingly, while others fought to keep power. Ghana won its independence from Britain peacefully. But Algeria, a former French colony, had to fight for its freedom.

**From Gold Coast to Ghana**   In the British West African colony of the Gold Coast, Kwame Nkrumah organized protests against British rule in the early 1950s. These protests took the peaceful form of strikes and boycotts. In a **boycott,** people refuse to buy or use certain products or services. The British threw Nkrumah in jail for his actions. But the protests continued without him. In 1957, he achieved his goal: independence for the Gold Coast. The country took the new name of Ghana, after the great trading kingdom that lasted until the 1200s. It was a name that recalled Africa's earlier greatness. Released from prison, Nkrumah became Ghana's first president in 1960.

**War in Algeria**   The French people who had settled in Algeria thought of it as more than a colony. To them, it was part of France. Algerians disagreed. They were willing to fight for the right to govern themselves. A bloody war began in Algeria in 1954. The eight-year struggle cost the lives of 100,000 Algerians and 10,000 French. But by 1962, the Algerians had won.

**The Challenges of Independence**   Africa's new leaders had spent many years working for independence. But they had little experience actually governing a country. The colonial powers had rarely allowed Africans to share in government. And even after agreeing to independence, the colonial powers did little to prepare the new leaders. As a result, some new governments in Africa were not very stable.

In some African countries, military leaders took control of the government by force. Military governments are not always fair. The people often have few rights. Further, citizens may be jailed if they protest. But this form of government has held together some African countries that otherwise would have been torn apart by war.

Other African countries have a long history of democracy. In a **democracy,** citizens help to make governmental decisions. Some countries have made traditional ways a part of governing. For example, in Botswana, lively political debates take place in "freedom squares." These outdoor meetings are like the traditional *kgotla* (KUHT luh), in which people talk with their leaders.

▼ Children wave goodbye to the British governor shortly after Ghana became independent.

## Gambians Celebrate Independence

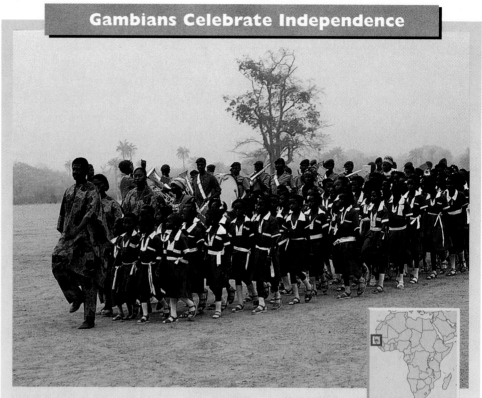

Gambia won its independence from Great Britain through peaceful elections in 1965. Schoolchildren celebrate Gambian independence every year. **Critical Thinking** How is this celebration similar to Fourth of July celebrations in the United States?

**READ ACTIVELY**

**Connect** The United States is a democratic country. How does democracy in the United States affect you?

Most African countries are less than 40 years old. In contrast, the stable, democratic country of the United States is over 200 years old. Many Africans feel that building stable countries will take time. One leader commented, "Let Africa be given the time to develop its own system of democracy."

## SECTION 4 REVIEW

1. **Define** (a) nationalism, (b) Pan-Africanism, (c) boycott (d) democracy.

2. **Identify** (a) Robert Mugabe, (b) Léopold Sédar Senghor, (c) Kwame Nkrumah.

3. Compare Ghana's road to independence to that of Algeria.

4. In what ways did colonial rule cause problems for African countries after independence?

**Critical Thinking**

5. **Recognizing Cause and Effect** How did World War II boost the independence movement in Africa?

**Activity**

6. **Writing to Learn** Research one African country that won its independence after 1950. Write a headline and a short article for a newspaper that might have appeared on the day your country became independent. Compile all the articles from your class to create a bulletin board display about African independence.

# Issues for Africa Today

BEFORE YOU READ

**Reach Into Your Background**
As you have grown, you have become more independent.

What challenges are you facing as you grow older? How have you met your challenges?

**Questions to Explore**
1. What challenges do African countries face today?
2. What actions may help Africans meet some of their challenges?

**Key Terms**
commercial farming
hybrid
literacy
life expectancy

**Key Places**
Niger
Senegal

In the past, nothing grew during the dry season in the Sahel. Farmers had to travel to cities to find work. Now, the West African country of Niger has a new irrigation program. This makes it possible for farmers to grow a second crop during the dry season. Farmer Adamou Sani (AH duh moo SAH nee) says that raising two crops a year means that he can stay on village land.

▼ Farmers in Niger use irrigation canals to bring water from the Niger River to their crops.

"Dry-season crops are such a normal practice now that everyone grows them. Before, each year after the harvest, I went to the city to look for work. But today, with the dry-season crops, I have work in the village. Truly it is a good thing."

Niger's irrigation program is one way Africans are improving their lives. Africans are also finding ways to meet economic, social, and environmental challenges.

## Economic Issues

The colonial powers saw Africa as a source of raw materials and a market for their own manufactured goods. They did little to build factories in Africa. African countries still have little industry. Most economies are based on farming and mining.

## A South African Gold Mine

South Africa's gold miners work day and night in a mammoth mine more than two miles underground. South Africa produces more than half the world's gold. The gold from this mine will make jewelry, coins—and even teeth—for people around the world. What do you think it would be like to work in a gold mine?

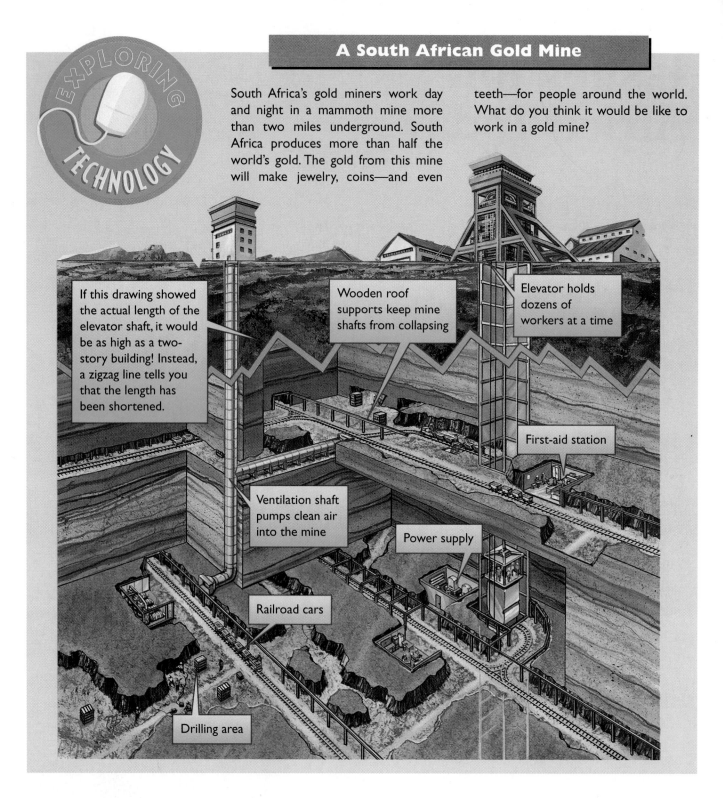

If this drawing showed the actual length of the elevator shaft, it would be as high as a two-story building! Instead, a zigzag line tells you that the length has been shortened.

Wooden roof supports keep mine shafts from collapsing

Elevator holds dozens of workers at a time

First-aid station

Ventilation shaft pumps clean air into the mine

Power supply

Railroad cars

Drilling area

**Farming and Mining** Farming is the most important activity in Africa. About 75 percent of workers are farmers. And more than half of what Africa sells overseas are farm goods. Africans practice two kinds of farming—subsistence and commercial. With subsistence farming, farmers work small plots of land. They raise just as much food as their families need. **Commercial farming** is the large-scale production of cash crops such as coffee, cocoa, and bananas for sale.

Many African nations have rich mineral resources. They export minerals to other countries. Nigeria has oil and coal. Zaire and Zambia have copper, while South Africa has gold. Look at the diagram on the previous page. How does South Africa produce its gold?

**Economic Challenges** About 75 percent of African countries have economies that depend on exporting one or two products. Gambia depends on peanuts, while Zambia relies on the export of copper. As a result, African economies are sensitive to the rise and fall of world prices. A fall in prices hurts economies that depend on the sale of one crop or mineral.

African countries are now trying to depend less on one export. They are trying to diversify their economies. For example, Senegal became independent in 1960. At the time, it earned more than 80 percent of its money by exporting peanuts. Today, Senegal has other industries such as fishing, fish processing, and mining. Peanuts account for only 25 percent of the money Senegal makes from exports.

### World Copper Prices

| Year | Cents Per Pound (kg) |
|------|----------------------|
| 1990 | 121.02 (266.27) |
| 1991 | 106.21 (233.69) |
| 1992 | 103.72 (228.21) |
| 1993 | 86.75 (190.87) |
| 1994 | 104.65 (230.25) |
| 1995 | 132.91 (292.43) |
| 1996 | 88.02 (193.66) |

**Chart Study** Zaire and Zambia both rely on copper mining for most of their income. Copper is used to make coins, wire, tubes, and jewelry, like the Tanzanian bracelet at right. **Critical Thinking** Based on these prices, what challenges do you think might face a country that gets most of its income from selling copper?

African nations face another economic problem—how to feed a growing population. Many governments are trying to help farmers grow more. One method they use is to develop hybrid plants. A **hybrid** is made by combining different types of the same plant. In the early 1980s, farmers in Zimbabwe who grew hybrid corn doubled their harvests. Today, most of Zimbabwe's corn comes from hybrids.

## Social Issues

African nations also must provide social services to a growing population. In the areas of health care and education, many African nations are working to keep their traditions alive while adapting to the modern world.

**Education** African children must often add to their family's income by working on family farms or selling goods in the market. When girls and boys go to school, families sacrifice. But many Africans gladly make this sacrifice in order to improve their lives.

READ ACTIVELY

**Predict** What problems do you think can arise when a nation depends on one crop or resource?

► How is this school in Zimbabwe similar to your school? How is it different?

In South Africa, parents often help to build new schools. The schools are often overcrowded. As a result, students take turns attending. The headmaster at one such school said that students "who couldn't cram into the desks knelt on the floor or stood on their toes so as not to miss a word the teacher was saying."

The number of people who can read and write varies from country to country. But in all countries, since independence, more people have learned to read. When the Portuguese left Mozambique in 1975, only 10 percent of the people in Mozambique were literate. **Literacy** is the ability to read and write. Today about 33 percent of the people are literate. In Tanzania, progress has been even more dramatic. At the time of independence only 15 percent of Tanzania's people were literate. Today, 90 percent of adult Tanzanians can read and write.

**Health**  Like literacy, **life expectancy**—how long an average person will live—differs from country to country. In Mali, life expectancy is less than 60 years. In Botswana, where most people live near health clinics, people are expected to live between 60 and 66 years.

In Africa's tropical climate, insects carry serious diseases. Research has helped control malaria and sleeping sickness. The World Health Organization has worked with African governments to end smallpox and reduce a disease called river blindness. Vaccination programs in Africa have also conquered typhoid. However, Africans are still working to overcome other widespread health problems.

## The Environment

Like the United States, Africa faces a number of environmental challenges. About two thirds of Africa is desert or dry land. And more and more of Africa is turning into desert. Forests are being cut down, which causes soil to wash away. This reduces the amount of land on which food can be grown. This, in turn, threatens many Africans with starvation.

**READ ACTIVELY**

**Ask Questions** What would you like to know about Africa's environment?

**Health Education in Nigeria**

This clinic is located in a rural area of Nigeria. Doctors here are teaching women the healthiest foods to feed young children. Health education programs focus on preventing sickness, rather than on curing it after it happens.

But science can help feed Africans and save Africa's environment. Irrigation projects, hybrids, and vegetation that holds water in the ground have all increased crop harvests. To fight soil erosion, farmers in Nigeria now plant food crops such as yams in long rows. Between the rows they plant trees that hold the soil in place. The trees can later be harvested for wood.

African nations still face many challenges. They are meeting them by using their resources, increasing education, and keeping traditions alive in a changing world.

## LINKS ACROSS THE WORLD

**Virtual Eritrea** Eritrea is a country in East Africa along the Red Sea. It won independence from Ethiopia in 1993. Now, Eritreans are using Internet technology to help them meet the challenges of self-rule. They have formed Dehai, an on-line community. Dehai is an Internet newsgroup. About 500 Eritreans living in other countries use Dehai to discuss issues related to Eritrea's new constitution.

## SECTION 5 REVIEW

1. **Define** (a) commercial farming, (b) hybrid, (c) literacy, (d) life expectancy.

2. **Identify** (a) Niger, (b) Senegal.

3. Why are African nations trying to diversify their economies?

4. List two challenges African countries face and describe the steps African countries are taking to meet these challenges.

**Critical Thinking**

5. **Drawing Conclusions** In what ways have Africans shown the high value they place on education?

**Activity**

6. **Writing to Learn** You are the economic adviser to the president of an African country. Write a brief report on some steps the president might take to improve the economy.

# Recognizing Bias

When Latisha got to class, she looked at the chalkboard. Every day, Mr. Copeland began class by writing something on the board to discuss:

*Life in West Africa is better than life in North Africa.*

"Well, class? What do you think about that?" Mr. Copeland asked.

Latisha wondered how someone decided what made life better in one place than another. She raised her hand.

"That statement does not tell the whole story! Whose life are you talking about? And when?"

Mr. Copeland smiled. "Latisha, you've hit the nail on the head. The statement on the board does not tell the whole story—it may even be completely untrue. It shows you an example of *bias*."

## Get Ready

To be biased is to lean to a particular point of view. Sometimes, people who write about something only know one side of the story.

935 8525

L'S NEWSSTAND

58

Other people leave out information on purpose to give their own viewpoint. Biased writing takes a side, even if at first it seems not to.

You need to be able to recognize bias in writing. It is the only way you can know whether you're getting a fair picture. When you read, you can look for certain clues that will point out a writer's bias.

## Try It Out

To determine if a writer is biased, do the following:

**A. Look for opinions.** Opinions are beliefs that cannot be proved. They are the opposite of facts, which can be proved. Biased writing often contains opinions disguised as facts. For example, the statement "Life in West Africa is better than life in North Africa" may sound like a fact, but it is an opinion.

**B. Look for loaded words and phrases.** Loaded words and phrases carry a hidden meaning. They give a positive or negative impression. Read this sentence: "The coastline of Nigeria is so beautiful it takes your breath away." The words "so beautiful it takes your breath away" are loaded. They give a very positive impression. However, this hidden meaning cannot be proved. It is not fact.

**C. Look for what isn't there.** Biased writers often leave out information that does not support their bias. For example, the writer might say "the Mali empire failed," but leave out the fact that before it declined, it succeeded for centuries.

◄ Everything you read was written by someone. You need to use your skills to sort out whether to believe what the writer says.

**D. Think about the tone.** Tone is the overall feeling of a piece of writing. It shows the writer's attitude toward the subject: "From burning desert to steamy tropics, the climates of Africa are unbearable." This sentence gives you the clear impression that the writer has negative feelings about the climates of Africa. Unbiased writing provides the facts and lets the reader form his or her own opinions.

## Apply the Skill

The selection in the box is a biased, one-paragraph description of the early African empire of Ghana. To spot the bias, follow steps A through D, at left. Consider these questions: Are there any opinions disguised as facts in the selection? What words give a positive or negative impression of the West African kingdoms? What important facts about West African kingdoms does the writer fail to include? How would you describe the tone of the writing? Positive? Negative? After you have finished, describe the West African kingdoms in one paragraph without bias.

### West African Kingdoms

Between the 3500s and the 1500s, West Africa was a terrible place to live. People couldn't even survive without salt. They were forced to trade their most precious gold just to get enough salt to stay alive. In the kingdom of Ghana, the kings forced people to pay money just to carry salt, gold, and other goods through the land. The Ghanaian kingdom became so weak that it fell to the crushing power of the kingdom of Mali.

# Review and Activities

## Reviewing Main Ideas

1. List some of the ways in which early Africans made a living.
2. What were Africa's earliest civilizations like?
3. List several effects of the Bantu migrations.
4. How did Africa's kingdoms and city-states become wealthy?
5. (a) How did the relationship of Europeans and Africans begin? (b) How did it change?
6. Explain two effects of the Atlantic slave trade on Africa.
7. What factors helped lead to independence for many African countries?
8. Describe two types of government used in African countries after independence.
9. How are Africans working to improve their economies?
10. How are Africans working to improve social conditions?

## Reviewing Key Terms

Use each key term below in a sentence that shows the meaning of the term.

1. hunter-gatherer
2. fertile
3. surplus
4. civilization
5. migrate
6. ethnic group
7. Quran
8. city-state
9. colonize
10. nationalism
11. Pan-Africanism
12. democracy
13. commercial farming
14. literacy
15. life expectancy

## Critical Thinking

1. **Recognizing Cause and Effect** Many of Africa's cities and countries are located along trade routes. How has trade affected Africa's history?

2. **Expressing Problems Clearly** The Atlantic slave trade lasted from the 1500s to the 1800s. Then the "scramble for Africa" began. How did the slave trade and the scramble for Africa affect traditional African cultures?

## Graphic Organizer

Copy the web onto a sheet of paper. Then fill in the empty spaces to complete a web of African history.

African History

# Map Activity

## Africa

For each place listed below, write the letter from the map that shows its location.

1. Senegal

2. Great Zimbabwe

3. Tombouctou

4. Cape of Good Hope

5. Kilwa

6. Kingdom of Mali

7. Nubia

8. Aksum

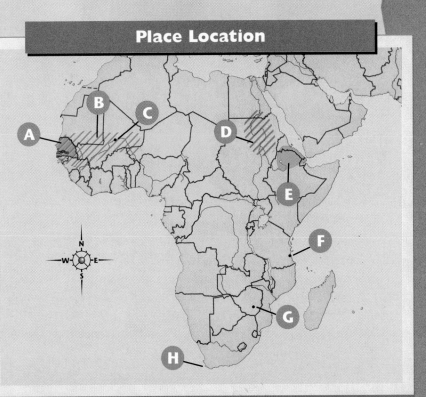

**Place Location**

# Writing Activity

## Writing a Speech

In the 1800s, many people in the United States spoke out against slavery. They were called abolitionists, because they wanted to abolish, or put an end to, slavery.

Pretend that you are an abolitionist living in the 1800s. Use what you have learned about the slave trade to write a speech that will help persuade people that slavery is wrong.

## Internet Activity

Use a search engine to find **AfricaOnline.** Choose **Kids Only** and then choose **Learn About Africa.** Click on the **People** icon. Read about notable Africans who have influenced Africa's history. Research one person. Send your report and illustration to AfricaOnline to be posted on their website.

# Skills Review

**Turn to the Skills Activity.**

Review the steps for recognizing bias. (a) In your own words, explain the difference between biased and unbiased writing. (b) How can you determine whether a writer is biased?

# How Am I Doing?

**Answer these questions to check your progress.**

1. Can I explain how early humans lived in Africa?

2. Can I identify the ancient civilizations of Africa and name their accomplishments?

3. Do I understand how European rule affected Africa?

4. Can I identify the challenges that African nations have faced since independence?

5. What information from this chapter can I use in my book project?

# CHAPTER
# 3

# Cultures of Africa

## PICTURE ACTIVITIES

*An African market brings together a wide variety of people and goods. Here you can buy baskets, spices, scarves, or a lamb. You can get a haircut, listen to a storyteller, or watch acrobatic dancers perform. To help you begin to understand Africa's cultures, do the following:*

### Look for clues
From this picture, what can you tell about how these Africans live? How do they dress? What kinds of products do they make and sell?

### Make a list of questions
Pick a person in the picture whose life you would like to know more about. Make a list of questions that you would ask this person if you could. As you read, see if some of your questions are answered.

# The Cultures of North Africa

## BEFORE YOU READ

### Reach Into Your Background

Suppose you have been given the assignment of describing your way of life to students in North Africa. How would you answer the following questions: What is a day in your life like? What is your school like? What is your home like? Think about your answers as you read this section.

### Questions to Explore

1. What is culture?
2. How does Islam influence life in North Africa?
3. How has its Mediterranean location affected the cultures of North Africa?

### Key Terms

culture
cultural diffusion

### Key Places

Sahara
Mediterranean Sea

---

**T**hirteen-year-old Meena lives in the city of Marrakech (muh RAH kehsh) in Morocco, a country in North Africa. Every morning she works in a factory, weaving carpets. She learned to weave carpets from her mother, who learned the skill from her mother. Carpets play an important role in Moroccan life. They are an export. And in some Moroccan homes, they serve as more than just floor coverings. They are used as chairs, beds, and prayer mats. In the afternoon, Meena leaves the factory to attend school. Her day ends at sunset, when she hears the crier who calls out from the nearby mosque, a Muslim house of worship. Muslims are followers of the religion of Islam. When she hears the call, Meena recites this prayer in Arabic: "There is no God but God, and Muhammad is His prophet."

## What Is Culture?

Meena's way of life is different in some ways from yours. That is partly because her culture is different.

▼ Moroccan weavers decorate their carpets with intricate designs. Which of these carpets would you buy? What would you use it for?

**Building With Adobe**
*Adobe* is an ancient Egyptian word. It refers to a brick made of earth and straw. Arabs brought adobe-making techniques to Spain. Later, the Spanish brought the use of adobe to what is now the south-western United States. People in the Southwest still build adobe homes.

▼ Adobe bricks fall apart if they are often exposed to cold or wet weather. They can only be used in hot, dry climates. The picture below shows adobe houses in Morocco.

**Culture** is the way of life of a group of people who share similar beliefs and customs.

Culture has many elements. Culture includes food, clothing, homes, jobs, language, and so on. It also includes things that are not so easy to see, such as how people view their world and what their religion is. These ideas shape the way people behave. Meena, for example, takes time from her activities to pray several times a day.

Cultures in different places have common elements. In many rural villages in Morocco, for example, houses are made of thick adobe, a type of brick made from sun-dried clay. Thick adobe walls help keep out the heat. Across the globe, in Mexico, and in the southwestern United States, many people in rural areas also live in adobe houses.

## The Influence of Islam

Religion is an important part of North African culture. Islam is the religion of most North Africans. More than 95 percent of North Africans are Muslims.

Like Jews and Christians, Muslims believe in one God. *Allah* is the Arabic word for God. Muslims believe that Muhammad, as well as the Old Testament prophets and Jesus, was God's messenger. The main duties of a Muslim are outlined in the Five Pillars of Islam, shown in the chart on the next page.

## The Five Pillars of Islam

| Duty | Description |
|------|-------------|
| Declaration of Faith | Declaring belief in one God and in Muhammad as God's final messenger |
| Prayer | Reciting prayers five times a day: at dawn, at midday, in the afternoon, at sunset, and in the evening |
| Almsgiving | Giving a portion of one's wealth to the needy |
| Fasting | Not eating or drinking from sunrise to sunset during the ninth month in the Muslim year, Ramadan |
| Pilgrimage | Making the *hajj*, or pilgrimage to Mecca, at least once in a lifetime if able |

38482

**Chart Study** Actions speak louder than words, so one form of Muslim worship is to do things to please God, like helping other people. Muslims must also perform the Five Pillars of Islam. **Critical Thinking** Which of the Five Pillars do you think is illustrated by the photo on the right?

## Five Pillars of Islam

The sacred book of Islam is the Quran. Besides teaching about God, the Quran provides a guide to life. Like the Bible, the Quran forbids lying, stealing, and murder. It also prohibits gambling, eating pork, and drinking alcohol.

The Islamic system of law is based on the Quran. Islamic law governs all aspects of life, including family life, business practices, banking, and government.

**Islam Unifies the People of North Africa**   Islam and the Arabic language unify the different peoples of North Africa. These peoples are spread out over a large area that includes the following countries: Egypt, Libya, Tunisia, Algeria, and Morocco. People here have many different backgrounds and ways of life.

An ethnic group is a group of people who share language, religion, or cultural traditions. Most North Africans are Arabs. But the region has other ethnic groups, too. The largest of these is the Berbers. About 20 million Berbers live in North Africa, mainly in Algeria and Morocco. Most Berbers speak Arabic as well as Berber. Some live in cities, but most live in small villages in rugged mountain areas. They make their living by herding and farming. The Tuareg (TWAH rehg) are a group of

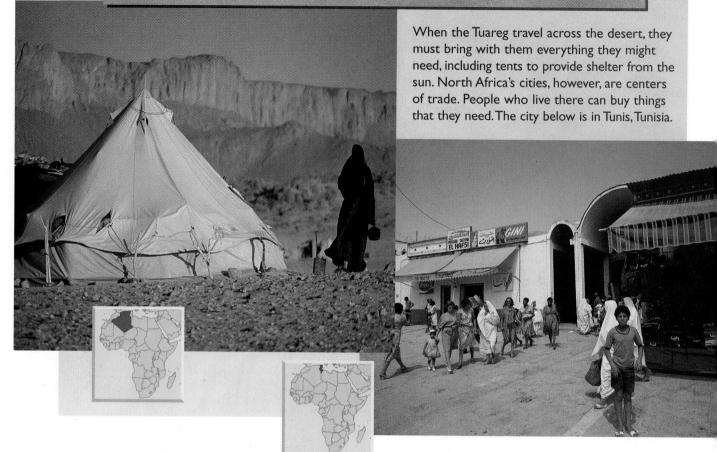

When the Tuareg travel across the desert, they must bring with them everything they might need, including tents to provide shelter from the sun. North Africa's cities, however, are centers of trade. People who live there can buy things that they need. The city below is in Tunis, Tunisia.

Berbers who live in the Sahara, the great desert that stretches across North Africa. The Tuareg herd camels, goats, and other livestock.

In parts of rural North Africa, some people live much as their parents and grandparents did. But traditional and modern ways of life mix in towns and large cities like Cairo (KY roh), Egypt, and Tunis, Tunisia. Like Meena, who weaves carpets, some city people work at traditional crafts. Others are architects, engineers, scientists, and bankers. Some sell baskets in outdoor markets. Others sell television sets in modern stores.

Arab and Berber, urban and rural, architect and herder—the peoples of North Africa live vastly different lives, yet almost all consider themselves fellow Muslims. Islam forms a common bond of culture among North Africans.

## Cultural Change in North Africa

North Africa's mix of traditional and modern ways of life shows that culture does not stay the same forever. It changes all the time.

**How Culture Spreads**   Cultural changes often occur when people travel. As they travel, people bring their customs and ideas with them. They also pick up new ideas and customs. In this way, customs

**READ ACTIVELY**

**Visualize** What sights might you see if you were walking through an outdoor market in a North African city? How would these sights be different from what you might see inside a modern skyscraper?

and ideas spread from one place to another. The movement of customs and ideas is called **cultural diffusion.** The word *diffuse* means "to spread out."

**A Mediterranean Outlook**  One factor that has aided the diffusion of culture in North Africa is location. Find North Africa on the map below. North Africans have long viewed their region as a gateway to three continents: Africa, Europe, and Asia. Can you see why? This Mediterranean outlook dates back to early history.

Because of its location, North Africa has been a hub of trade. Throughout history, the people of North Africa have traded with people in Europe, Asia, and other parts of Africa. Thus, they have influenced, and been influenced by, cultures in all these places.

The mixing of cultures in North Africa did not occur only through trade. It also occurred through conquest. North Africa is home to one of the world's oldest civilizations—ancient Egypt. The ancient Egyptians developed trade links with ancient civilizations in both Europe and Southwest Asia. They both conquered and were conquered by other empires. These conquests helped bring about cultural diffusion.

**Connect** What cities in the United States are centers of trade?

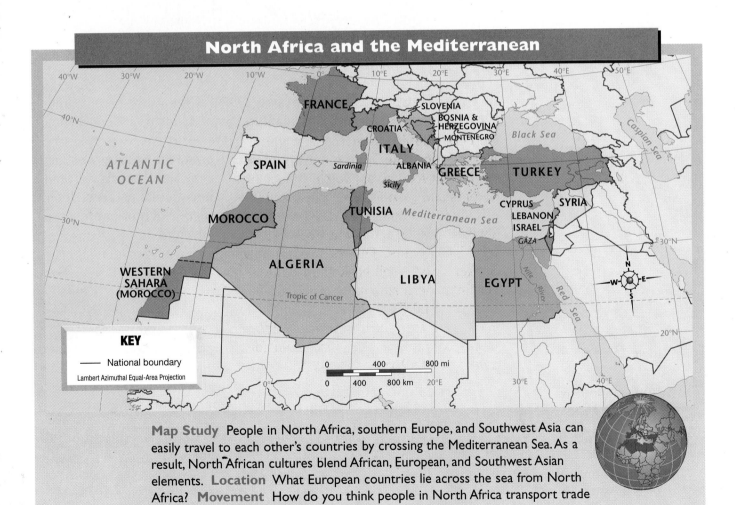

## North Africa and the Mediterranean

**KEY**

— National boundary

Lambert Azimuthal Equal-Area Projection

**Map Study** People in North Africa, southern Europe, and Southwest Asia can easily travel to each other's countries by crossing the Mediterranean Sea. As a result, North African cultures blend African, European, and Southwest Asian elements. **Location** What European countries lie across the sea from North Africa? **Movement** How do you think people in North Africa transport trade goods to other countries?

► Muslims often build a large, empty space into the middle of their mosques. Why? In countries with more than one culture and religion, Muslims use mosques as community centers. The empty space can be used for many different kinds of activities, including education.

**Preserving Muslim Culture**  One of the more recent influences on North Africa is Western culture. Some Muslims are concerned that their countries are becoming too Western. More people are wearing Western clothes, buying Western products, seeing Western films, and adapting Western ideas. Some Muslims fear that this will lead to the loss of Muslim values and traditions. They want to preserve their way of life. All over Africa, people face the challenge of how to preserve the traditions they value as their countries modernize.

## SECTION 1 REVIEW

1. **Define** (a) culture, (b) cultural diffusion.

2. **Identify** (a) Sahara, (b) Mediterranean Sea.

3. How does Islam affect everyday life in North Africa?

4. How has North Africa's location contributed to cultural diffusion?

**Critical Thinking**

5. **Making Comparisons** Which aspects of North African culture are similar to and which are different from your culture? Make a list of the similarities and differences.

**Activity**

6. **Writing to Learn** What traditions in your culture do you think are worth preserving? Write an essay describing the customs you value most.

# The Cultures of West Africa

## BEFORE YOU READ

**Reach Into Your Background**

How much do you know about different ethnic groups in the United States? Make a list of three or four groups. Jot down notes about each group's culture. Does the group speak a language other than English? What special customs or beliefs does the group have?

**Questions to Explore**

**1.** Why does West Africa have such a variety of cultures?

**2.** What effects do family ties have on West African culture?

**3.** How has urbanization affected the cultures of West Africa?

**Key Terms**

cultural diversity
lineage
kinship
clan
nuclear family
griot
extended family

In Mauritania, North Africa meets West Africa. Here, the Sahara merges into the savanna, or grasslands. Hamadi (hah MAH dee) is a teacher in a small village school in southern Mauritania. Although the country's official language is Arabic, Hamadi teaches French in the school. But at home, he speaks Poular, the language of the Halpoular, one of Mauritania's main ethnic groups.

▼ Children in Mauritania do not always have paper and pencils, but that doesn't stop them from learning. Instead, they use slates and chalk.

## Cultural Diversity of West Africa

Being able to speak more than one language is useful in Africa, and especially in West Africa. Seventeen countries make up this region. West Africa also has hundreds of ethnic groups. Because of its many ethnic groups, West Africa is famous for its **cultural diversity**—it has a wide variety of cultures. Unlike the ethnic groups of North Africa, West Africans are not united by a single religion or a common language.

**Predict** How do you think the cultural diversity of West Africa affects the lives of its people?

**West Africans Speak Many Languages** Think about your community. Imagine that the people who live nearby speak a different language. How would you communicate with them? Suppose you wanted to shop in a store, eat in a restaurant, or attend a sports event in the next town. It might seem like visiting another country.

This situation is real for many West Africans. The hundreds of ethnic groups in West Africa speak different languages. Sometimes groups in neighboring villages speak different languages.

To communicate, most West Africans speak more than one language. Many speak four or five languages. They use these different languages when they travel or conduct business. This practice helps unify countries with many ethnic groups.

**West Africans Have Many Ways of Making a Living** West Africa's ethnic groups differ in more than just the language they speak. Like North Africans, West Africans have many ways of making of a living. Most West Africans live in rural areas. A typical village consists of a group of homes surrounded by farmland. The village people grow food for themselves and cash crops to sell.

In the Sahara and the dry Sahel just south of the Sahara, many people herd cattle, goats, sheep, or camels. Along the coast, most West Africans make a living by fishing. Some West Africans live in large cities where they may work in hospitals, hotels, or office buildings.

## A Market in Dakar, Senegal

At this open-air market in Dakar, Senegal, customers can buy many kinds of groceries, including fresh fish. Dakar is a wealthy port city on Senegal's Atlantic coast. Senegal has built up its fishing industry so much that fish are its most important export. **Critical Thinking** Besides the people who catch the fish, who benefits from Dakar's fishing industry?

Ways of making a living in West Africa vary from country to country. Most people in Mali (below left) make a living growing crops such as grains, corn, potatoes, yams, and cassava. But in some countries, such as Côte d'Ivoire, almost half the people live and work in cities. The University of Côte d'Ivoire (below right), in the capital city of Yamoussoukro (yahm uh soo kroh), employs hundreds of people.

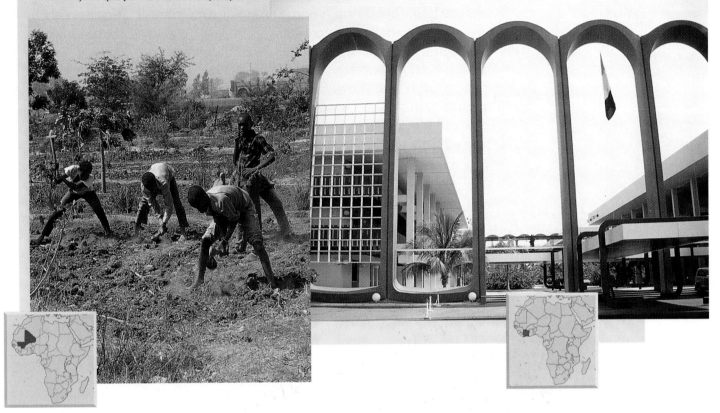

# Belonging to Groups

Like North Africans, West Africans see themselves as members of a number of groups. Just as you belong to a family, an ethnic group, and a country, so do West Africans.

**The Strong Ties of Kinship**   One of the strongest bonds West Africans have is **kinship,** which refers to a family relationship. The first level of kinship is the **nuclear family,** which consists of parents and their children. The next level is the **extended family,** which includes other relatives besides parents and children. It may include grandparents, aunts, uncles, and cousins. Many West Africans live in extended families.

Extended families work together and take care of each other. Family members care for the elderly and those who are sick or less well-off. They make decisions together. And they watch over all the children in the village. This custom is reflected in the well-known African proverb, "It takes a village to raise a child." Neighbors always pitch in and help one another. Thus, kinship adds to a strong sense of community.

**READ ACTIVELY**

**Connect** How do people outside your immediate family help to raise you?

**Larger Groups: Lineages and Clans**   In many rural areas, kinship reaches beyond extended families. A group of families may trace their descent back to a common ancestor. Such a group forms a **lineage.** Several lineages form a **clan.** The people in a clan all have roots back to an even earlier ancestor.

**Tracing Lineage**   Different traditions also govern the way groups trace their lineage. Some groups are matrilineal. They trace their lineage through women ancestors. Property is passed on to children through the female side of a family. In a matrilineal society, if people marry outside the clan, the husband comes to live with the wife's clan. The result is that the village has a core of women who live there. The men they marry are newcomers, who move into the homes of the local women. Most groups, however, are patrilineal. They trace their descent through the male side of a family.

## Changes in Family Life

Although traditional family ties remain strong in West Africa, family life is changing. More people are moving from rural villages to urban areas, or cities. This trend, called urbanization, is occurring throughout Africa and the world.

▼ In places like Tombouctou, Mali, where the climate is hot, some families in rural areas do many household chores outside.

Bus drivers must find their way carefully through the crowded streets of Lagos, Nigeria. Like people all over Africa, many of these people have come to Lagos to find work. **Critical Thinking** Why do you think it would be easier to find a job in a city than in a rural area?

Many young men come to West Africa's cities to find jobs. The women often stay in the rural homes. They raise the children and farm the land. The men come home from time to time to visit their families and to share what they have earned.

## Keeping Traditions Alive

In West Africa today, people are adapting to change in various ways. But most West Africans still keep strong family ties. People still pass their history, values, and traditions on to the young.

One important way in which West African traditions are being preserved is through storytelling. Traditional West African stories are spoken rather than written. The stories teach children cultural values. A storyteller called a **griot** (GREE oh) passes this oral tradition from one generation to another. The oral tradition of West Africa tells the histories of ethnic groups and kinships. Stories of tricksters, animal fables, proverbs, riddles, and songs are also part of West Africa's oral tradition. This Yoruba proverb reflects the value placed on passing on traditions: "The young can't teach traditions to the old."

### LINKS TO LANGUAGE ARTS

**West African Folk Tales** West Africa has a rich tradition of folk tales. One type of tale is the escape story, in which a clever person thinks of a way out of an impossible situation. One tale from Benin is about a cruel king who orders his people to build him a new palace. He tells them that they must start at the top and build down. The people despair. Then a wise old man invites the king to begin by setting the first stone in place. The people are saved.

When a griot tells a story, it can take all night or even several days. The audience does not mind, because the stories are usually scary, funny, or exciting. This griot, from Côte d'Ivoire, is telling these children a legend from their history. The children pay careful attention, because the griot acts out parts of the story as he goes along.

West African traditions have greatly influenced other cultures, especially American culture. About half of the enslaved Africans who were brought to the United States came from West Africa. They brought with them the only things they could: their ideas, stories, dances, music, and customs. The stories of Brer Rabbit as well as blues and jazz music have their roots in West Africa. Today, West African culture—the stories, music, dances, art, cooking, clothing—is more popular than ever. Griot guitarists and other musicians from West Africa have international followings. In recent years, three Nobel Prize winners for literature have been African. One of them, Wole Soyinka (WOH lay shaw YING kah), is from the West African country of Nigeria.

## SECTION 2 REVIEW

1. **Define** (a) cultural diversity, (b) kinship, (c) nuclear family, (d) extended family, (e) lineage, (f) clan, (g) griot.

2. In what ways is West Africa culturally diverse?

3. Describe the importance of family ties to West Africans.

4. How has urbanization changed the lives of West Africans?

**Critical Thinking**

5. **Drawing Conclusions** How has the extended family helped to develop a sense of community among West Africans?

**Activity**

6. **Writing to Learn** Imagine that you live in a small village in an extended family in West Africa. Make a list of the advantages and disadvantages of your way of life.

# The Cultures of East Africa

**BEFORE YOU READ**

**Reach Into Your Background**
Think about the language you speak. How many words can you identify that come from another language? What about the words *banjo, canyon,* or *succotash? Banjo* comes from an African language, possibly Kimbundu. *Canyon* comes from Spanish. *Succotash* comes from Narragansett, a Native American language. See if you can find other examples.

**Questions to Explore**
1. How has location affected the development of East African cultures?
2. What role does the Swahili language play in East African cultures?
3. How and why are ideas about land ownership changing in East Africa?

**Key Terms**
plantation

**Key People and Places**
Julius Nyerere
East Africa

Alemeseged Taddesse Mekonnen (ah LEM uh seh ged tah DAY say meh KOH nen) is an Ethiopian who works in a bakery in St. Louis, Missouri. Before coming to the United States, he lived with his extended family in Gonder, a city in northern Ethiopia. His father owned a large store there. Mekonnen speaks three languages: Amharic, Arabic, and English. At home, in Ethiopia, Amharic was his first language. Because he is Muslim, he learned Arabic to study the Quran. And he learned English in school, as other Ethiopians do.

Mekonnen misses life with his close-knit family in Ethiopia. "At home we ate every meal together. If anyone was missing, we waited until they came home," he says. Mekonnen hopes to return home someday. He lives in the United States, but his heart is in Ethiopia.

▼ Shown below is the city of Gonder, in northern Ethiopia. Ethiopia is one of the countries in East Africa.

75

# Living Along the Indian Ocean

Knowing three languages is not unusual for an East African, just as it is not for a West African. In Ethiopia alone, more than 70 different languages are spoken. Like West Africa, East Africa has many ethnic groups who speak different languages. The region has great cultural diversity.

East Africa's diversity is the result of its location. Many ethnic groups have migrated to East Africa from other regions of the continent. For example, about 2,000 years ago, Bantu-speaking peoples migrated to East Africa from West Africa. In addition, East Africa has a long coastline along the Indian Ocean. The ocean connects the people of East Africa to people living across the ocean to the east. These people include Arabs, Indians, and other Asians. The connection extends even to countries as far away as China and Malaysia.

This link dates back to early times. Arab traders began to settle in the coastal villages of East Africa nearly 2,000 years ago. They brought Arab culture into East Africa, where it mixed with various African cultures. This mixture produced the Swahili culture.

## Lunch Time for a Kenyan Family

Shown above is a family from Kenya. Families in East Africa traditionally eat their meals together, using one bowl or plate. In the traditional style, they use their fingers rather than forks and spoons. **Critical Thinking** What foods do people in the United States share from one plate or bowl?

Kampala is Uganda's largest city and leading trade center. It is a religious center as well. You can find Muslim mosques, Hindu temples, and Christian churches here.

## Swahili Culture

The Swahili are Africans who have mixed African and Arab ancestry. They live along the east coast of Africa from Somalia to Mozambique. Their language is also called Swahili. It is a Bantu language, but it contains many Arabic words. The Swahili are just one of hundreds of ethnic groups in East Africa. But their language is widely used for business and communication among many ethnic groups throughout the region.

Swahili is the first language of about 49 million people worldwide. It also serves as the second language of millions of East Africans. Swahili is the official language of Kenya and Tanzania. In Tanzania, children are educated in Swahili through the primary grades. Later, they learn English as well. By promoting the use of Swahili, these nations are trying to preserve their African heritage.

## A Mixture of Religions

Like languages, religious beliefs in East Africa reflect the cultural diversity of the region. Both Islam and Christianity have large followings in the region. Islam was introduced into East Africa by Arab traders. The Romans introduced Christianity into some of their North African territories. Later, it spread into Ethiopia. In the 1800s,

### LINKS ACROSS THE WORLD

**Kwanzaa** Swahili culture and language have also come to the United States. Many African Americans celebrate Kwanzaa (KWAN zah), a holiday based on a traditional African harvest festival. The word *Kwanzaa* is related to the Swahili word for "first." Kwanzaa is based on a set of values that also have Swahili names. These include *umoja* (oo MOH juh), or unity; *kuumba* (koo OOM buh), or creativity; and *imani* (ee MAHN ee), or faith.

Europeans pushed into Africa and spread Christianity farther. In addition, traditional religions remain alive in East Africa and throughout the continent.

## Changing Ideas About Land

In East Africa, as in the rest of Africa, most people live in rural areas, where they farm and tend livestock. The ways in which they view and work the land are part of the culture of East Africans.

**Before Land Was Owned**   Before Europeans took over parts of Africa in the 1800s, individual Africans did not own land. People did not buy or sell land. The very idea of owning land did not exist. Families had the right to farm plots of land near the village, but the actual plots might vary in size and location over time.

Traditionally, extended families farmed the land to produce food for the whole group. Men cleared the land and broke up the soil. Women then planted the seed, tended the fields, and harvested the crops. Meanwhile, the men herded livestock or traded goods. This division of roles still exists in many parts of Africa today.

**The Rise and Fall of Plantations**   The idea of privately owned land was introduced into many parts of Africa by European settlers. In parts of East Africa, the British set up plantations. A plantation is a large farm where cash crops are grown. When many African countries became independent, they broke up the old colonial plantations. They sold the land to individual Africans.

Some land in East Africa is still available to buy. But much of it is poor farmland in areas where few people live. In fertile areas like the Ethiopian Highlands and the Rift Valley, land for farming is scarce. Many people live in these areas where the farmland is fertile. In densely populated countries, such as Rwanda and Burundi, conflicts have developed over land.

## Where Is Home?

Traditionally, Africans feel a strong bond to the land where they grew up. Like the rest of Africa, East Africa is becoming increasingly urban. Yet even people who spend most of their time in a city do not call it home. If asked where home is, an East African will name the village of his or her family or clan. Most people consider their life in the city temporary. They expect to return to their villages at some time.

Tanzania's former president Julius Nyerere (nyuh RAIR ay) is one example. Nyerere continues to be involved in world affairs, but he now lives far from Dar es Salaam, the capital city of Tanzania. After he

**READ ACTIVELY**

**Connect** How do you feel when you return home after being away for a long time?

◀ The coastal city of Mombasa, Kenya, began as a trading center in the 1200s. One of its chief exports was ivory. Today, metal arches shaped like elephant tusks memorialize Kenya's ivory trade. While cities like Mombasa can be beautiful and exciting, to most East Africans a city can never really be home.

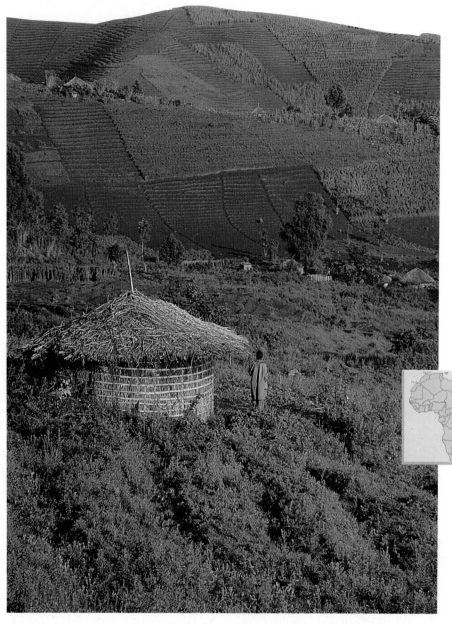

stepped down as president in 1985, Nyerere moved back to his home village. There, he grows corn and millet on his farm. He spends his mornings working in the fields. In an interview in 1996, Nyerere said: "In a sense I am a very rural person. I grew up here, and [working in] Dar es Salaam was a duty. I did my duty and after retiring in 1985, I came back here and said, 'Ah, it's good to be back.'"

Other East Africans feel the same. They may do their duty by earning money in the city. But their homes—and their hearts—are in their rural villages.

◄ On his family farm in Rwanda, this farmer grows potatoes, corn, beans, and cabbage. East Africans sometimes move away from their farms, but they almost always hope to return to them one day.

## SECTION 3 REVIEW

1. **Define** plantation.

2. **Identify** (a) Julius Nyerere, (b) East Africa.

3. **Describe** some ways in which East Africa's location along the Indian Ocean has affected its cultures.

4. Why is Swahili spoken by so many people in East Africa?

5. Explain the changes in ideas about land ownership in East Africa.

**Critical Thinking**

6. **Making Comparisons** How did traditional East African ideas about land differ from the ideas of Europeans who took over parts of Africa?

**Activity**

7. **Writing to Learn** Write a description of the place that you consider home. Tell what it means to you and explain why.

# The Cultures of Central and Southern Africa

## BEFORE YOU READ

### Reach Into Your Background

Think of a goal you had to work hard to achieve at home or at school. Why was it important to you to achieve your goal? Think about the plan you made and the strategies you used to achieve your goal. What obstacles did you have to overcome? How did you feel when you finally succeeded?

### Questions to Explore

1. How has the country of South Africa influenced the entire region of Southern Africa?
2. How did migrant labor give rise to a new group identity among the peoples of Southern Africa?
3. How does Central Africa reflect the cultural diversity of all of Africa?

### Key Terms

migrant worker

### Key Places

Republic of South Africa
Southern Africa
Central Africa
Zaire

The African National Congress (ANC), a political party in the Republic of South Africa, played a key role in gaining political and civil rights for all South Africans. Until 1991, Europeans in South Africa had denied equal rights to blacks, who make up a majority of the population. Three countries—Tanzania, Zambia, and Zimbabwe—adopted the ANC anthem for their national anthems. Here are the words to the ANC anthem:

> "Bless, O Lord, our land of Africa
> Lift its name and make its people free.
> Take the gifts we offer unto Thee
> Hear us, faithful sons.
> Hear us, faithful sons."

▼ These teenagers sang the ANC anthem for the opening of Parliament in Cape Town, South Africa.

# The Pull of South Africa

South Africa is just one country in Southern Africa, but it has had, by far, the greatest impact on the region. Its political and economic influence has touched the lives of millions of people.

**Ask Questions** What questions do you have about South Africa's influence on the rest of southern Africa?

**Political Influence of South Africa**   Until the 1990s, a European minority ruled South Africa. In 1923, they separated South Africans into categories based on skin color. People of African descent were classified as black, people of European descent as white, and people of mixed ancestry as colored. Asians, who were mostly from India, formed the fourth category. Blacks, coloreds, and Asians could not vote and did not have other basic rights. For nearly 70 years, these groups struggled to gain their rights.

The struggle for basic rights created a sense of nationalism among black South Africans. White settlers, not blacks, had established the nation of South Africa. But as blacks struggled to gain political rights, they began to think of themselves as members of the nation. They wanted to take part as equal citizens in running the nation. The struggle for majority rule in South Africa lasted so long that it inspired similar movements in Namibia and what is now Zimbabwe.

**Economic Influence of South Africa**   South Africa is the richest and most industrialized country on the continent of Africa. It produces two fifths of the manufactured goods, half of the minerals, and one fifth of the agricultural products of the entire continent. Its economic power and needs have affected all of Southern Africa because its demand for labor has been so great. To provide a labor force for the mines, South African companies used workers from throughout Southern Africa.

To get jobs in South Africa, hundreds of thousands of workers migrated from nearby countries. Workers were allowed to stay in South Africa for only a short time. New workers were always needed. A large force of **migrant workers,** people who move from place to place to find work, was soon created.

## A South African Gold Miner

This miner commutes to work by crawling through cramped tunnels until he reaches this room, where he does not have space to stand up. **Critical Thinking** What do you think a work day for this gold miner would be like?

In 1912, South African blacks organized the African National Congress (ANC) to fight for equality. The ANC used boycotts, rallies, and work strikes to force the government to reform its laws. Many ANC members, including Nelson Mandela, were jailed for their actions. Mandela spent almost 30 years in jail. The struggle finally paid off. In the 1990s, South Africa ended its discriminatory laws and gave nonwhite South Africans the right to vote for the first time. Mandela became South Africa's president.

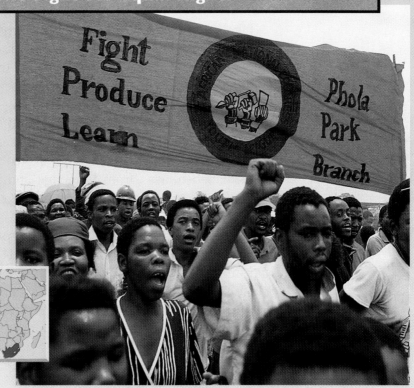

# Migrant Workers Form a New Group Identity

Mine workers in South Africa were from many countries. They lived together in compounds, or fenced-in groups of homes. They were far from their families, clans, and ethnic groups. They worked long hours in dangerous conditions for low wages.

**A Person Is a Person Because of People**   The migrant mine workers came to rely on one another. They began to think of themselves as a group—as workers. This kind of group identity was new for Southern Africans. It was not based on family or ethnic group. Group identity is very important in Africa. This is reflected in the African proverb "A person is a person because of people." It means that a person is who he or she is because of his or her relationships with other people. The migrant workers formed a new identity based on how they related to each other as workers.

**Mine Workers Form a Union**   In the 1980s, the mine workers in South Africa formed a union—the National Union of Mineworkers. This union was illegal at the time. But it played a leading role in the drive for equal rights. The union workers sometimes went on strike in support of their causes. Thus, the new identity of the mine workers led them to take group action.

**READ ACTIVELY**

Predict How do you think South Africa's mines affected its culture?

# Tradition and Change in Central Africa

Like people in Southern Africa and the rest of Africa, Central Africans have gone through many cultural changes in the 1900s. But many people in the region also follow old traditions. Like the rest of the continent, Central Africa displays great cultural diversity. The country of Zaire, alone, has about 200 ethnic groups.

One ethnic group in Zaire is the Mbuti (em BOO tee), who live in the rain forests. The Mbuti are unique because they live much as their ancestors did. In forest camps of 10 to 25 families, they make their dome-shaped houses from branches and leaves. For food, they hunt wild animals and gather wild plants. The culture of the Mbuti is more than 3,000 years old.

In contrast, millions of people live in crowded shantytowns or cinder-block apartments in Kinshasa, the largest city in Zaire. They walk or take buses or trucks to work in factories, offices, and hotels. Some people are Roman Catholics or Protestants. Others practice religions that blend Christian and traditional African beliefs. Still others are Muslims. On Saturday evenings, many people dance and listen to Zairian jazz in city dance halls.

**LINKS TO ART**

**Barkcloth Art** The Mbuti of Zaire use only renewable resources. For example, they make some of their cloth out of tree bark. Men pound the bark with mallets until it is almost as soft as velvet. Then women draw shapes and patterns on the cloth. Many art galleries in the United States and Europe collect Mbuti barkcloth drawings.

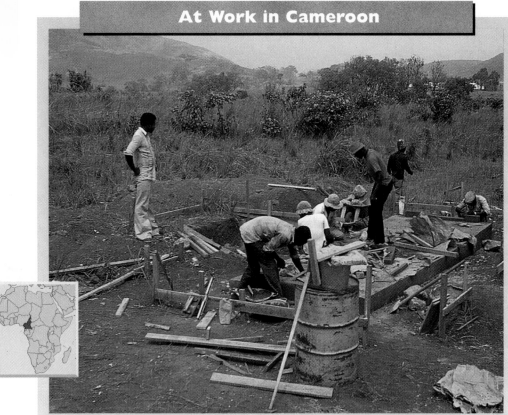

## At Work in Cameroon

Cameroon is a country in northwest Central Africa. Most people in Cameroon live in rural areas and make a living by farming or by herding cattle. These men are building farm structures used in taking care of cattle.

## A Modern City in an Old Location

Kinshasa is Zaire's capital. People have lived here since the late 1400s, making a living by fishing or trading on the Congo River. Today, people still fish on the Congo River, and it remains an important source of transportation. However, Kinshasa is also a center of government and industry.

What one writer said about North Africa applies to Southern Africa as well. To define the real North African, he said, "you have to define which one you mean: the rich or the poor, the Berber women of the mountains or the college girls on motorbikes...." Old, new, and mixtures of the two live on in all regions of Africa.

## SECTION 4 REVIEW

1. **Define** migrant worker.

2. **Identify** (a) Republic of South Africa, (b) Southern Africa, (c) Central Africa, (d) Zaire.

3. Describe the political and economic effects South Africa has had on the entire region of Southern Africa.

4. What was unusual about migrant workers in South Africa forming a group identity as workers?

5. In what ways are the cultures of Central Africa like those in other parts of Africa?

**Critical Thinking**

6. **Recognizing Cause and Effect** What positive and/or negative effects might South Africa's labor needs have had on the economies of nearby countries?

**Activity**

7. **Writing to Learn** Consider the life of a mine worker in a South African gold mine in the 1970s. Write the first verse of a song protesting miners' living and working conditions and wages.

# SKILLS ACTIVITY

# Assessing Your Understanding

Imagine you have a pen pal, a student your age from Africa. In one of her letters, she asks you this question: "What is your school like?" How would you answer?

You might describe it as a large school, or a small one. You could say whether it is in a rural area or in the heart of a big city. You could describe your school building, the classes you take, your teachers, your friends, and so on. This would be easy for you, because school is such a big part of your life. The classes you take, the people you see, and the books you read all seem normal to you.

But have you ever wondered what school is like for a person your age in Africa? You could ask your pen pal. Depending on where your pen pal lives, though, the answer would be different. A school in a big city in Egypt is very different from a school in rural Uganda. But every school in Africa has at least one thing in common with your school—students are there to learn. Like other students, if you want to study new things, you must learn to assess your understanding.

## Get Ready

What does "assessing your understanding" mean? It means checking to see how well you understand something you are reading or studying. If you assess your understanding as you go along, you will know what areas you need to read or think more about to make sure you understand. You can concentrate on studying those things. This can help you to get better grades. For example, by assessing your understanding before a test, you can predict what grade you will get on the test. And you will know exactly what you need to study if you want to get a higher grade. It can help you get more out of your reading. If you realize something does not make sense to you, you can use some strategies such as rereading or making a graphic organizer to help you understand the information.

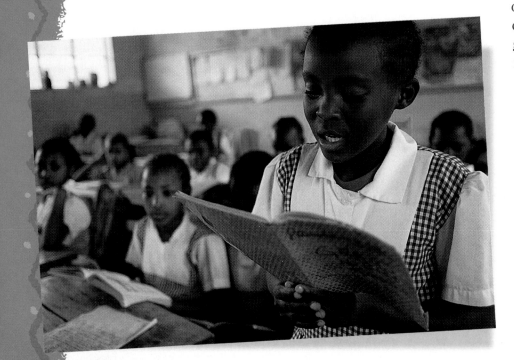

## Try It Out

A good way of assessing your understanding is to play a simple game called "Do I Understand?" To play, choose one assignment you completed recently. Then ask yourself the questions on the checklist.

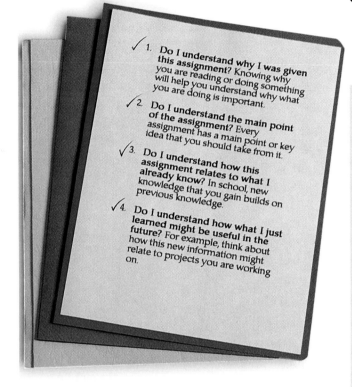

1. Do I understand why I was given this assignment? Knowing why you are reading or doing something will help you understand why what you are doing is important.

2. Do I understand the main point of the assignment? Every assignment has a main point or key idea that you should take from it.

3. Do I understand how this assignment relates to what I already know? In school, new knowledge that you gain builds on previous knowledge.

4. Do I understand how what I just learned might be useful in the future? For example, think about how this new information might relate to projects you are working on.

## Apply the Skill

Practice assessing your understanding with the short reading assignment in the box, "An African School" by David Lamb.

1. Now, reread Question 1 in the list above. Why is it worthwhile to learn about a school in Kenya? What key ideas about the school does the writer try to communicate?

2. Reread Question 2. What do you think is the main point of "An African School"?

3. Reread Question 3. How does the writer's description fit with what you have already learned about Africa? Consider such things as languages, climate, and the condition of the school. Does anything in the reading assignment surprise you, or is it what you expected?

4. Look at Question 4. What are two ways that the knowledge you have just gained could help you in the future?

### An African School

The Njumbi primary school [is] not far from the town of Karai in Kenya. . . . The headmaster, Michael Mathini, an energetic . . . man of thirty who rides a bicycle to work, greeted us at the door. He led us into his office and pointed with great pride to a wall graph showing that his students scored above the national average in the annual. . .examination.

The school has 620 students . . . and seventeen teachers who earned from $80 to $135 a month. . . . In the first-grade classroom across from Mathini's office, thirty or forty boys and girls were learning to count. . . They applauded . . . each time one of them gave the teacher the right answer. . . an ancient wooden radio sat on another teacher's desk and the dozen or so teenagers there strained through the heavy static to hear the creative writing lesson being broadcast in English from Nairobi.

# CHAPTER 3 — Review and Activities

## Reviewing Main Ideas

1. Describe how Islam has influenced the culture of North Africa.
2. What factor has greatly aided cultural diffusion in North Africa?
3. How is West Africa culturally diverse?
4. What role do family ties play in West African culture?
5. Explain how location has affected East African cultures.
6. How does the language of Swahili help unite the people of East Africa?
7. Why is the idea of privately owned land fairly new to East Africans?
8. How has South Africa affected the cultures of the entire region of Southern Africa?
9. What major effect did migrant labor have on the people of Southern Africa?
10. How is Central Africa like other parts of Africa?

## Reviewing Key Terms

Use each key term below in a sentence that shows the meaning of the term.

1. culture
2. cultural diffusion
3. cultural diversity
4. kinship
5. nuclear family
6. extended family
7. lineage
8. clan
9. griot
10. plantation
11. migrant worker

## Critical Thinking

1. **Identifying Central Issues** Explain why the proverb "A person is a person because of people" is particularly suited to African culture.
2. **Drawing Conclusions** What benefits and problems have come with modernization in Africa?

## Graphic Organizer

Copy the chart onto a sheet of paper. Then complete the chart by describing one or more key features of the cultures of each region.

| The Cultures of Africa | | | | |
|---|---|---|---|---|
| Region | North Africa | West Africa | East Africa | Central and Southern Africa |
| Culture | | | | |

# Map Activity

## Africa

For each place listed below, write the letter from the map that shows its location.

1. Mediterranean Sea
2. North Africa
3. West Africa
4. East Africa
5. Central and Southern Africa

# Writing Activity

## Writing a Dialogue

An exchange student from an African country has come to stay at your home for six weeks. You and your family are sharing your first dinner with the visitor. Write a dialogue in which you ask your visitor about African culture. Use what you have learned in this chapter to write your visitor's answers.

## Internet Activity

Use a search engine to find the **Africa Stories Project.** Read about the project. Then read the stories and the African reviewers' comments. Choose a story and research the culture, folk stories, history, and geography of the country where the story was set. Use what you learned about the country or region to write your own fictional Africa story.

# Skills Review

Turn to the Skills Activity.

Review the steps for assessing your understanding. Then look at the Writing Activity on this page. Ask yourself questions to assess whether you understand the reason for this writing assignment.

# How Am I Doing?

Answer these questions to check your progress.

1. Can I describe the cultural diversity of Africa?

2. Do I understand the role of kinship in African cultures?

3. Can I explain how urbanization has changed the way of life of many Africans?

4. What information from this chapter can I use in my unit project?

# The Language of Music

In the United States, you can hear music at parties, in concerts, on the radio, or even in supermarkets. It has many purposes. Music also has many roles in the cultures of African countries. Music may be used to send messages or to tell a story. It may organize work or celebrate a special occasion. In the United States, it is not uncommon to perform music by itself. People in African countries, however, rarely play music by itself. Most often, they combine music with dance, theater, words, games, or visual art.

Traditional African instruments include xylophones, lutes, harps, horns, flutes, clarinets, bells, and drums. Musicians can study for years to master their art, just as they do in the United States. In many African cultures, drums play an important role in traditional and modern music.

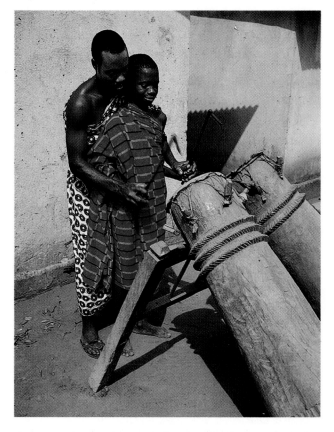

## Purpose

In this activity, you will research traditional African drums and make your own drum. As you work on this activity, you will learn how Africans make and use drums.

## Research African Drums

Traditionally, drums have been the most important instrument in African music. There are many types of drums, including the slit drum, the obodo, and the kettle drum. Use the information on this page to get you started. Then use encyclopedias, the Internet, and other resources to find out more about traditional African drums and how they differ. When you do research, look under subject headings such as African Arts, African Music, and Musical Instruments. You should also search under the names of specific drums.

Write down the names of several African drums. Then choose one drum to model your own after. Learn as much as you can about this kind of drum, including what materials it is made from, how it is played, how it is used, and where it is used.

# Build Your Own Drum

Once you have chosen a traditional African drum as a model, you can build your own drum. You may want to use items such as buckets, cans, or cartons for the body of your drum. For the head of the drum, you might use cloth, plastic, or paper. Also consider the following questions:

- How will you attach the head of the drum to the body?
- Is one side of the drum open or are both sides covered?
- How will you strike your drum?

If possible, use materials that are similar to the materials the traditional drums are made from. Experiment with different methods to see which sounds best.

# Play Your Drum

Figure out how you can use your drum in a way similar to the one you are modeling. For example, if the drum you are modeling was used to communicate messages across a long distance, think of a rhythmic code you can use to play a message to your classmates across the playground. If the drum was used as part of a drum group, you may want to write a short piece of music and play it with your classmates. If the drum accompanied a chant or song telling

## Links to Other Subjects

| | |
|---|---|
| Researching African instruments | **Music** |
| Researching traditional materials | **Life Science** |
| Building a drum | **Physical Science** |
| Communicating over distance | **Language Arts** |
| Using a drum as part of a drum group | **Math (rhythms), Music** |
| Writing a chant to accompany a drum | **Language Arts, Music** |
| Writing a paragraph comparing drums | **Language Arts** |

the history of a community, write a song telling a story about something that has happened to you or someone you know.

# Compare Drums

After you have built your drum and practiced with it, write a paragraph comparing your drum to its African model. You may want to present your work to the class and perform a piece of music.

Write a summary that describes how you built and used your drum. Be sure to answer the following questions in the summary.

1. How is your drum similar to and different from the African drum you used as a model?

2. What factors affect the way your drum sounds?

3. How did you adapt the original uses of the model drum?

**CHAPTER**

# 4

# Exploring North Africa

**SECTION 1**

## Egypt

HEARING THE CALL
OF ISLAM

**SECTION 2**

## Algeria

THE CASBAH AND
THE COUNTRYSIDE

**KEY**

— National boundary

⊛ National capital

• Other city

Lambert Azimuthal Equal-Area Projection

0     400     800 mi

0     400     800 km

# MAP ACTIVITIES

*Six countries make up the region of North Africa. Find them on the map above. To help you get to know this region, do the following:*

## Size up the region

Which country in the region looks the largest? Which country looks the smallest? What body of water lies on the region's northern boundary?

## Consider the location

Find the major cities of North Africa shown on this map. How close are they to the Mediterranean Sea? How do you think that nearness to the sea might have affected North Africa's cultures?

# Egypt

## HEARING THE CALL OF ISLAM

**Reach Into Your Background**

You probably have a favorite holiday that you look forward to all year. Think about what you do during the holiday. What special foods do you eat? What different songs do you sing? Why do you and your family celebrate on that holiday?

**Questions to Explore**

1. How does religion affect Egypt's culture?

2. How has the role of Islam in Egypt changed in recent times?

**Key Terms**
bazaar
fellaheen

**Key Places**
Cairo

At noon, the restaurants in Cairo stand empty. Egyptian teenagers try not to think about pita bread or sweet dates. Only certain people, such as the very young or those who are sick, eat regular meals. Is there a food shortage in Egypt? No, it's the Muslim holiday of Ramadan (ram uh DAHN). Muslims are followers of the religion of Islam. For a month, Muslims fast from dawn to dusk. A fast is a period when people go without food. During Ramadan, Muslims eat only when the sun is down.

But Muslims do more than fast during Ramadan. They also think of those who are less fortunate than themselves. And they try not to get angry when things go wrong.

## Islam in Egypt

Egypt is located in North Africa, where many of the world's Muslims live. Egypt is across the Red Sea from Saudi Arabia, where the messenger of Islam, Muhammad, was born. Islam spread from Saudi Arabia across North Africa. Today, the countries in this area have populations that are mostly Muslim. Look at the Country Profile on the next page. You can see that Islam is the major religion in Egypt. In fact, it is the country's official religion.

▼ More people live in Cairo than in any other city in Africa. Most of the people who live here are Muslim Arabs.

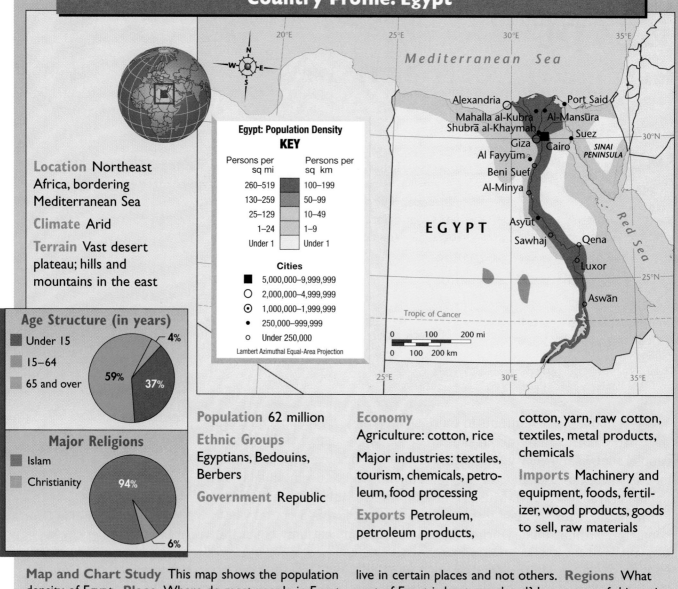

**Location** Northeast Africa, bordering Mediterranean Sea

**Climate** Arid

**Terrain** Vast desert plateau; hills and mountains in the east

**Egypt: Population Density**
**KEY**

| Persons per sq mi | Persons per sq km |
| --- | --- |
| 260–519 | 100–199 |
| 130–259 | 50–99 |
| 25–129 | 10–49 |
| 1–24 | 1–9 |
| Under 1 | Under 1 |

**Cities**
- ■ 5,000,000–9,999,999
- ○ 2,000,000–4,999,999
- ◉ 1,000,000–1,999,999
- • 250,000–999,999
- ○ Under 250,000

Lambert Azimuthal Equal-Area Projection

**Age Structure (in years)**
- Under 15
- 15–64
- 65 and over

4%
59%
37%

**Major Religions**
- Islam
- Christianity

94%
6%

**Population** 62 million

**Ethnic Groups** Egyptians, Bedouins, Berbers

**Government** Republic

**Economy**

Agriculture: cotton, rice

Major industries: textiles, tourism, chemicals, petroleum, food processing

**Exports** Petroleum, petroleum products, cotton, yarn, raw cotton, textiles, metal products, chemicals

**Imports** Machinery and equipment, foods, fertilizer, wood products, goods to sell, raw materials

**Map and Chart Study** This map shows the population density of Egypt. **Place** Where do most people in Egypt live? What are Egypt's three largest cities? **Interaction** Read the information in the Country Profile. Using this information, think of two reasons why people in Egypt live in certain places and not others. **Regions** What part of Egypt is least populated? Is any part of this region densely populated? Explain why. **Critical Thinking** Look at the chart of Egypt's major religions. What religion is most common in Egypt?

**Teachings and Practices** The Quran is the sacred book of the Muslims. It contains the basic teachings of Islam. Muslims believe that the Quran contains the words of God, which were revealed to Muhammad during the month of Ramadan. Muslims also believe that the Jewish Torah and the Christian Bible are the word of God.

Recordings of the Quran have become very popular in Egypt. As Ahmed Abdel Rahman (AH med AHB del RAHK mahn), a record store manager in Cairo, says, "You can get bored by a song after a few days. But no one gets bored listening to the Quran." During the day, many Egyptians listen to the recordings on audiotapes or on the government radio station.

Muslim scholars do not limit themselves to studying the Quran. From the 600s on, Muslims have studied art, literature, philosophy, math, astronomy, and medicine. Muslim mathematicians invented algebra, and Muslim astronomers accurately mapped the locations of the stars. A Muslim astronomer drew this illustration of a comet in the 1500s. **Critical Thinking** What practical purpose do you think Muslim scholars may have had for studying astronomy?

"I have two ears," says Saad Eddin Saleh (SAH ahd EH deen SAH leh), a carpenter in Cairo, "one for work, and one for listening to the Quran."

The Quran requires that Muslims pray five times a day. Many Egyptians pray in a mosque, a building used for Muslim worship. During prayer, Muslims face in the direction of Mecca, Saudi Arabia, where Islam's holiest shrine is located. A mosque may also offer religious training for schoolchildren. The young students who attend these schools learn to read and memorize the Quran.

**An Islamic Renewal**  The Quran is one of the main sources of Sharia (sha REE ah), or Islamic law. The Sharia is also based on the words and deeds of Muhammad, and on comments written by Muslim scholars and lawmakers. Muslims in North Africa and Southwest Asia try to renew their faith by living each day according to Sharia.

Praying and fasting are two of the ways that Egyptian Muslims have brought their religion into their daily lives. But the Quran includes many teachings that govern day-to-day life. It stresses the importance of honesty, honor, and giving to others. It also requires Muslims to love and respect their families.

Most Muslims in Egypt agree that the laws of Egypt should be based on Islamic law. In 1978, Egypt's government studied its laws and discovered that most already were in agreement with Sharia. But in recent years, some Egyptians have said that all of Egypt's laws should match Islamic law. And this has led to disagreements among Egyptian Muslims.

**READ ACTIVELY**

**Ask Questions** What else would you like to know about the religion of Islam?

**King Tut's Clothes**

Scientists are studying the clothes of Pharaoh Tutankhamen, the boy who became ruler of Egypt at the age of nine, in about 1333 B.C. They have learned that Egyptian clothing had no hooks or buttons. King Tut had to tuck, wrap, and tie his clothes on. Because of their clothing, ancient Egyptians had to take small steps and walk carefully.

▼ Some Egyptian women veil their faces, while others do not. Why do you think a woman would choose to veil her face? Why might she not?

**Dressing Modestly**   One part of the debate about Sharia has centered on how women should dress in public. Muhammad taught that men and women are equal in the eyes of God. And Islamic law requires that both men and women dress modestly in public. Men and women must wear loose-fitting clothing that covers most of the body. Sharia requires that women cover all parts of their body except their hands, face, and feet.

However, some Muslims believe that women should also veil their faces, except for the eyes. They believe that covering the face is an important way for women to show their Muslim faith. Many other Muslims, including some government leaders, disagree. In 1994, these leaders banned female public school students from veiling their faces. This upset many Egyptians who were not strongly religious. They feel that the kind of veil a woman wears should be a matter of individual choice.

# Life in Egypt

People in Egypt's cities and villages alike practice Islam. However, except for the time they spend in prayer, people in the cities and the villages live very different lives.

**City Life**   About half of all Egyptians live in cities. Cairo, the nation's capital and largest city, is home to about six million Egyptians. More people live in Cairo than in Los Angeles and Chicago combined. It is the largest city in Africa. Some

**A Traffic Jam in Cairo**

Some people think that Cairo is the loudest city in the world because of its honking horns and roar of car engines. More than 13 million people live in the city, but even more drive or take buses and trains in from the suburbs during the day. At night the streets are empty, but it can be difficult to find even one open parking space.

parts of Cairo are more than 1,000 years old. Other parts of Cairo look just like a Western city. Most people live in apartment buildings with electric fans or air-conditioning. However, they often shop in traditional open-air markets called **bazaars.**

Many people move to the cities from rural areas. They hope to find jobs and better education. As a result, Cairo is very crowded. There are traffic jams and housing shortages. Some people live in tents that they have set up on rowboats on the Nile. Others live in homes they have built in the huge graveyards on the outskirts of Cairo. So many people live in the graveyards that they are considered suburbs of the city, and the government has provided the graveyards with electricity.

**Rural Life** Most of the people in Egypt's rural areas live in villages along the Nile River or the Suez Canal. In Egyptian villages, most of the people make their living by farming. Egypt's rural farmers are called *fellaheen* (fel uh HEEN). Most of the fellaheen do not own land. Land is scarce because the river banks are so narrow. Some fellaheen farm small, rented plots of land. Others work in the fields of rich landowners.

Many of the fellaheen live in homes built of mud bricks or stones. Most of these homes are small. They have one to three rooms and a courtyard that the family often shares with its animals. The roofs of village houses are flat. The fellaheen use their roofs as places to store food and firewood, spread dates out to dry, and dry wet clothes.

**READ ACTIVELY**

**Connect** How does urban life differ from rural life in the United States?

▲ With power from a water buffalo, a fellaheen woman runs a traditional machine that separates the seeds of grain from the plants.

Egypt's people differ from each other in many ways. Some live in cities, while others live in rural areas. Some people make a living by programming computers, while others farm using ancient techniques. Despite their differences, however, most Egyptians are unified by one thing—their faith in Islam. Egyptian Muslims hope that renewing their faith every day will help them to maintain traditional values and customs in a modern age.

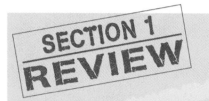

# SECTION 1 REVIEW

1. **Define** (a) bazaar, (b) fellaheen.
2. **Identify** Cairo.
3. Give two examples of how Islam affects everyday life in Egypt.

4. Compare the lives of city and village dwellers in Egypt.

**Critical Thinking**

5. **Identifying Central Issues** How have Egyptian Muslims tried to renew their faith?

**Activity**

6. **Writing to Learn** In a journal entry, describe how the clothes people wear and the music they listen to may reflect their beliefs. Use examples from your own experience as well as from this section.

# Algeria

## THE CASBAH AND THE COUNTRYSIDE

## BEFORE YOU READ

**Reach Into Your Background**

How do you adapt to the climate in your area? How do you change your schedule or your choice of clothing based on the weather?

**Questions to Explore**

1. What are some differences and similarities between the Berbers and the Arabs of Algeria?

2. How is life in Algerian cities different from life in the villages?

**Key Terms**

terrace
souq
casbah

**Key People and Places**

Sahara
Berber
Arab

L ike people in many parts of the world, Algerians adapt to their climate by resting during the hottest hours of the day. Journalist William Langewiesche described part of his visit to Adrar, an oasis city in the Algerian Sahara, as follows:

"We . . . waited out the hot midday hours, drinking brown water from a plastic jug. The water was brown because Miloud had mixed in cade oil. The cade is an evergreen bush that grows in the Atlas Mountains. Saharan nomads use its oil to seal the inside of goatskin water bags. Miloud did not have a goatskin, but he came from a long line of desert travelers. He bought the oil in small bottles and added it to his water for flavor and good health. The mixture smelled of pine sap and tasted of clay. . . . But I would have drunk anything. I had been for a walk."

▼ The Tuareg, a nomadic Berber group, normally relax under tents during the hottest hours of the day. This Tuareg man is brewing green tea.

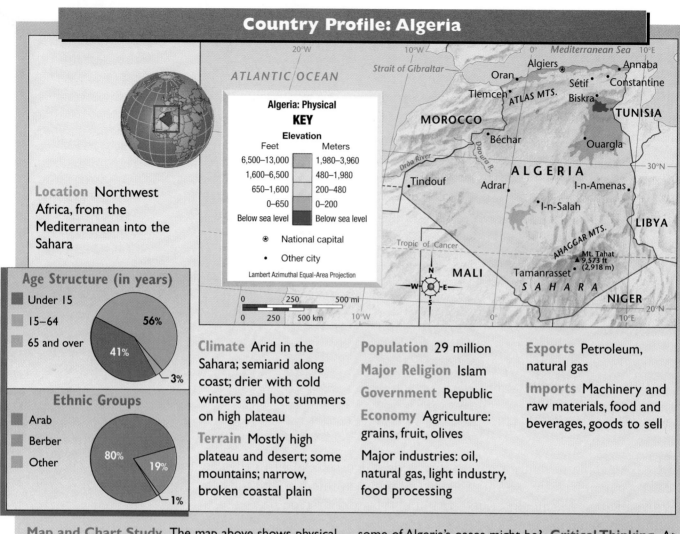

# Country Profile: Algeria

**Location** Northwest Africa, from the Mediterranean into the Sahara

**Algeria: Physical**
**KEY**

**Elevation**

| Feet | Meters |
|---|---|
| 6,500–13,000 | 1,980–3,960 |
| 1,600–6,500 | 480–1,980 |
| 650–1,600 | 200–480 |
| 0–650 | 0–200 |
| Below sea level | Below sea level |

⊛ National capital

• Other city

Lambert Azimuthal Equal-Area Projection

**Age Structure (in years)**
- Under 15
- 15–64
- 65 and over

56%
41%
3%

**Ethnic Groups**
- Arab
- Berber
- Other

80%
19%
1%

**Climate** Arid in the Sahara; semiarid along coast; drier with cold winters and hot summers on high plateau

**Terrain** Mostly high plateau and desert; some mountains; narrow, broken coastal plain

**Population** 29 million

**Major Religion** Islam

**Government** Republic

**Economy** Agriculture: grains, fruit, olives

Major industries: oil, natural gas, light industry, food processing

**Exports** Petroleum, natural gas

**Imports** Machinery and raw materials, food and beverages, goods to sell

**Map and Chart Study** The map above shows physical features of Algeria. **Regions** What parts of Algeria contain mountains? What areas are a part of the Sahara? **Location** The Sahara is dotted with oases. Cities in the Sahara are often located at oases. Where do you think some of Algeria's oases might be? **Critical Thinking** At one time, only Berbers lived in Algeria. Look at the chart of Algeria's ethnic groups. What ethnic group is the largest in Algeria today?

# Algeria's People

The temperature outside while Langewiesche was walking was 124°F (51°C). To survive in that heat, people must drink enough water to produce 2 to 4 gallons (8 to 16 l) of sweat a day. Look at the map in the Country Profile. The Sahara covers all of Algeria south of the Atlas Mountains. Water is in short supply in this area. For this reason, fewer than three percent of Algeria's people live here. But because of their resourcefulness, Berber and Arab nomads have survived in the Sahara for hundreds of years.

**The Berbers** The Berbers and the Arabs are Algeria's two main ethnic groups. The Berbers have lived in North Africa since at least 3000 B.C. No one knows exactly where they came from, but many

**READ ACTIVELY**

**Predict** How do you think people in Algeria make a living?

historians think they migrated from Southwest Asia. They settled in the Atlas Mountains and on plains near Algeria's coast. More than 90 percent of Algerians still live near the coast, where the weather is milder than in the Sahara.

Some Berbers live in Algeria's cities. Most, however, live in villages in rural areas. Many Berbers continue to follow traditional ways of life. Berber households form an extended family, which includes more relatives than just a mother, a father, and their children. Each Berber house has an open courtyard in the back. The windows in the house face the courtyard, not the street. Each married couple in a family has its own home, opening onto the family courtyard. In this way, grandparents, parents, sons, daughters, and cousins can all live close together.

Family is so important to the Berbers that their village governments are based on it. The head of each family is a member of the village assembly, which makes laws for the village.

Most families in Berber villages make a living by farming and herding. They get up as soon as it is light. In the middle of the day, when the sun is hottest, people rest for several hours. Then they work until dark. Farmers use wooden plows drawn by camels. They grow wheat and barley and raise livestock. In the mountains, the Berbers build **terraces,** or platforms cut into the mountainside, for their crops. The terraces increase the amount of farmland and stop the soil from washing away when it rains.

**The Professional Poet**
Many Berber villages have a professional poet. The poet is always a woman who improvises songs in one of the Berber languages. A chorus of women accompany the poet with their voices and with small drums.

## A Desert Lifestyle

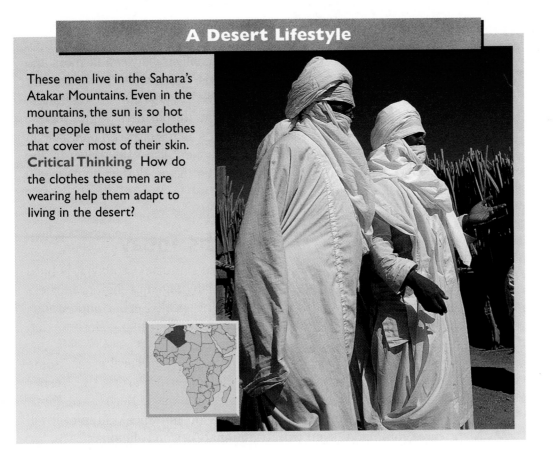

These men live in the Sahara's Atakar Mountains. Even in the mountains, the sun is so hot that people must wear clothes that cover most of their skin. **Critical Thinking** How do the clothes these men are wearing help them adapt to living in the desert?

**Arabs in Algeria** The Berber way of life changed in the A.D. 600s, when Arabs spread across North Africa. The Arabs conquered North Africa gradually, over hundreds of years. Peace in the region came about when most Berbers accepted the religion of Islam.

Arab traditions are like Berber traditions in many ways. For example, both Muslim Arabs and non-Muslim Berbers traditionally live with extended families. However, Arabs and Berbers do differ.

Muslim Arabs created a central government in Algeria that is based on Islam. The Berber tradition is for each village to govern itself. But Berbers adapted to Arab rule by keeping their own governments along with the new one.

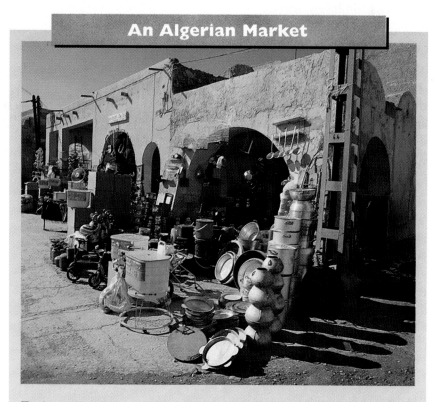

**An Algerian Market**

Traditionally, Algerians bought goods in open-air markets. Shopkeepers in Algeria today still put some of their goods outside their stores, so that Algerians can continue to enjoy shopping in the open air. This shop is in the town of El Dued.

Another difference between the Berbers and the Arabs was that most Arabs were nomads. They usually camped near a well or stream in the summer and herded animals across the desert during the rest of the year. As a result of Arab influence, many Berbers of the hills and plains changed from a farming to a nomadic lifestyle. Sometimes there were conflicts between farmers and nomads. More often, however, they achieved peaceful settlement. Usually, the farmers would let the nomads' herds graze on their land in exchange for livestock and goods. The farmers also sold grains to the nomads. Most Berbers today are farmers, but some Berber nomads still migrate across the Sahara.

## Berbers and Arabs Today

Berbers and Arabs have mixed over the centuries. Today, it is hard to recognize a Berber or an Arab based on language or religion. Berbers and Arabs alike are Muslim. Most Berbers speak Berber and Arabic. Because France ruled Algeria for part of its history, many Berbers and Arabs also speak French.

Most Berbers and many Arabs in Algeria live in rural areas. Some are farmers, while others are nomads. In some rural areas, the Berber way of life has hardly been touched by Arab ways. Berbers in these areas speak Berber languages, and some do not speak Arabic at all. Many have combined Islam with traditional African religions.

**READ ACTIVELY**

**Visualize** Visualize yourself walking through a village in rural Algeria. What would you see? What might you see along a city street?

Algiers, the capital of Algeria, has a modern section of high-rise buildings, shown at the left. The old section of the city (above) is called the Casbah. What clue shows that the Casbah was not built in the 1900s?

**Life in the Cities** Berbers and Arabs who live in Algeria's cities have the most in common with each other. About half of Algeria's people live in cities, and most speak Arabic. Mosques and open-air marketplaces called *souqs* (sooks) fill the cities. Older parts of the cities are called *casbahs* (KAHZ bahz). The houses and stores here are close to each other on narrow, winding streets. Newer parts of the cities look like cities in Europe and the United States. They have tall buildings and wide streets.

The Berbers and the Arabs of Algeria have had many conflicts in the past. However, there have also been long periods during which they learned from each other peacefully. Algeria's future will continue to mix Berber and Arab, old and new.

## SECTION 2 REVIEW

1. **Define** (a) terrace, (b) souq, (c) casbah.

2. **Identify** (a) Sahara, (b) Berber, (c) Arab.

3. How did the Berber way of life change when Arabs came to North Africa?

4. How are Arabs and Berbers similar today?

**Critical Thinking**

5. **Drawing Conclusions** What differences might have caused conflicts between Berbers and Arabs? How did Berbers and Arabs sometimes overcome their differences?

**Activity**

6. **Writing to Learn** Suppose that you were a member of a Berber village assembly at the time that the Arabs first came to North Africa. Write a speech in which you discuss the possible impact of this change on your community.

# SKILLS ACTIVITY

# Using Regional Maps

**H**ave you ever seen anyone try to drive around town with a map of the whole world?

It would never work. A world map is useful for looking at the world as a whole. You can easily see the shapes and locations of the continents and oceans. They do not show you street names, however. Because they cover such a large area, world maps lack the detail to show much about a specific part of the world.

That is why we have regional maps. You already know that a region is an area of the Earth that shares some common characteristics. A regional map is a map of a region. Regional maps are probably the most common type of map. Road maps and bus maps are regional maps. So are the weather maps you see on the news. Throughout your life, you will see regional maps in newspapers and magazines, in textbooks and on television. It pays to know how to use them.

regional maps. But if you learn how to read one type of regional map, you can use your skills to help you read others.

## Try It Out

Follow these steps to read the map in column two on the next page.

**A. Identify the region.** What region is shown on the map? What defines the region?

**B. Use the map key to learn about the region.** What basic information is shown on the map? What do the solid lines represent? What do the single dots represent?

## Get Ready

Regional maps focus on one part of the world, showing it in greater detail. Because of this detail, you can learn a lot about the region that is shown on the map. Since regions can be defined by many different characteristics—landforms, economies, political boundaries, and so on—there are many different types of

**C. Use the regional map as a tool.** What landforms can be found on either side of the Nile River valley? Where are most cities in the Nile River valley located?

**D. Extend your learning.** Why might the Nile River be important to people in Egypt? How is the Nile related to the location of Egyptian cities?

## Apply the Skill

The map below is a regional map of North Africa. Work independently to apply the four basic regional map reading skills to this map.

**1 Identify the region.** What region is shown on the map? What defines the region?

**2 Use the map key to learn about the region.** What basic information is shown on the map? What physical features are identified on this map?

**3 Use the regional map as a tool.** How many countries are in North Africa? Which countries are they? Do you see any bodies of water in North Africa?

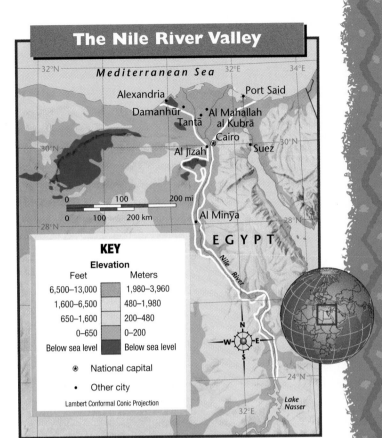

**The Nile River Valley**

**4 Extend your learning.** Why would this map be useful in learning about the ways of life of this region? How might it help you understand the history of the region? What do you think might have been very important to people of this region?

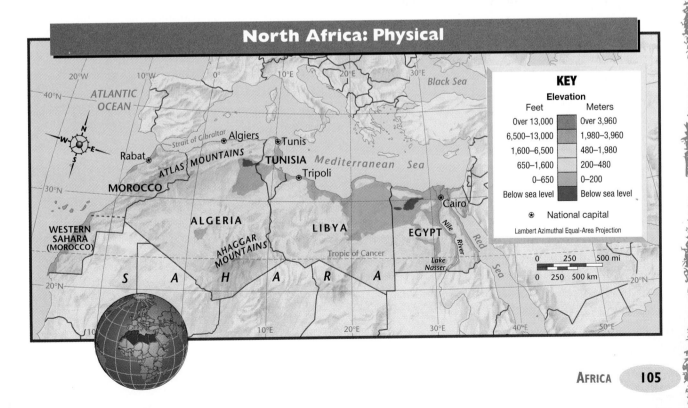

**North Africa: Physical**

# CHAPTER 4

# Review and Activities

## Reviewing Main Ideas

1. Why do most Muslims study and memorize parts of the Quran?

2. How do Egyptians show their faith in Islam in their daily lives?

3. How does life in Egypt's cities differ from life in Egypt's rural areas?

4. Explain what Berbers and Arabs in Algeria have in common and what sets them apart.

5. How does Algeria's geography affect the people who live there?

6. How do Algeria's cities blend the old and the new?

## Reviewing Key Terms

Decide whether each statement is true or false. If it is true, write "true." If it is false, change the underlined term to make the statement true.

1. A traditional Egyptian open-air market is called a <u>casbah</u>.

2. Egypt's rural farmers are called <u>fellaheen</u>.

3. <u>Souqs</u> are platforms cut into the side of a mountain.

4. In Algeria, an open-air market may be called a <u>nomad</u>.

5. The old section of Algiers is called the <u>Sharia</u>.

## Critical Thinking

1. **Recognizing Cause and Effect** Why do you think that the Berbers who lived in isolated areas maintained their language and traditions after Arabs came to Algeria?

2. **Drawing Conclusions** How do you think religion affects the way people in Egypt and Algeria feel about their communities?

## Graphic Organizer

Copy the web onto a sheet of paper and then complete it. Narrow your focus each time you move to a new level on the web. Fill in the web with as many people and ideas as you can.

## Map Activity

### North Africa
For each place listed below, write the letter from the map that shows its location.

1. Cairo

2. Algeria

3. Mediterranean Sea

4. Egypt

5. Sahara

## Writing Activity

### Writing a Poem
The Berber languages are rarely written down. Most Berber history is preserved by professional poets. Pretend that you are a professional poet living in the 600s, when Arabs first came to North Africa. Write a poem explaining some of the differences and similarities between Arabs and Berbers.

### Internet Activity
Use a search engine to find the **Library of Congress Country Studies.** Scroll down and choose **Algeria.** Choose several links to explore. Write a report about what you found most interesting.

## Skills Review

**Turn to the Skills Activity.**

Review the steps for using regional maps. Then answer the following questions: (a) How can you use the map key to help you learn about a region? (b) How can you use a regional map as a tool?

## How Am I Doing?

**Answer these questions to check your progress.**

1. Do I understand how Islam has influenced life in both Egypt and Algeria?

2. Can I identify some historic events that have shaped the modern cultures of North Africa?

3. Do I understand how cultures in North Africa compare to other African cultures I have studied?

4. What information from this chapter can I use in my book project?

# Exploring West Africa

KEY

— National boundary

⊛ National capital

• Other city

Lambert Azimuthal Equal-Area Projection

## MAP ACTIVITIES

*Seventeen countries make up the region of West Africa. To help you get to know this region, do the following.*

### Consider the location
What ocean do many of West Africa's countries border? What capitals of West African countries are close to rivers and lakes? What cities are far from rivers and lakes?

### Think about the cities
Where are most of West Africa's cities? What factors might explain the locations of West African cities?

### Consider the climate
Nearness to the Equator is one factor that can influence a country's climate. Where does most of West Africa lie in relation to the Equator and the Tropic of Cancer? Based on West Africa's location, what do you think its climate might be like?

# Nigeria

## ONE COUNTRY, MANY IDENTITIES

**BEFORE YOU READ**

**Reach Into Your Background**
Think about the ways in which you use language in daily life.

How would you communicate with people who do not speak your language?

**Questions to Explore**
1. What are Nigeria's main ethnic groups?
2. How are Nigeria's main ethnic groups similar to and different from each other?

**Key Terms**
multiethnic
census

**Key Places**
Lagos
Abuja
Kano

The language of England is English. The language of Spain is Spanish. The language of Greece is Greek. But the language of Nigeria is not Nigerian. In fact, there is no such language as Nigerian. Nigerians speak more than 250 languages!

The languages of Nigeria match its ethnic groups. Nigeria's three most widely spoken languages are Hausa, Yoruba, and Ibo. There are places called Hausaland, Yorubaland, and Iboland. Most people in Hausaland are Hausa and speak Hausa. Most people in Yorubaland are Yoruba and speak Yoruba. And most people in Iboland are Ibo and speak Ibo. But these places are not countries. In fact, Hausaland and Yorubaland both lie partly in Nigeria and partly in other countries.

## Nigeria's History

Why are there so many ethnic groups and languages within one country? Before Europeans arrived, what is now Nigeria was ruled by many ethnic groups, including the Hausa, the Yoruba, and the Ibo. But when Europeans drew Nigeria's borders, they did not think about ethnic groups. Look at the map in the Country Profile. You can see that Nigeria's borders do not match the borders of any one ethnic group.

Nigeria contains so many ethnic groups in part because it is so big. Nigeria is about as big as the states of California, Arizona, and New Mexico combined. More people live in Nigeria than in any other country in Africa. About one out of five Africans lives here. And Nigeria is **multiethnic,** which means that many ethnic groups live within its borders.

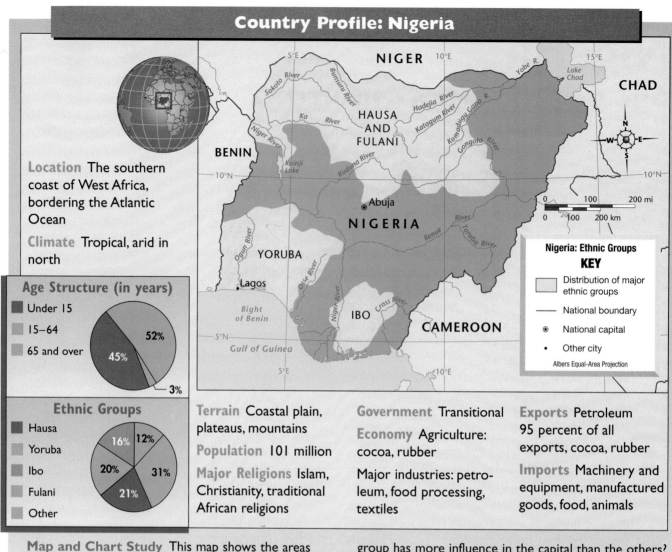

**Location** The southern coast of West Africa, bordering the Atlantic Ocean

**Climate** Tropical, arid in north

**Age Structure (in years)**
- Under 15
- 15–64
- 65 and over

52%
45%
3%

**Ethnic Groups**
- Hausa
- Yoruba
- Ibo
- Fulani
- Other

12%
16%
31%
20%
21%

**Nigeria: Ethnic Groups**
**KEY**
- Distribution of major ethnic groups
- National boundary
- ⊛ National capital
- • Other city

Albers Equal-Area Projection

**Terrain** Coastal plain, plateaus, mountains

**Population** 101 million

**Major Religions** Islam, Christianity, traditional African religions

**Government** Transitional

**Economy** Agriculture: cocoa, rubber

Major industries: petroleum, food processing, textiles

**Exports** Petroleum 95 percent of all exports, cocoa, rubber

**Imports** Machinery and equipment, manufactured goods, food, animals

**Map and Chart Study** This map shows the areas where Nigeria's three major ethnic groups—the Hausa-Fulani, the Yoruba, and the Ibo—are in the majority. **Location** Find Abuja, Nigeria's capital, on the map. Based on its location, do you think that any one ethnic group has more influence in the capital than the others? Why or why not? **Critical Thinking** There are many other ethnic groups in Nigeria besides the Hausa-Fulani, the Yoruba, and the Ibo, but these groups are by far the largest. What is Nigeria's largest ethnic group?

**The Colonial Legacy** The Hausa, the Fulani (FOO lah nee), the Yoruba, and the Ibo were each governing their own regions when Europeans arrived. In the late 1400s, Portugal began to buy slaves in West Africa. Later, Great Britain, the Netherlands, and other countries entered the slave trade.

By 1914, Great Britain had taken over the government of Nigeria. The borders of the British colony of Nigeria included part of Hausaland, part of Yorubaland, and Iboland.

Nigeria became independent in 1960. Ethnic groups that had always lived separately then worked together to create one nation. To help unify the country, in 1991 the government moved the nation's capital from Lagos, in the south, to Abuja (ah BOO jah). The new capital is located in the central portion of the country, where several ethnic groups live.

# Three Different Ways of Life

Making Abuja the capital helped bring Nigeria together, because it meant that the capital would be close to more than one ethnic group. The Hausa, the Fulani, the Ibo, and the Yoruba each live in different regions. Most Hausa and Fulani live in the north. The Ibo live mainly in the southeast, and the Yoruba in the southwest. Many smaller ethnic groups live in central Nigeria and throughout the country.

**The Hausa and Fulani: Traders of the North**  Both the Hausa and the Fulani built city-states in northern Nigeria. The Fulani conquered Hausaland in the early 1800s. Many Hausa and Fulani have intermarried since that time. The Hausa and the Fulani make up about 33 percent of Nigeria's people. Together, they are called the Hausa-Fulani. Most Hausa and Fulani are Muslims.

For hundreds of years, the Hausa-Fulani have made an important part of their living by trading. Hausa-Fulani traders dealt in goods from as far away as Spain, Italy, and Egypt. The Hausa-Fulani built cities at the crossroads of trade routes. Each of these cities had its own ruler, was enclosed by walls, and had a central market. Kano, the oldest city in West Africa, is a Hausa city. Kano has been a center of trade for over 1,000 years. The Kurmi Market in Kano is one of the largest trading centers in Africa. People from around the world visit its thousands of stalls. These stalls sell everything from fabrics and dyes to electric appliances.

**LINKS TO LANGUAGE ARTS**

**Pidgin** How do people talk to each other when they speak different languages? One way is to create a language that includes a little of each language. This kind of language is called pidgin. Nigerian pidgin mixes English words with the grammar of Nigerian languages. Enslaved Africans and their captors may have been the first people in Africa to use pidgin.

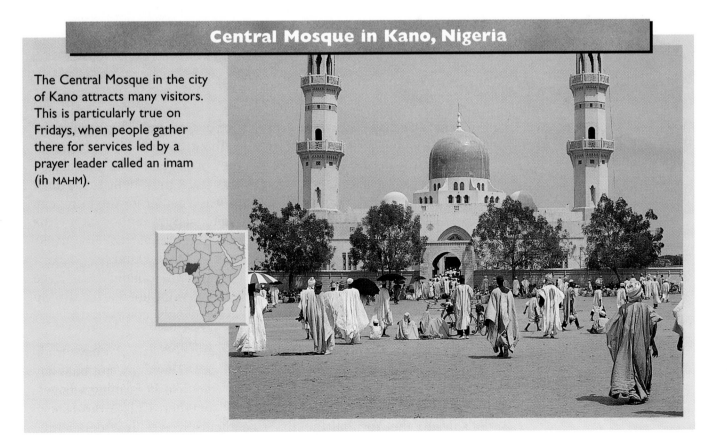

## Central Mosque in Kano, Nigeria

The Central Mosque in the city of Kano attracts many visitors. This is particularly true on Fridays, when people gather there for services led by a prayer leader called an imam (ih MAHM).

## Calabash Carver in Kurmi Market

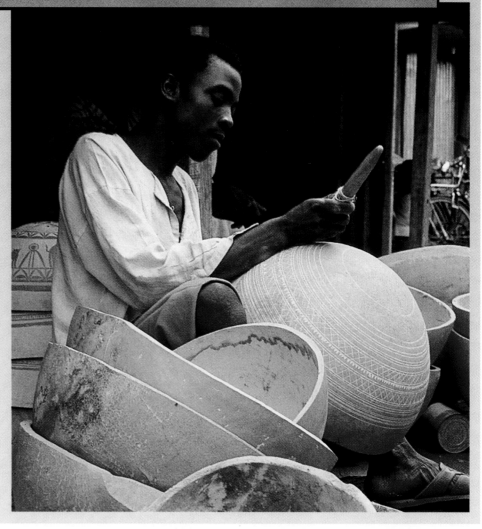

A carver decorates a calabash, or empty gourd, at his stall in Kano's Kurmi Market. A plain calabash makes a light and inexpensive bowl. A highly decorated calabash may, in time, become very valuable. At the Kurmi Market, you can buy crafts from not only Nigeria, but also many other African countries.

**READ ACTIVELY**

**Ask Questions** What would you like to know about the differences among the Hausa-Fulani, the Yoruba, and the Ibo?

**The Yoruba: Farmers Near the Coast**   The Yoruba are Nigeria's second largest ethnic group. About 20 percent of Nigeria's people are Yoruba. By about A.D. 1100, the Yoruba had built several city-states. Many Yoruba still live in the city-state they built more than 500 years ago, Lagos. In the 1800s, Lagos was a center for the European slave trade. Many Yoruba were sold into slavery and sent to the Americas. But today, Lagos is a more peaceful center of trade. Its streets are lined with hundreds of small shops that sell many kinds of goods.

Most Yoruba are farmers. They live with their families in large compounds. Each compound has several houses grouped around a big yard. A Yoruba community is made up of many such compounds.

**The Ibo: A Tradition of Democracy**   The Ibo have traditionally lived as rural farmers in the southeast. They have not built any large cities like Kano or Lagos. Instead, they live in farming villages. The people in each village work closely together. Unlike the Hausa-Fulani and the Yoruba, the Ibo rule themselves with a democratic council of elders. Instead of one or two leaders making decisions for an entire village, members of the council work together to solve problems.

The southeast was the first area of Nigeria to be affected by the arrival of Europeans. During colonial times, the Ibo were often educated by Christian missionaries. Many people in the south converted, or changed their religion, to Christianity. During British rule, some Ibo attended European or American universities and became teachers, doctors, and lawyers. Today, many Ibo have left rural villages and work in Nigeria's towns and cities.

Tensions sometimes arise between the Ibo and the other two major groups. In 1967, the Ibo tried to leave Nigeria to start their own country. For two and a half years the country was torn by war. In the end, Nigeria stayed united, and people tried to put the war behind them.

**Counting Heads**  It is hard to know exactly how many people belong to each ethnic group. Nigeria has tried to count its people. A count of all the people in a country is called a **census.** In Nigeria,

▼▲Cities like Lagos (below) are not new to Nigeria. The skyscraper below dates from the late 1900s, but the Yoruba built Lagos in the 1400s. The Yoruba traditionally trade in cities and farm (above) in rural areas.

▶ Kano's airport was closed for three days during Nigeria's 1991 census. No one could fly in or out of the country.

whenever a census is taken, it causes debate. This is because the largest ethnic group will have the most power in Nigeria's government.

In 1991, Nigeria conducted an unusual census. On November 26, the country was cut off from the outside world. No one could enter or leave the country for three days. And no one in Nigeria was allowed to move from one place to another between 7 A.M. and 7 P.M. Hundreds of thousands of census takers went from house to house, making a count of the people. The census showed that over 88 million people live in Nigeria, and that the Hausa-Fulani are the country's largest ethnic group. This gives them more political power than other groups.

Over the years, many Nigerians have challenged the census results. In 1963 and 1973, for example, some ethnic groups charged that other ethnic groups had reported too large a number of people. Nigerians hope that by taking accurate censuses, they will be able to hold the many ethnic groups together.

## SECTION 1 REVIEW

1. **Define** (a) multiethnic, (b) census.
2. **Identify** (a) Lagos, (b) Abuja, (c) Kano.
3. What are the three largest ethnic groups in Nigeria, and where does each group live?
4. Why might taking a census create tension in Nigeria?

**Critical Thinking**
5. **Cause and Effect** How did the arrival of Europeans in Nigeria affect the ethnic groups that live in the region?

**Activity**
6. **Writing to Learn** Currently, Nigeria does not have one national language. Based on what you have learned about this country, do you think a national language might be useful? Why or why not? Write a paragraph explaining your opinion.

# Ghana

## FIRST IN INDEPENDENCE

**BEFORE YOU READ**

**Reach Into Your Background**

Think about a turning point in your own life, such as moving to a new community or beginning a new school. What was different after that turning point? What remained the same?

**Questions to Explore**

1. What changes did Kwame Nkrumah bring to Ghana?
2. How has life in Ghana changed since independence?

**Key Terms**

sovereignty
coup

**Key People**

Kwame Nkrumah
Jerry Rawlings

In 1935, Kwame Nkrumah, a 26-year-old student, sailed from Ghana to the United States. At that time, Ghana was called the Gold Coast. It had been ruled by Great Britain for over 60 years. Nkrumah's visit to the United States was a turning point in his life. He was well aware that the people of his country did not have true freedom or equality. When Nkrumah saw the Statue of Liberty for the first time, it made him determined to bring freedom not only to his country, but to the whole continent. As he looked at the statue, he thought, "I shall never rest until I have carried your message to Africa."

## Moving Toward Independence

In 1947, Nkrumah returned to the Gold Coast. The Gold Coast was named for its gold, which is one of the country's most important natural resources. The Country Profile on the next page shows the country's other important resources. But while the Gold Coast had many resources, most of its people were poor. Nkrumah believed that the people should benefit from the wealth of their own country. He began traveling all over the country. He convinced the people to demand independence from Great Britain.

▼ Kwame Nkrumah, the first leader of independent Ghana, showed his respect for African traditions by wearing traditional clothing.

# Country Profile: Ghana

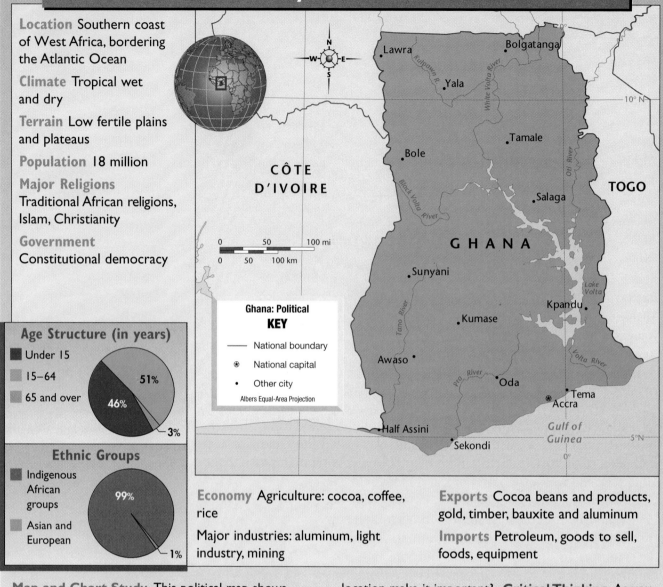

**Location** Southern coast of West Africa, bordering the Atlantic Ocean

**Climate** Tropical wet and dry

**Terrain** Low fertile plains and plateaus

**Population** 18 million

**Major Religions** Traditional African religions, Islam, Christianity

**Government** Constitutional democracy

### Age Structure (in years)
- Under 15
- 15–64 — 51%
- 65 and over — 3%
- 46%

### Ethnic Groups
- Indigenous African groups — 99%
- Asian and European — 1%

**Economy** Agriculture: cocoa, coffee, rice

Major industries: aluminum, light industry, mining

**Exports** Cocoa beans and products, gold, timber, bauxite and aluminum

**Imports** Petroleum, goods to sell, foods, equipment

**Map and Chart Study** This political map shows Ghana's major cities and waterways. Study Ghana's river systems. Which rivers flow into Lake Volta? **Location** Find Ghana's capital, Accra, on the map. Why does its location make it important? **Critical Thinking** As you can see from the top chart, Ghana has a large number of young people. How might this fact affect education and jobs?

**Traditional Government in Ghana** During the 1900s, Africans who were ruled by European countries pushed to become independent. But the European countries did not want to give up their colonies. Some Europeans claimed that the colonies were not ready to rule themselves. Kwame Nkrumah answered this with a question.

"Wasn't the African who is now unprepared to govern himself governing himself before the advent [arrival] of Europeans?"

The Akan are the largest ethnic group in Ghana. When the Akan give power to a new leader, they also give a warning:

> "Tell him that
> We do not wish greediness
> We do not wish that he should curse us
> We do not wish that his ears should be hard of hearing
> We do not wish that he should call people fools
> We do not wish that he should act on his own initiative
> We do not wish that it should ever be said 'I have no time. I have no time.'
> We do not wish personal abuse
> We do not wish personal violence."

If the leader does not rule fairly, the people can give power to a new ruler. In this way, the Akan are democratic. The people have control over who rules them.

While the Europeans were trading in gold and slaves on the coast, some Akan groups formed the Asante kingdom. This kingdom became very rich from trade. It controlled parts of the northern savanna and the coastal south. The Asante used all their power to try to stop the Europeans from taking over West Africa.

**The Influence of Colonialism** In 1874, Great Britain made the Gold Coast a colony. But it let the leaders of various ethnic groups continue to rule their people. Even today, there are at least 75 ethnic groups in Ghana, and their leaders are powerful people.

**To Be a Leader** The Asante did not submit to colonial rule without a fight. In 1900, Asante Queen Yaa Asantewa led a war against the British. Although the British were armed with modern rifles and machine guns, it took them more than three months to defeat the queen and her troops. Because of Yaa Asantewa's rebellion, the British began to treat the Asante more respectfully. In her memory, Asante children still sing a song about "Yaa Asantewa, the warrior woman who carries a gun and a sword of state into battle."

## All That Glitters is Gold

The current Asantehene, the leader of the Asante, has ruled for more than 25 years. His power is symbolized by the Golden Stool, which sits in a place of honor on a chair beside him. If a leader does something wrong, the people may take the stool away. The Golden Stool is made of wood and decorated with real gold. **Critical Thinking** What does this picture tell you about the economic status of the Asante?

The British were most interested in controlling the economy of the Gold Coast. They encouraged farmers to grow cocoa. Then, the British sent the cocoa to factories in Britain, where it was made into chocolate. The British also exported timber and gold. As these raw materials left the country, goods from other countries were shipped in. This led to a problem that was typical of much of colonial Africa. People grew fewer food crops because growing cash crops like cocoa brought in more money. Food, therefore, had to be imported. People also spent more time on farming and less on traditional crafts. The British sold food and factory-made goods to the people of the Gold Coast. Soon, they began to depend on these imports.

The British also built schools in the Gold Coast. Foreign missionaries ran the schools. Christianity began to replace traditional religions. By the time Ghana became independent in 1957, many new ideas and lifestyles had come to traditional communities. Many people blended the new ways and the old African ways. Kwame Nkrumah, for example, was a Christian. But he also believed in parts of the traditional African religion. Nkrumah's respect for old and new ways helped him govern when Ghana became independent.

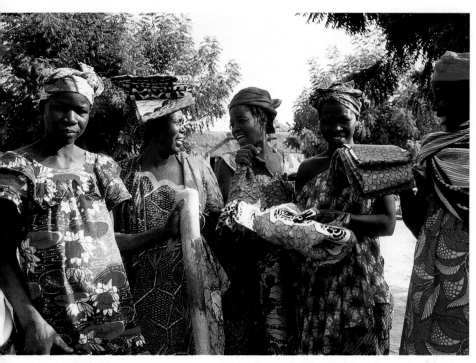

▼ Since colonization, many Ghanaian women purchase machine-made cotton fabrics, instead of traditional kente cloth, for everyday dresses and head scarves.

READ ACTIVELY

**Connect** How does your community blend traditional ways of life with modern ways?

## Independence

In 1957, some 22 years after making his pledge to the Statue of Liberty, Nkrumah gave a moving speech to his people. Great Britain, he said, had finally agreed to grant them **sovereignty** (SAHV run tee), or political independence. Cheering, the people carried Nkrumah through the streets. Crowds sang victory songs to celebrate a dream come true.

Nkrumah became the leader of the new country. Later, he became the president. The government changed the country's name from the Gold Coast to Ghana, after an African kingdom that had ruled the region hundreds of years ago. Ghana was the first African colony south of the Sahara to become independent.

Since independence, Ghana has worked to balance new technology with traditional culture. Modern health care, electricity, transportation, and education are things that most Ghanaians want. Sometimes, however, these changes happened too quickly.

**Nkrumah's Government Is Overthrown**  Nine years after being carried through the streets as a hero, Nkrumah was thrown out of office by a military coup (koo), or takeover. Army officers led the coup. Most Ghanaian citizens did not protest. In fact, many celebrated. People pulled down statues of Nkrumah.

How did this hero become an enemy? Nkrumah had big plans for Ghana. He borrowed huge amounts of money to make those plans happen fast. He spent millions of dollars to build a conference center. He spent millions more to build a super-highway. In addition, he made a deal with an American company to build a dam on the Volta River. The dam was to provide electricity and irrigation for people in rural areas. But when world prices for cocoa, Ghana's chief export, fell, Ghana could not pay back its loans. Many people blamed Nkrumah for the country's economic problems.

Nkrumah's downfall did not end Ghana's problems. The country alternated between military and democratically elected governments. Few were successful. In the meantime, people began to think better of Nkrumah. Many felt that he had done his best to help the country. When he died in 1972, he was hailed as a national hero. Leaders around the world mourned his death.

**Ghana's Economy and Culture Today**  In the 1980s, Ghana's president, Jerry Rawlings, tried to reform Ghana's politics and economy. Rawlings stressed the traditional African values of hard work and sacrifice. Ghanaians supported Rawlings, and as a result, Ghana's economy began to grow.

Ghana is still dependent on the sale of cocoa. Even so, the economy has grown so much that Ghana has been able to build better roads and irrigation systems. The government plans to improve education and health care. People have formed groups so they can voice concerns about issues that affect their lives.

Ghana's culture, as well as its economy, has benefited from Rawlings's renewal of traditional values. Ghana has special centers that have been

**Nkrumah Toppled**

Pulled down by angry citizens, the headless statue of Kwame Nkrumah lies on the grounds of the central police station in Accra. Nkrumah was out of the country when he was overthrown, in February 1966. He never returned to Ghana, but lived in exile in the nearby country of Guinea.

set up to keep the country's traditional culture alive. People who visit Ghana may bring new ideas, but they also learn from Ghana's rich traditional culture. Art from Ghana is valued around the world. Ghana's culture can also be seen in daily life. Most people in Ghana live in small villages. Traditional dancing can be found even in the most modern dance clubs. In all forms, traditional Ghanaian culture exists alongside new ideas.

▼ Ghanaian crafts are popular all over the world. Below right is stamped adinkra cloth and woven kente cloth. Below left are hand-crafted beeswax candles.

## SECTION 2 REVIEW

1. **Define** (a) sovereignty, (b) coup.

2. **Identify** (a) Kwame Nkrumah, (b) Jerry Rawlings.

3. How did colonization affect Ghana's economy?

4. Why did Kwame Nkrumah believe that Ghana should be independent?

**Critical Thinking**

5. **Recognizing Cause and Effect** Kwame Nkrumah went from being a Ghanaian hero to an unpopular figure. What caused this change in people's attitudes?

**Activity**

6. **Writing to Learn** Write about one or two changes you would like to see in your country or community. What obstacles might be in the way of this change? How could those obstacles be overcome?

# Mali

## THE DESERT IS COMING

### Reach Into Your Background

Think about how the environment you live in affects your daily life. How does the clothing you wear reflect the climate? Are there sports or other activities that take place in only certain seasons?

### Questions to Explore

1. How does the environment in Mali affect the country's economy?
2. How are the challenges faced by Mali typical of the challenges faced by other countries in the Sahel?

### Key Terms

desertification
drought
erode

### Key Places

Tombouctou
Sahara
Sahel

O utside the Hotel Bouctou in Tombouctou, Mali, sand piles up against buildings. It coats the fur of camels. It gives a yellowish tint to everything in sight. Inside, manager Boubacar Toure (boo buh CAR too RAY) sits in a lobby that is covered with a fine layer of red sand. Only 4 of his hotel's 29 rooms are taken. He is waiting for the river to rise, hoping that it will bring customers.

But each year, the river rises a little later. "Ten years ago the first boat arrived on July 1," says Tombouctou politician Moulaye Haidara (moo LAH ee HY dah rah). "Five years ago it was July 15. Now, we're lucky it's here by early August. In another five years, who knows?"

## Mali's Environment

Tombouctou wasn't always so empty. From the 1300s to the end of the 1500s, Tombouctou was an important trade center. Caravans from North Africa crossed the Sahara to trade goods at Tombouctou. The Sahara covers much of West Africa, and it is getting bigger. The Sahara covers almost 60 percent of Mali. Few people live in the Sahara, however. Some Malians live in the savanna, the one area of the country that gets enough rain for farming. Other Malians live in the Sahel, the partly dry lands south of the Sahara. Tombouctou is in the Sahel.

▼ Tombouctou's narrow streets used to attract crowds of tourists and traders. Now the city is slowly being covered with sand.

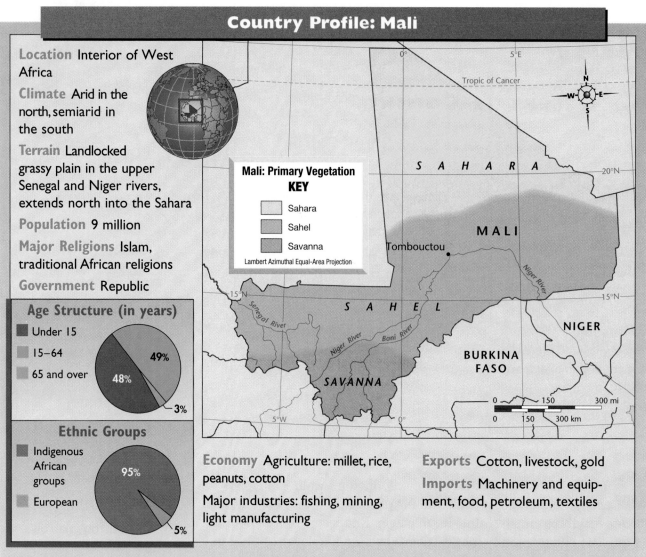

# Country Profile: Mali

**Location** Interior of West Africa

**Climate** Arid in the north, semiarid in the south

**Terrain** Landlocked grassy plain in the upper Senegal and Niger rivers, extends north into the Sahara

**Population** 9 million

**Major Religions** Islam, traditional African religions

**Government** Republic

**Mali: Primary Vegetation**
**KEY**
- Sahara
- Sahel
- Savanna

Lambert Azimuthal Equal-Area Projection

### Age Structure (in years)
- Under 15
- 15–64
- 65 and over

49%
48%
3%

### Ethnic Groups
- Indigenous African groups
- European

95%
5%

**Economy** Agriculture: millet, rice, peanuts, cotton

Major industries: fishing, mining, light manufacturing

**Exports** Cotton, livestock, gold

**Imports** Machinery and equipment, food, petroleum, textiles

**Map and Chart Study** This map shows Mali's major vegetation regions. What part of the country is most liveable? Why do you think the population is so small in a country so large? **Location** Find Mali's major city, Tombouctou. How do you think the city's location contributed to its importance as a trading crossroads? **Critical Thinking** Like many other African countries, Mali has a very young population as the top chart shows. What do you think it would be like to live in a country where almost half the people are under the age of 15?

**READ ACTIVELY**

**Ask Questions** What would you like to know about life in the Sahel?

**Life in the Sahel** The Sahel is a zone between the desert and the savanna. Eleven African countries lie partly in the Sahel. The Sahel stretches through the middle of Mali. Look at the map in the Activity Atlas. What other countries are in the Sahel? The large, dry Sahel affects the economy of every country it touches. But people who live in the region have long used the resources of the Sahel to earn their living.

People have lived in the Sahel for thousands of years. For a long time, they did very well and even grew rich. The region's grasslands provide food for animal herds. And the Sahel's location between the Sahara and the savanna is important. People traveling south must pass through the Sahel before reaching the savanna. For this reason, Tombouctou became a wealthy center of learning and business.

Once European ships began trading along Africa's coast, trade through the Sahara decreased. Tombouctou and other trade cities declined. But life in Tombouctou still follows certain traditional patterns. As in past times, caravans still carry huge blocks of salt into Tombouctou. And women still bake bread in outdoor ovens in the traditional way.

**The Desert Comes Closer** Mali has little industry. Most people make their living by trading, farming, and herding. However, all of these kinds of work are being threatened by **desertification,** the change of fertile land into land that is too dry or damaged to support life. In Mali and other countries of the Sahel, the desert is spreading south. Even the wetter lands in southwest Mali are in danger.

The region facing the greatest threat is the Sahel. The people of the Sahel whose way of life is most affected by desertification may be the Tuareg (TWAR ehg). The Tuareg have lived in the desert and the Sahel for hundreds of years. Wrapped from head to toe in blue cloth, with only their eyes showing, the Tuareg gallop across the land on fast camels. They live a nomadic life, moving their herds of goats, sheep, and camels

**Dogon Granary Doors**
The Dogon live in a wetter part of Mali. They work as farmers. They use granaries to store grain. These granaries are made of twigs and mud but have very stylized wood doors. The Dogon believe the tree from which the wood came contains a spirit that protects the stored grain. Although the rain and sun often wear down the granaries, the Dogon transfer the symbolic door from one granary to another.

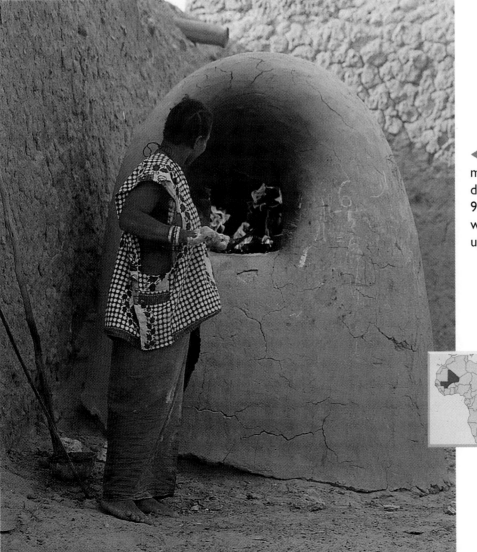

◀ Baking bread outside makes sense when average daily temperatures exceed 90°F (32°C). An oven inside would only heat your house up more.

south in the dry season and north in the wet season. Most Tuareg have never lived permanently in one place. The desertification of countries like Mali and Niger is threatening their way of life.

**A Change in Lifestyle** Major droughts in the 1970s and 1980s made life very difficult for the Tuareg. A **drought** is a time when there is little or no rain. Facing water and food shortages, some Tuareg settled on farms or in cities. Others built camps outside Tombouctou.

Ibrahim Ag Abdullah and his wife Fatimata are Tuareg. They live in a camp near Tombouctou. In the morning, Ibrahim Abdullah rides his camel into the city. Instead of tending his herds, Ibrahim Abdullah now sells camel rides to tourists. Fatimata Abdullah draws water from a well built by the government and grows vegetables. But the Abdullahs want to return to their nomadic life. "Each time I earn a little money, I buy a goat or a sheep. I save up so I can have enough animals to return to the desert," says Ibrahim Abdullah. But this way of life will only be possible if the Sahel's grasslands are maintained.

▼ This picture shows a Tuareg man dressed in traditional style. The Tuaregs' name for themselves means "free people." Clustered in small groups throughout the southwest Sahara, these nomads resist being controlled by any government. The Tuareg practice their own form of Islam, which keeps many elements of their original religion.

# Preserving the Environment

Many people around the world are worried about the Sahel. The United Nations has created a committee to fight desertification. First people must understand why the fertile land changes into unusable desert.

Some environmentalists think that overgrazing can cause desertification. They say that grazing large herds of animals **erodes** the soil, or wears it away. That allows the desert to take over. When there are no roots to hold soil in place, the fierce winds of the Sahel blow it around. Yellow dust clouds fill the air. This loose soil is one reason that Tombouctou is slowly being covered in sand.

Other environmentalists say that grazing does not increase desertification. They think that grazing may actually help grasses grow once the area gets enough rain. These scientists think that long periods of

## Desertification and the Economy

This is the West Africa Regional Bank in Bamako, Mali's capital and largest city. Desertification has hurt Mali's economy by making it harder for farmers to grow cash crops. Now Mali's government is trying to encourage people to start their own businesses, as well as encouraging existing businesses to come to Mali.

drought turn land into desert. Over the last 25 years, the Sahel has had much less rain than it did in the 70 years before. If these scientists are right, a few years of good rainfall could stop desertification. The Tuareg would not have to change their way of life.

Currently, Mali's government is studying the problem. Mali is working with the United Nations to educate people in rural areas about better ways to use land. The government is also irrigating and planting in some areas to create a greenbelt. It hopes to have its plan for tackling desertification operating by the year 2000.

## SECTION 3 REVIEW

1. **Define** (a) desertification, (b) drought, (c) erode.

2. **Identify** (a) Tombouctou, (b) Sahara, (c) Sahel.

3. How does Mali's geography affect how people make a living?

4. How does desertification affect the people who live in the Sahel?

**Critical Thinking**

5. **Drawing Conclusions** Many Tuareg living around Tombouctou are now depending on the tourist trade for income. Based on what you have learned about Tombouctou, what will be some of the challenges of this new occupation?

**Activity**

6. **Writing to Learn** Overgrazing may contribute to the desertification of the Sahel. What common North American activities may present a threat to the environment? Do you think those activities should be discouraged? Why or why not?

# Using Distribution Maps

**D**o you think in pictures? Most people do. They try to visualize what they read about. For example, if you read a story about a trip along the Niger River, you may imagine a wide river with dense forest along its banks. You may try to picture, in your own mind, what the writer saw. Thinking in pictures is a natural way to make sense of the world.

Geographers think in pictures, too. For them, of course, the pictures are often maps. There is an old saying: "A picture is worth a thousand words." This is especially true when the picture is a distribution map.

## Get Ready

A distribution map is a map that shows how something is distributed. In other words, it shows where something is located. A "population distribution map" shows where people live. It is one of the most common distribution maps. A "resource distribution map" shows where resources are found. You can make a distribution map that shows how nearly anything is distributed. The location of ethnic groups, languages, vegetation, schools—and almost anything else you can think of—can all be indicated on distribution maps.

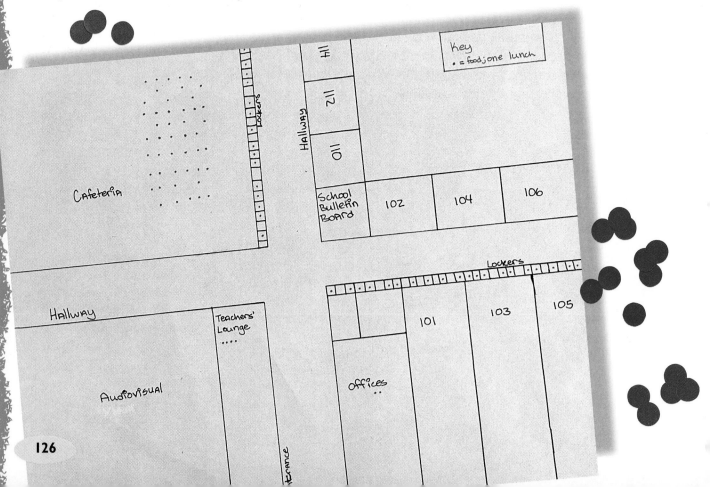

## Try It Out

Imagine a map of your school. What would a "food distribution map" of your school look like? Chances are, it would indicate that food is located in the cafeteria, in student lunchboxes, and perhaps in the teacher's lounge.

How would this work exactly? To find out, make that map. Sketch a map, or floor plan, of your school. Make a map key that uses a symbol to indicate "food." One symbol on the map will indicate one food item, two symbols will represent two food items, and so on. Now mark the map with the symbols. When you're done, you'll probably have a map with many symbols in the cafeteria and some others scattered throughout the school.

Every distribution map tells you three basic things:

**A. What is distributed** Your map shows the distribution of food.

**B. Where it is distributed** By looking at the symbols, you can see where the food is located.

**C. How many are distributed** Because each symbol represents a certain number of food items, the map tells you approximately how many food items are located in each room in the house.

## Apply the Skill

Now that you see how distribution maps are made and what three things they tell you, you can use what you have learned to read a real distribution map. Use the distribution map on the right to answer the following questions.

① **Determine what is distributed.** What resource does this map show the distribution of?

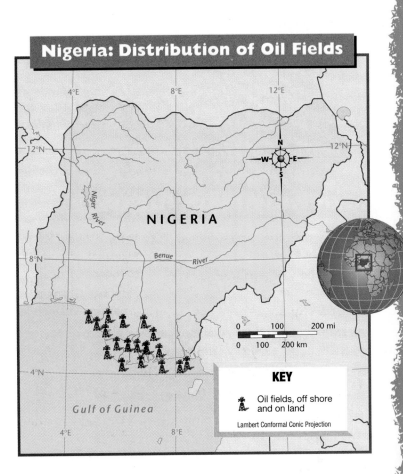

**Nigeria: Distribution of Oil Fields**

**KEY**

Oil fields, off shore and on land

Lambert Conformal Conic Projection

② **Determine where it is distributed.** How is the distribution indicated on the map? In what part or parts of Nigeria is this resource located?

③ **Determine how many are distributed.** How many symbols are shown on the map?

④ **Organize what you have learned.** Using the map as a guide, write a paragraph that explains the information on the map. After you have completed your paragraph, write another paragraph explaining whether or not you think the map is a more useful way of communicating this information than writing.

⑤ **Make a connection to the real world.** Explain why this map would be useful to each of the following people: the president of an oil company, an officer in the Nigerian armed forces, a member of the Nigerian government, a member of the government of neighboring Cameroon.

# Review and Activities

## Reviewing Main Ideas

1. Identify the three largest ethnic groups of Nigeria.
2. Explain how Nigeria's census affects politics.
3. What role did Kwame Nkrumah play in Ghana's move to independence?
4. How has Ghana changed since it became independent?
5. How has desertification affected the life of the Tuareg?
6. Describe two possible causes of desertification.

## Reviewing Key Terms

Match the definitions in Column I with the key terms in Column II.

**Column I**

1. to wear away
2. composed of many ethnic groups
3. a group distinguished by race, language, religion, or cultural traditions
4. the change of fertile land into land that is too dry or damaged to support life
5. a long period of little or no rainfall
6. a systematic counting of the population
7. a sudden overthrow of a ruler or government
8. a country's freedom and power to decide on policies and actions

**Column II**

a. drought

b. erode

c. census

d. ethnic group

e. multiethnic

f. coup

g. desertification

h. sovereignty

## Critical Thinking

1. **Making Comparisons** Compare Ghana's geography to that of Mali. How do you think each country's geography has affected its history?
2. **Recognizing Cause and Effect** How did the colonial histories of Nigeria and Ghana affect those countries after independence?

## Graphic Organizer

Copy the chart onto a sheet of paper. Fill it in to show how Nigeria's Hausa-Fulani, Yoruba, and Ibo groups are similar and different.

| | Hausa-Fulani | Yoruba | Ibo |
|---|---|---|---|
| Region of Nigeria | | | |
| Ways of Making a Living | | | |

# Map Activity

**West Africa**
For each place listed below, write the letter from the map that shows its location.

1. Nigeria

2. Ghana

3. Sahara

4. Tombouctou

5. Lagos

6. Abuja

7. Sahel

8. Mali

# Writing Activity

**Writing a News Report**
Choose one of the recent events described in this chapter and write a news report about it. Remember to describe these five things for your readers: who, what, where, when, and why.

## Internet Activity

Use a search engine to find **Cyberkids.** Click on **Reading Room** and then choose **Previous Issues.** Choose Issue 5. Then click on **TOC.** Choose **My Trip to Ghana.** Read about a girl's trip to her parents' homeland, Ghana. According to the author, how is life in Ghana different from life in the United States?

# Skills Review

**Turn to the Skills Activity.**

Review the three basic types of information a distribution map provides. Then answer the following questions: (a) What would a vegetation distribution map of Mali tell you? (b) What would a natural resources distribution map tell you about Ghana?

## How Am I Doing?

Answer these questions to check your progress.

1. Can I describe the main geographic features of West Africa?

2. Do I understand how cultures in West Africa compare to other African cultures I've studied?

3. Can I identify some historic events that have shaped the modern cultures of West Africa?

4. What information from this chapter can I use in my book project?

# ACTIVITY SHOP Desertification

**D**esertification occurs when land that was once fertile becomes a desert. The land becomes dry and salty, underground water dries up, erosion occurs, and plant life dies. Changes in climate, such as a long drought, can cause desertification. So can people. For example, people sometimes allow animals to graze so much that most plants are killed.

## Purpose

The Sahara is expanding into the edge of the savanna, or the Sahel. The desertification of the Sahel affects not only the environment, but also the people living there. In this activity, you will explore one cause of desertification.

## Materials

- three-sided box
- blow-dryer
- piece of sod as wide as the box
- sand
- goggles

## Procedure

**STEP ONE**

**Set up your experiment.** Place the box so that the open end is in front of you. Put on your goggles. Lay the sod in the box, with some space between the sod and the back of the box.

Pour the sand in a pile across the open end of the box, directly in front of the sod. Hold the blow-dryer at the open end of the box so that it will blow across the sand toward the sod.

### STEP TWO

**Create a windstorm over good land.** Use the blow-dryer to create "wind." Lift handfuls of sand and let it sift through your fingers in front of the blow-dryer, so that the sand is blown across the grass. This represents the sandy winds that blow across the desert and over grassy lands. Do this for about one minute, holding the blow-dryer no higher than the top of the sod. Note how much sand gets caught in the grass.

### STEP THREE

**Begin the desertification process.** Thin the vegetation by removing about half of the grass in the sod. This is similar to what happens when vegetation is grazed or dies from climate change. Use the blow-dryer and handfuls of sand to create another windstorm, again for one minute. How much sand is in the sod this time? How does the grass look?

### STEP FOUR

**Continue the desertification process.** This time remove almost all of the grass in the sod. This represents more overgrazing and the death of vegetation. Make a final one-minute windstorm. How much sand is in the sod now? How does the sand affect the soil?

## Observations

**1** What happened to the sand as it blew across the grass?

**2** What happened to the remaining grass and topsoil as the sand blew across the "overgrazed" sod?

**3** Imagine you are a cattle herder who needs to feed your cattle. You know that if you let your animals graze, you might contribute to

desertification. But if your animals do not eat, they will die. What would you do? The agricultural officials in your region want to know your decision. Write them a letter explaining your decision.

# ANALYSIS AND CONCLUSION

**1.** Why do you think that it is important to people living in the Sahel to slow desertification?

**2.** Pretend you are a journalist on a photo shoot. You see a farmer allowing animals to feed in an area where there is little vegetation. You know the farmer has no other place to let the animals graze. You take a photograph. Write an article to accompany your photograph.

# The Distant Talking Drum

## POEMS FROM NIGERIA
## BY ISAAC OLALEYE

**Visualize** How can people make light using palm oil?

gourd *n.*: a fruit with a hard skin, such as a melon or a pumpkin
radiant *adj.*: bright

## My Village

Èrín is the name
Of my African village.
Laughter is what Èrín means
In the Yoruba language.

In streams,
Women and children
Still collect water in gourds
    and clay pots,
Which they balance on their
    heads.

Electric light has not shone in
    my village.
With ruby-red palm oil
Poured into a clay vessel
We see at night.

My village of Èrín is peaceful,
Like a hidden world.
It's ringed by radiant green
And surrounded by five
    streams.

Like a stream,
The love
For my village
Flows.

## Village Weavers

Men and women
Weave cloth
From yarns
Dyed in herbs
In colors of green, blue,
    black, and red.

Thick and heavy cloth
They weave.
Cloth thick for the sun,
Tough for the field,
And fancy for feasts.

In alleys,
Or under the shadow of
    trees,
From morning to evening
Their hands and feet
Are busy weaving.

They work happily,
Singing and laughing,
So their mouths
Also keep busy.

**Connect** Do you like to keep your mouth busy talking when your hands are busy working? Why or why not?

◀ This Nigerian man is weaving in a workshop.

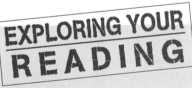

## EXPLORING YOUR READING

### Look Back

**1.** How do the people of the village use the cloth that the weavers weave?

### Think It Over

**2.** Do you think the people in the poems live in rural or urban Nigeria? Why?

**3.** Why do you think that the author describes Èrín as peaceful?

**4.** How do you think the people in the village spend most of their time? Why?

### Go Beyond

**5.** No electricity means no televisions, no light bulbs, and no air conditioning. How would your life be different without electricity? How would your life be the same? For example, you would not watch television, but you would still play with your friends. Think of other examples.

### Ideas for Writing: Hometown Poem

**6.** If you were going to write a book of poems about your hometown, what topics would you write about? Make a list. Then choose one topic from your list and write a poem. Use Olaleye's poems as a model.

# Exploring East Africa

## MAP ACTIVITIES

*The borders of many East African countries were set by the Europeans who started colonies there. Borders often follow rivers and mountains. To get to know this region, do the following:*

### Rename a lake
Find Lake Victoria on the map. It was named after Queen Victoria of England, who ruled at the end of the 1800s. At that time, Tanganyika and Kenya were ruled by Great Britain. (Tanganyika later became part of the country of Tanzania.) Use features on the map or ideas of your own to help you rename the lake.

### Consider location
The countries of East Africa are located between the Red Sea, the Gulf of Aden, and the Indian Ocean. How do you think East Africa's location might have affected its history and cultures?

# Ethiopia

## CHURCHES AND MOSQUES

**Reach Into Your Background**

Think about the subjects you study in school. Why is it important for you to be able to read and write? Why is it important for you to learn history and math? What might your life be like if you could not go to school? What kind of jobs could you do if you did not go to school?

**Questions to Explore**

1. What religions can be found in Ethiopia?

2. Why did Christianity in Ethiopia develop in a unique way?

**Key Terms**

monastery

**Key Places**

Lalibela

Addis Ababa

As a young boy, Iyasus Moa (ee YAH soos MOH uh) went to school and learned to read and write. But he dreamed of studying music and painting. He also wanted to learn another language, so Iyasus traveled to Tigray (TEE gray), in northern Ethiopia. He walked a distance that today would take three days to drive. Did he plan to enter a university in Tigray? No. The year was A.D. 1220, and there were no universities in Ethiopia. Iyasus entered a Christian **monastery.** This is a place where priests live, work, and study. A priest who lives in a monastery is called a monk.

Iyasus studied hard for many years. He became a monk. He also became a famous teacher and artist. His students built monasteries and schools all over the country.

## Religions of Ethiopia

Iyasus Moa lived in Ethiopia, a country in East Africa. He studied Geez (gee EZ), one of the world's oldest languages. Geez is an ancient form of the language spoken by the Amhara, one of Ethiopia's larger ethnic groups. The Amhara were writing their language by 500 B.C. Ethiopia and

▼ The Debre Bizen monastery sits about 8,000 feet (2,438 m) up in the mountains of Eritrea, which was part of Ethiopia until 1993.

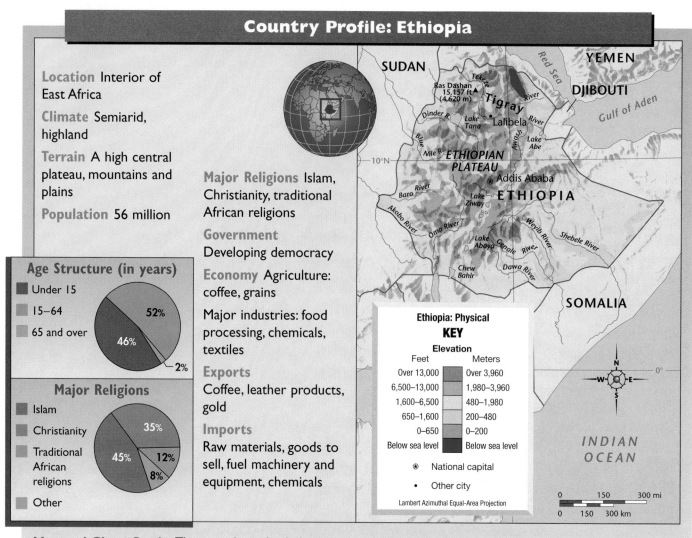

**Location** Interior of East Africa

**Climate** Semiarid, highland

**Terrain** A high central plateau, mountains and plains

**Population** 56 million

**Major Religions** Islam, Christianity, traditional African religions

**Government** Developing democracy

**Economy** Agriculture: coffee, grains

Major industries: food processing, chemicals, textiles

**Exports** Coffee, leather products, gold

**Imports** Raw materials, goods to sell, fuel machinery and equipment, chemicals

### Age Structure (in years)
- Under 15
- 15–64
- 65 and over

52%
46%
2%

### Major Religions
- Islam
- Christianity
- Traditional African religions
- Other

35%
45%
12%
8%

**Ethiopia: Physical**
**KEY**
**Elevation**

| Feet | | Meters |
|---|---|---|
| Over 13,000 | | Over 3,960 |
| 6,500–13,000 | | 1,980–3,960 |
| 1,600–6,500 | | 480–1,980 |
| 650–1,600 | | 200–480 |
| 0–650 | | 0–200 |
| Below sea level | | Below sea level |

⊛ National capital
• Other city

Lambert Azimuthal Equal-Area Projection

0   150   300 mi
0   150   300 km

**Map and Chart Study** This map shows land elevation in Ethiopia. **Location** What area of Ethiopia has the highest elevations? **Place** Where are most of Ethiopia's rivers located? **Movement** What physical features might make it hard to travel between western and eastern Ethiopia? **Critical Thinking** Look at the graph of Ethiopia's major religions. What two religions have the most followers?

**Church History** The Egyptian Coptic Church was one of the first to leave the rest of the Christian Church. Later, the Christian Church divided even more. Today, there are many denominations, or types, of Christian churches.

Egypt are the only African countries that have a written history dating back to ancient times. Much of Ethiopia's history was preserved by monks like Iyasus, who copied books by hand.

The religion Iyasus studied was also very old. It had spread to Ethiopia along trade routes. Ethiopia was a center of trade. Look at the map in the Country Profile. Find the Nile River and the Red Sea. The main source of the Nile River is in Ethiopia's highlands. Ethiopia used to include the countries that today are Eritrea, Djibouti, and Somalia. These countries border the Red Sea. As people traded goods along the Nile River and the Red Sea, they also learned about each other's religions.

**Ethiopian Christianity** Alexandria, a city in Egypt, was one of the first centers of Christianity. Over time, Christians in Alexandria came to differ with Christians in Rome and Constantinople. In A.D. 451,

Egyptian Christians separated from the rest of the Christian Church. They formed the Coptic Christian Church. Coptic Christianity slowly spread from Egypt to Ethiopia.

Ethiopian Christians were isolated from Christians in other parts of the world. Ethiopia's mountains made it hard for people in the interior to travel to other areas. Some people traveled along the Nile River and the Red Sea. With the spread of Islam, however, these travel routes were cut off to Ethiopian Christians.

**Islam**   In the 600s, Arabs began to spread across North Africa. They brought their religion, Islam, with them. Muslim Arabs did not take over Ethiopia, but they moved into the areas around it. Over time, Arab traders built cities along trade routes. Eventually, Muslim Arabs came to control trade in the entire region. And, in time, some Ethiopians adopted the Muslim faith.

**Christians and Muslims**   As Muslim Arabs took control of Ethiopia's coastal regions, Ethiopian Christians began moving inland. Finally, Christian Ethiopia was landlocked. It was surrounded by Muslim-controlled areas. As a result, Christians in Ethiopia had little contact with Christians elsewhere. The Ethiopian Christian Church developed into a unique form of Christianity. The Ethiopian Church still uses its own traditions and literary language, Geez.

Throughout Ethiopia's history, Christians and Muslims have sometimes fought over religious issues. They were at war with each other in the 1500s. But, for the most part, Christians and Muslims have lived together peacefully in Ethiopia. Today, about 35 percent of Ethiopians are Christians, and some 45 percent are Muslims. The rest practice traditional African religions.

**READ ACTIVELY**

**Ask Questions** What questions do you have about the spread of Islam to Ethiopia?

▼ Ethiopian Christians and Muslims both have histories that are rich in literature and education. The page at left is from the Quran and the page at right is from a hand-painted Christian document.

Most churches are built from the bottom up. In the 1100s, however, Ethiopians carved 11 churches from the top down. Workers carved the roof first. They worked their way from the top of the church to the bottom. They always left enough rock in place so that they could stand on it and still reach the area, inside or outside, that they were carving. How might carving a church starting at the top be easier than starting at the bottom? How might it be harder?

Because the churches at Lalibela were underground, Ethiopian Christians were able to hide them from invaders by piling earth on the roofs.

Workers carved the roof, windows, and floors of each church on a slight incline, to allow the heavy summer rains to run off.

Each church is connected to other churches by underground passages carved out of rock.

Workers used hand tools to carve each church out of solid underground rock. Some churches took 150 years to complete.

# Contrasting Ways of Life

Most Ethiopians, regardless of their religious background, live in rural areas. What is life like for rural Ethiopians? A look at the town of Lalibela (lah lih BEL uh) provides some clues.

**Lalibela** Lalibela was the capital of Christian Ethiopia for about 300 years. Rural Ethiopia also has many towns with Muslim shrines and tombs.

Services such as electricity and running water are rare in rural Ethiopia. No one in Lalibela has electricity or a telephone, and the town has only one car. The people who live around Lalibela make a living by farming. In some areas, people make a living by herding cattle or fishing. Some families specialize in jobs such as woodworking and beekeeping.

**Addis Ababa** Some 200 miles (322 km) south of Lalibela lies Ethiopia's capital city, Addis Ababa (ad uh SAB uh buh). It has all the conveniences of city life—running water, electricity, and modern hospitals. The city also has a more traditional, rural side. In some areas, houses are made not of concrete and stone, but of wood and dried mud. And some families still wash their clothes in the river, leaving them to dry on the riverbanks.

Addis Ababa's mix of modern and traditional ways of living illustrates the outlook of many Ethiopians. While expressing great pride in their past, they look toward the future with confidence.

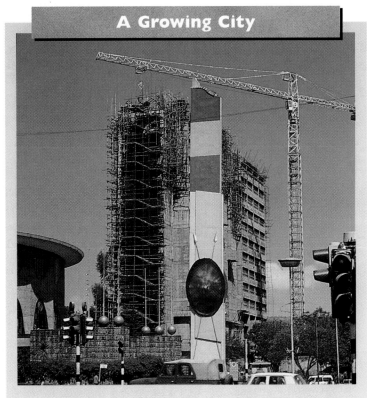

### A Growing City

The population of Addis Ababa is growing. New buildings are always being constructed. This one lies near the center of the city.

**READ ACTIVELY**

**Connect** How is your community a mix of old and new?

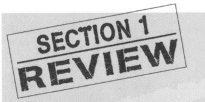

# SECTION 1 REVIEW

1. **Define** monastery.

2. **Identify** (a) Lalibela, (b) Addis Ababa.

3. How did Ethiopia's geography affect its role in the ancient world?

4. Why did Christian beliefs in Ethiopia differ from those of Christians in the rest of the world?

**Critical Thinking**

5. **Making Comparisons** How is life in Ethiopia's rural areas different from life in Addis Ababa? How is life similar in both areas?

**Activity**

6. **Writing to Learn** Write a paragraph encouraging travelers to visit the historic churches of Ethiopia. In your paragraph, explain how the Ethiopian Christian Church has been affected by the country's history.

# Tanzania
## WHEN PEOPLE COOPERATE

▼ In October 1995, happy citizens rallied in Tanzania's capital, Dar es Salaam, as the country prepared to hold its first multiparty general elections.

In October 1995, the capital of Tanzania, Dar es Salaam, looked ready for a celebration. Flags hung from almost every building. Crowds of people chanted and sang in the streets. Why all this joy? Was it a special holiday? Had a Tanzanian sports team won a championship? Neither. An election was about to start. It would be the first election in over 30 years to include more than one political party. Finally, voters would have a real choice among candidates with differing views.

Tanzanians felt joyful, but they did not know what the future might hold. Their feelings were rooted in Tanzania's history.

## Tanzania's History

Look at the map of Tanzania in the Country Profile. You can see that Tanzania lies on the Indian Ocean. Its location has made this area a center for trade. The people on the coast of East Africa traded with the ancient Greeks, Romans, Arabs, and Persians.

In the last 2,000 years, this part of East Africa has been ruled mostly by Arabs, who settled here, and by the Germans and the British, who did not. The British named the area Tanganyika. Tanganyika became independent in 1961. In 1964, it joined with the island of Zanzibar to form the nation of Tanzania.

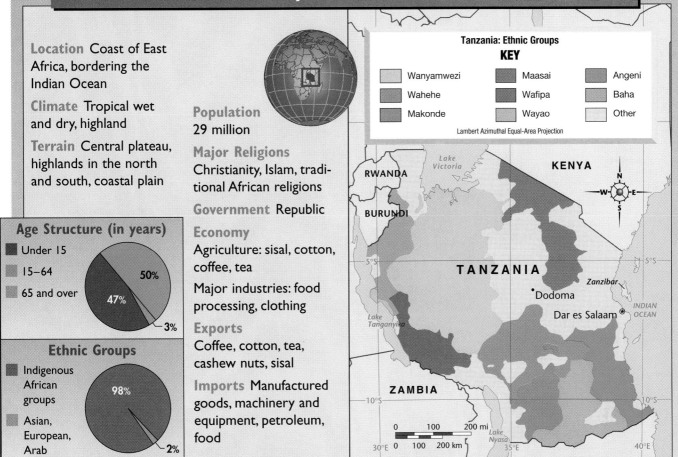

**Location** Coast of East Africa, bordering the Indian Ocean

**Climate** Tropical wet and dry, highland

**Terrain** Central plateau, highlands in the north and south, coastal plain

**Population** 29 million

**Major Religions** Christianity, Islam, traditional African religions

**Government** Republic

**Economy** Agriculture: sisal, cotton, coffee, tea

Major industries: food processing, clothing

**Exports** Coffee, cotton, tea, cashew nuts, sisal

**Imports** Manufactured goods, machinery and equipment, petroleum, food

### Age Structure (in years)
- Under 15
- 15–64
- 65 and over

50%
47%
3%

### Ethnic Groups
- Indigenous African groups
- Asian, European, Arab

98%
2%

**Tanzania: Ethnic Groups**
**KEY**
- Wanyamwezi
- Wahehe
- Makonde
- Maasai
- Wafipa
- Wayao
- Angeni
- Baha
- Other

Lambert Azimuthal Equal-Area Projection

**Map and Chart Study** Compare the chart of Tanzania's ethnic groups with the map. Although most Tanzanians are descended from Africans, they come from many different African ethnic groups. **Regions** Tanzania has two capitals because it is moving its capital from Dar es Salaam to Dodoma. Based on the distribution of ethnic groups, why do you think the government of Tanzania decided to move its capital?

## Nyerere's Changes

When Tanzania became independent, most of its people were poor. Few were literate. Literacy is the ability to read and write. Tanzania's new president was Julius Nyerere. According to Nyerere, the new republic had serious problems:

> "We had 12 medical doctors in a population of 9 million. About 45 percent of children of school-going age were going to school, and 85 percent of the population was illiterate."

Nyerere also worried about keeping the peace among Tanzania's 120 ethnic groups. In many African nations, ethnic groups fought each other after independence. Nyerere wanted to make sure that would not happen in Tanzania.

**Working Together** When Tanzania became independent, it did not have enough educated citizens to run the government. Many people had to moonlight, or work more than one job. For example, Amri Abedi was the mayor of Dar es Salaam, the leader of a regional government, and the Minister of Justice—all at the same time.

After Julius Nyerere became Tanzania's first president, he also became famous for living simply. He drove a tiny compact car and would accept only a small salary. He now lives in a simple home on his family farm.

## LINKS TO LANGUAGE ARTS

**English and Swahili**
Swahili is spoken as a lingua franca by people whose first languages are different. As a result, it contains words from several languages. English, too, contains words from several languages and is used as a lingua franca in some countries. Nyerere called English "the 'Swahili' of the world."

**Swahili**   To help all the ethnic groups feel like part of one country, Nyerere made Swahili the national language. Swahili is a mix of Arab and African words. It is the language of East African trade. Swahili culture mixes African and Arab cultures. As a result, adopting Swahili as the national language made it less likely that the government would be controlled by just one ethnic group.

Many Tanzanians speak Swahili as a second language. It is the country's *lingua franca.* This means that Tanzanians can use it to talk to each other if they speak different first languages.

**The One-Party System**   Nyerere also feared that political parties in Tanzania would be based on ethnic groups. Then, to win an election, a candidate from one party might promote hatred toward an ethnic group whose members belonged to another party. This had happened in other newly independent African nations.

To avoid this situation, Nyerere pushed to have only one political party. In Nyerere's one-party system, voters still chose from more than one candidate. But all the candidates were members of the same party.

**Improving the Economy**   Next, Nyerere turned to the economy. He told Tanzanians that independence meant *uhuru na kazi* (oo HOO roo nah KAH zee)—"freedom and work." This was his way of saying that only hard work could end poverty. Nyerere said that Tanzania should be self-reliant and not depend on other nations.

One part of self-reliance was *ujamaa* (oo JAH mah), which is Swahili for "togetherness" or "being a family." Tanzania's economy is based on farming. Most Tanzanian farmers work on family homesteads. Nyerere asked these farmers to move to ujamaa villages. He knew that it would be easier for the government to provide clean water and education in a few locations, rather than in many scattered places. At first, many people volunteered to move to the villages. Later, many others were forced to move.

**Nyerere's Successes and Failures** Nyerere's social policies worked. He kept peace in Tanzania. He also greatly improved education. Nyerere was proud of his success. He commented:

> "When I stepped down, 91 percent of the adult population was literate, 100 percent of the children of schoolgoing age were going to school, not just for four years, but for seven years. We did not have enough engineers, but we had thousands of engineers trained by ourselves. We did not have enough doctors, but we had many more than twelve, we had thousands trained by ourselves. That is what we were able to do ourselves in a short period of independence."

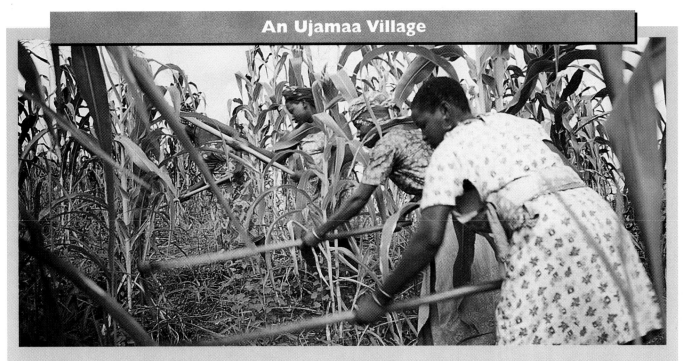

**An Ujamaa Village**

The ujamaa villages were supposed to boost farm production. Communities could then sell their surplus produce. Some people, like the women hoeing corn above, were glad to take part in ujamaa. Many other Tanzanians, however, resisted leaving the small family farms where their ancestors were buried. In the long run, Tanzania ended the ujamaa program.

However, Nyerere's ujamaa program failed. Many farm families refused to live in ujamaa villages. They wanted to work their own land. Few crops were produced. Meanwhile, factories produced fewer products, and world prices for many of Tanzania's products fell. By the mid-1980s, the country was poorer than it had been at independence.

## Tanzania Today

Nyerere retired in 1985. Now he works with leaders from other countries to study the challenges that face the continent. In 1996, he led an effort to stop a civil war in a nearby country, Burundi.

**The End of Ujamaa**   After Nyerere left office, Tanzania's new leaders changed some of his unsuccessful programs. To begin with, they ended ujamaa. They also decided that farms should put more effort into producing cash crops to sell. They also asked foreign countries for more help. Tanzania is still very poor. It has a huge **foreign debt,** or money owed to foreign countries. But the economy is improving.

**A Multiparty System**   Tanzania's new leaders also changed the election system. In 1992, the government started to allow new political parties to form. When a country has two or more political parties, it has a **multiparty system.** The first elections under the multiparty system were held in October 1995. Members of more than 10 parties

Connect How are elections in the United States like elections in Tanzania today?

### A Cash Crop That Smells Sweet

Tanzania's island of Zanzibar is the biggest producer of cloves in the world. People use cloves as a spice. A clove tree must grow for five years before it will begin to flower (right). When it does, farmers pick the buds by hand before the flowers open. They dry the cloves in the sun until they turn dark brown (below).

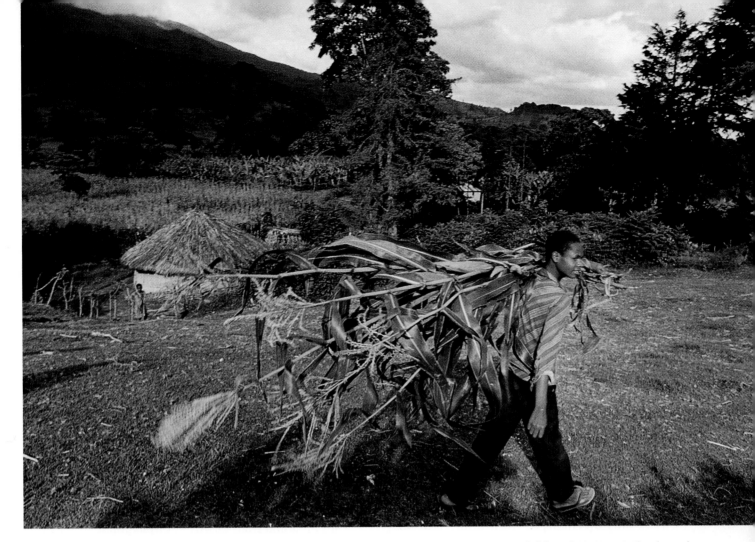

ran for office. In the end, Nyerere's party won the most votes. But the election raised some issues that divided people. For example, one party suggested that Zanzibar should leave the union with Tanzania. This is exactly what Nyerere worried about.

As Tanzania's leaders face new challenges, they may keep in mind Nyerere's words: "There is a time for planting and a time for harvesting. I am afraid for us it is still a time for planting."

▲ New farming methods and seeds are helping some Tanzanian farmers to grow more than they could in the past. Changes like these are helping to improve Tanzania's economy.

## SECTION 2 REVIEW

1. **Define** (a) lingua franca, (b) foreign debt, (c) multiparty system.

2. **Identify** (a) Julius Nyerere, (b) Dar es Salaam, (c) Zanzibar.

3. What changes did Julius Nyerere bring to Tanzania?

4. What challenges faced Tanzania in the 1990s?

**Critical Thinking**

5. **Identifying Central Issues** Why did Julius Nyerere want a one-party system? Do you think he was right? Why or why not?

**Activity**

6. **Writing to Learn** How does Nyerere's slogan, "uhuru na kazi," or freedom and work, apply to the kind of independence that comes from growing up? Write a paragraph explaining how you have experienced uhuru na kazi as you have grown older.

# SKILLS ACTIVITY

# Using Isolines to Show Elevation

**"W**hat on Earth is this?"

Alicia stared at the map. She could not imagine the purpose of the strange lines she was looking at.

"Those are isolines," her teacher, Ms. Washington, answered. "And they are not really on Earth. They are imaginary lines that people draw on maps. Think about the borders of countries. You can't see borders in the real world—there are no big, painted lines on the ground. Isolines are like that. They exist only on maps, to show information."

"Okay," Alicia said. "What do they show?"

"These isolines show elevation. By understanding isolines, you can make a flat map stand up! Let me show you how to figure them out."

## Get Ready

Ms. Washington is right. Isolines do make flat maps stand up, in a way. How? Start with the word *isolines* itself. It comes from the Greek word *iso,* which means "equal," and the English word *lines.* Isolines outline equal parts of a map. When isolines are used to show elevation, they outline different parts of the map at the same elevation. Isolines that show elevation are also called contour lines because their pattern shows the contour, or shape, of the land. If you understand how to read isolines, you can see a two-dimensional map in three dimensions!

### Mt. Kenya: Contour Map

**KEY**
Contour interval = 2,000 ft
Mercator Projection

Look at the opposite page. The picture on the left shows how a landform looks from the side. To the right, the landform is represented by isolines. Do you see how they match? Where the land is steeper, the isolines are closer together. Where the land is flatter, the isolines are farther apart.

## Try It Out

You can learn to read isolines by playing a game. All you need are notecards, pens, and a partner.

**A. Deal the cards.** Deal six notecards to your partner and six to yourself.

**B. Draw landforms.** You and your partner should each draw a profile, or sideways view, of an imaginary landform on each of your cards.

**C. Draw isolines.** Now, on your remaining three cards, you and your partner should each draw isolines that represent different imaginary landforms, one per card. The isolines can be any shape you want.

**D. Trade Cards.** Work with your partner's cards. Draw a profile of the landform based on your partner's isolines, and isolines based on your partner's landforms. When you have finished, check each other's work.

## Apply the Skill

The map on this page shows isolines of Ethiopia. Use the map to complete the steps that follow, and try to visualize the contour of the land of Ethiopia.

1 **Remember that isolines connect places of equal elevation.** The isolines on this map are labeled to show elevation. What is the lowest elevation in Ethiopia? What is the highest? What is the difference between each pair of isolines?

2 **Use the isolines to get an idea of landscape.** How would you describe the Ethiopian landscape—hilly, mountainous, flat? Where are the highest parts of the country? Which part of the country is the most rugged?

3 **Use isolines to find the elevation near bodies of water.** Look at the isolines around Lake Tana and Ethiopia's other bodies of water. Which is on higher land, Lake Tana or the rivers in the southeastern part of Ethiopia?

**Ethiopia: Contour Map**

KEY

• City

Isolines in meters

Lambert Azimuthal Equal-Area Projection

0    100    200 mi
0   100   200 km

# Kenya

## SKYSCRAPERS IN THE SAVANNA

BEFORE YOU READ

**Reach Into Your Background**

How do you stay in touch with friends and family members after one of you moves? How do you cope with feeling homesick when you are away from home?

**Questions to Explore**

1. How do Kenyans who move to Nairobi from rural areas maintain ties to their homes and families?

2. Why do many more Kenyan men than women move from the country to the city?

**Key Terms**
harambee

**Key People and Places**
Jomo Kenyatta
Mount Kenya
Nairobi

---

▼ This series of buildings is called a shamba. It was built by members of Kenya's Kikuyu ethnic group. The whole shamba is considered the family home.

"**W**here is your *shamba*?" This is a question that two Kenyans usually ask each other when they first meet. A shamba is a small farm owned and run by a Kenyan family. Even Kenyans who live in the city think of the piece of land where they were born as home. They return to it throughout their lives. Land is very important to Kenyans.

## Kenya's Geography and People

Kenya is a country in central East Africa. Mount Kenya, Kenya's highest mountain, lies just south of the Equator. But its twin peaks are covered with snow all year. Find Mount Kenya in the Country Profile map. Southwest of Mount Kenya is a region of highlands. This region has a high elevation. Its average temperature is 67°F (19°C). The area also gets plenty of rain, so the land is good for farming. Most of Kenya's people are farmers, and they live in shambas dotting the countryside in the highlands.

**Location** East Africa, bordering Indian Ocean

**Climate** Semiarid, highland

**Terrain** Low coastal plain and plateau to the south. The Great Rift Valley enters country north-south flanked by high mountains.

**Population** 29 million

**Major Religions** Christianity, traditional African religions

**Government** Republic

**Economy**
Agriculture: coffee, corn, tea

Major industries: tourism, light manufacturing, petroleum products

**Exports** Tea, coffee, petroleum products

**Imports** Machinery and equipment, petroleum and petroleum products, iron and steel, raw materials, food, goods to sell

### Age Structure (in years)
- Under 15
- 15–64
- 65 and over

50%
48%
2%

### Ethnic Groups
- Indigenous African groups
- Asian, European, Arab

99%
1%

**Kenya: Physical**
**KEY**
Elevation

| Feet | Meters |
| --- | --- |
| Over 13,000 | Over 3,960 |
| 6,500–13,000 | 1,980–3,960 |
| 1,600–6,500 | 480–1,980 |
| 650–1,600 | 200–480 |
| 0–650 | 0–200 |
| Below sea level | Below sea level |

⊛ National capital

Mercator Projection

0    100    200 mi
0    100    200 km

**Map and Chart Study** This map shows land elevation in Kenya. **Location** What areas of Kenya have the highest elevation? **Interaction** Look at the information about Kenya's economy. What parts of the country might be suited to agriculture? **Critical Thinking** Look at the chart showing the age structure of Kenya's population. If you had to guess, what percentage of people in your community would you say are under age 15? How is your community similar to or different from Kenya?

The land near the coast is warmer than the highlands, but the area also has good farmland. Farther inland, plains stretch across Kenya. Here there is little rainfall. Because of this lack of rain, the plains support only bushes, small trees, and grasses. North of the plains lie deserts, where the temperature can sometimes climb as high as 135°F (57°C).

**The Diversity of Kenya's People** Nearly all of Kenya's people are indigenous Africans. A few of Kenya's people are of European or Asian descent. Kenyans belong to more than 40 different ethnic groups. Each group has its own culture and language. Most Kenyans are Christian or Muslim.

## A Typical Day for Young Kenyans

| Time | Activity | Time | Activity |
|------|----------|------|----------|
| 5:45 A.M. | Get up, wash, and dress. | 4:00 P.M. | Lessons end. Help clean the school or work on the school shamba. |
| 6:15 A.M. | Eat breakfast. | | |
| 6:30 A.M. | Start walking to school. | | |
| 7:00 A.M. | Arrive at school. Help clean the school. | 5:00 P.M. | Start walking home. |
| | | 5:30 P.M. | Reach home. Wash uniforms. Lock up goats and sheep. Help prepare supper. |
| 7:30 A.M. | Prepare for lessons. | | |
| 7:45 A.M. | Assembly. Sing national anthem. | | |
| 8:00 A.M. | Lessons start. | 7:00 P.M. | Eat supper. |
| 10:20 A.M. | Break | 7:30 P.M. | Wash up. |
| 11:00 A.M. | Lessons | 8:00 P.M. | Do homework every night. |
| 12:45 P.M. | Lunch break. Children bring their own lunch. | | |
| | | 8:30 P.M. | Wash and prepare for bed. |
| 1:00 P.M. | Play. | 9:00 P.M. | Go to bed. |
| 2:00 P.M. | Lessons start. | | |

**Chart Study** Like you, Kenyan children spend most of each day in school. **Critical Thinking** Compare your schedule with this one. How would your day be different if you lived in Kenya? How would it be similar?

**LINKS ACROSS THE WORLD**

**Running from Kenya to Boston** Kenyan runners work together to train for athletic events—and it pays off. Kenyan runners won the Boston Marathon four times in a row, from 1992 to 1995. In 1995, they placed first, second, and third. And Kenyan athletes have won numerous Olympic medals. No one is sure why Kenyan runners are so good at their sport, but some people think that training in Kenya's high elevations gives runners more endurance.

Despite the differences among Kenya's people, they have many things in common. As much as they value the land, Kenyans also value their families. Many families have six or more children. People also consider their cousins to be almost like brothers and sisters. An uncle may be called "my other father."

**Harambee—Working Together** After Kenya gained independence in 1963, the new president, Jomo Kenyatta (JOH moh ken YAH tuh), began a campaign he called *harambee* (hah RAHM bay). The word is Swahili for "let's pull together." One example of harambee is Kenyatta's approach to education. The government pays for some of a child's education, but not all of it. As a result, in many villages, the people have worked together to build and support schools.

# Rural Kenya

The people who live in the rural areas of Kenya are farmers. Most of Kenya's farmers, like farmers all over Africa, are women. They grow fruits and vegetables to eat. They also herd livestock. Men also farm, but they usually raise cash crops, such as coffee and tea. Some women also grow cash crops.

**Farming in the Highlands**  The Kikuyu (ki KOO yoo) are Kenya's largest ethnic group. Many Kikuyu live in shambas on the highlands near Mount Kenya. They build round homes with mud walls and thatched roofs. The Kikuyu grow food and cash crops such as coffee and sisal, which is used to make rope.

Children in a farming village have more responsibilities than most children in the United States. They may begin their day by carrying water from a stream to the village. They milk the cattle or goats and clean their homes before going to school. For fun, Kenyan boys play soccer, and the girls play dodgeball. Kenyan children also make toy cars, dolls, and other toys. Occasionally, someone will bring a truck with a generator, a film projector, and a screen to the village, and the people will enjoy a movie. To see what a typical day is like for a Kenyan child, look at the schedule on the previous page.

Visualize Kenyan children spend about half an hour walking to school in the morning. Visualize the scenes they might see on their way to school.

## Moving to the City

The way of life of many Kenyans is changing. As the population increases, many men and some women are moving to the city to find work. Most women and children, however, stay in the rural areas. Women are the primary caretakers for children, and it is expensive for women with children to move from the country to the city. Many find it easier to support their families by farming.

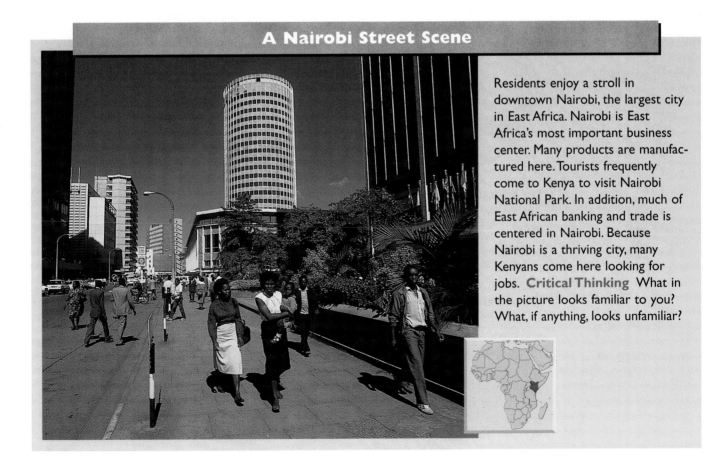

### A Nairobi Street Scene

Residents enjoy a stroll in downtown Nairobi, the largest city in East Africa. Nairobi is East Africa's most important business center. Many products are manufactured here. Tourists frequently come to Kenya to visit Nairobi National Park. In addition, much of East African banking and trade is centered in Nairobi. Because Nairobi is a thriving city, many Kenyans come here looking for jobs. **Critical Thinking** What in the picture looks familiar to you? What, if anything, looks unfamiliar?

**Ask Questions** What more would you like to know about what it's like to live in Nairobi?

**Nairobi: Kenya's Capital City** Every day, people arrive in Nairobi (ny ROH bee) by train, bus, or *matatu* (muh TAH too)—a minibus. They are new residents of the city. Nairobi's population grew from one million in 1985 to three million in 1995, making it bigger than the city of Chicago in the United States. By the year 2000, the city is expected to have more than four million residents. Many of Nairobi's newcomers walk to their jobs in the city from the outskirts of town. They may walk as far as 10 miles to work, because they cannot afford the few cents that it costs to take the bus.

When men move to Nairobi without their families, they often feel homesick for their loved ones in rural villages. Meanwhile, the women who are left behind in the villages must do twice as much work. Many people in Kenya have responded to this situation in the spirit of harambee—working together.

**Women's Self-Help Groups** One of the best examples of harambee in rural Kenya are women's self-help groups. Women in rural areas all over Kenya have formed these groups to solve problems in their communities. The women grow cash crops in addition to the crops they grow for their families to eat. Then they sell the cash crops and save the money as a group. The women meet to decide what to do with the money they have saved.

**Matatu Ride**

**Ian Kamau**
**Age 16**
*Kenya*

Look carefully at the painting. Notice that, like the British, Kenyans drive on the left side of the road and have their steering wheels on the right side of vehicles. That's because Kenya used to be a colony of Great Britain. **Critical Thinking** This matatu is bound for Nairobi. Do you think the artist considers a visit to Nairobi a happy event? Why or why not?

In Mitero, a village in the mountains north of Nairobi, Kikuyu women's groups have built a nursery school and installed water pipes for the community. They also loan money to women who want to start small businesses. Sometimes they give money to women who need to buy such things as a cow or a water tank. They also save money individually and use it to educate their children.

However, it is not easy to grow cash crops, grow vegetables for the family, chop firewood, haul water, and take care of children all in one day. One woman commented, "My children were educated through the sweat of my brow."

**Men in the City**  Men who move to the city also work hard. Many are saving money to buy land in the countryside. Men in Nairobi who are from the same ethnic group often welcome each other, share rooms, and help each other.

Moses Mpoke (MOH zuz uhm POHK ay) is a Maasai. The Maasai of Kenya traditionally make a living farming and herding. Mpoke finished high school and now works in Nairobi. He has land in his home village. But the land is too dry for farming, and he could not move his livestock to find good grazing. He left the village to find work.

Now Mpoke is a filing clerk in the city. Mpoke lives outside the city, where he shares a room with two other Maasai. Their friendship makes his life in the city bearable. Like Mpoke, most newcomers to the city are made welcome by relatives or other members of their ethnic group.

Every weekend, Mpoke returns to his village to see his family and friends. Once, as Mpoke sat in his village home, a visitor asked him which was the real Moses Mpoke, the one in the city or the one in the village. He answered:

> **"T**his is the real Moses Mpoke, but the other is also me. In the week, I can live in the city and be comfortable. At weekends, I can live here and be comfortable. The city has not stopped me from being a Maasai."

**SECTION 3 REVIEW**

1. **Define**  harambee.

2. **Identify**  (a) Jomo Kenyatta, (b) Mount Kenya, (c) Nairobi.

3. Describe the daily life of a child in a rural Kenyan village.

4. Why do so many Kenyan men move to Nairobi?

**Critical Thinking**

5. **Expressing Problems Clearly**  How are women in rural villages affected when men move to the city?

**Activity**

6. **Writing to Learn**  Describe an example of harambee in your community.

# Review and Activities

## Reviewing Main Ideas

**1.** What are the main religions in Ethiopia? How did they get there?

**2.** Compare life in Ethiopia's cities with life in its rural communities.

**3.** Did Nyerere's one-party system achieve its goals? Why or why not?

**4.** Explain the purpose of an ujamaa village.

**5.** How do men's and women's lives change when men move to Nairobi?

**6.** How are Kenyans in rural areas working together to improve their lives?

## Reviewing Key Terms

Decide whether each statement is true or false. If it is true, write "true." If it is false, change the underlined term to make the statement true.

**1.** The Swahili word that means "let's pull together" is <u>shamba</u>.

**2.** Tanzania owes a huge <u>foreign debt</u> to other countries.

**3.** A building where priests live and work is a <u>multiparty system</u>.

**4.** People who speak different languages often communicate by speaking a <u>lingua franca</u>.

**5.** A country with two or more political parties has a <u>harambee</u>.

## Critical Thinking

**1. Making Comparisons** What do you think would be the advantages of a one-party political system? What would be the advantages of a multiparty political system?

**2. Recognizing Cause and Effect** How did the spread of Islam cause Ethiopian Christians to become more isolated?

## Graphic Organizer

Copy the web onto a sheet of paper. Then complete the web by filling in the empty circles with the ways that President Nyerere planned to help Tanzania to be self-reliant.

Self-reliance in Tanzania

# Map Activity

## East Africa
For each place listed below, write the letter from the map that shows its location.

1. Ethiopia
2. Nairobi
3. Tanzania
4. Dar es Salaam
5. Zanzibar
6. Kenya
7. Addis Ababa
8. Lalibela

# Writing Activity

### Writing a Newspaper Opinion Article
Think about your community. Is it growing or getting smaller? Hypothesize about why your community has developed in the way that it has. Is it developing in a way that benefits its citizens? What are some good things about the change in growth in your community? What are some bad things? Write a newspaper opinion article explaining your view.

# Internet Activity
Use a search engine to find **AfricaOnline.** Choose **Kids Only** and then choose **Learn About Africa.** Click on the **Land** icon. Click **Next** two times to get to the **Cities** page. Take an on-line quiz about African cities. Then click **Next** to learn about Kenya. Compare and contrast the top 10 things kids do in Kenya with what kids do in your city or town.

# Skills Review

### Turn to the Skills Activity.
Review the steps for using isolines. Then complete the following: (a) Explain what information you can discover by using the isolines on a map. (b) How are isolines used on water maps?

# How Am I Doing?
Answer these questions to check your progress.

1. Can I identify the main religions of Ethiopia?
2. Can I explain some of the ways Tanzania's government has changed in recent years?
3. Do I understand why men in Kenya are moving to the cities? Can I explain how their move affects people throughout the country?
4. What information from this chapter can I use in my book project?

# A Promise to the Sun

## BY TOLOLWA M. MOLLEL

**BEFORE YOU READ**

**Reach Into Your Background**

What does a promise mean to you? Have you ever made a promise that you later discovered you could not keep?

Promises are famous around the world for being easy to make but hard to keep. Making a promise is a serious matter, because a person who accepts a promise trusts that it will be kept. In most cultures, breaking a promise is the same as betraying a person's trust. This Maasai story from East Africa is about just such a broken promise.

**Questions to Explore**

1. What can you learn from this story about how people in East Africa make a living?
2. What does this story tell you about the values of the Maasai people?

maize *n.:* a type of corn

shrivel *v.:* to wrinkle as moisture is lost

wilt *v.:* to droop

withered *adj.:* shriveled and shrunken from drying out

Long ago, when the world was new, a severe drought hit the land of the birds. The savannah turned brown, and streams dried up. Maize plants died, and banana trees shriveled in the sun, their broad leaves wilting away. Even the nearby forest grew withered and pale.

The birds held a meeting and decided to send someone in search of rain. They drew lots to choose who would go on the journey. And they told the Bat, their distant cousin who was visiting, that she must draw, too. "You might not be a bird," they said, "but for now you're one of us."

Everyone took a lot, and as luck would have it, the task fell to the Bat.

Over the trees and the mountains flew the Bat, to the Moon. There she cried, "Earth has no rain, Earth has no food, Earth asks for rain!"

The Moon smiled. "I can't bring rain. My task is to wash and oil the night's face. But you can try the Stars."

On flew the Bat, until she found the Stars at play. "Away with you!" they snapped, angry at being interrupted. "If you want rain, go to the Clouds!"

The Clouds were asleep but awoke at the sound of the Bat

arriving. "We can bring rain," they yawned, "but the Winds must first blow us together, to hang over the Earth in one big lump."

At the approach of the Bat, the Winds howled to a stop.

"We'll blow the Clouds together," they said, "but not before the Sun has brought up steam to the sky."

As the Bat flew toward the Sun, a sudden scream shook the sky:

"Stop where you are, foolish Bat, before I burn off your little wings!"

The Bat shrank back in terror, and the Sun smothered its fire in rolls of clouds. Quickly the Bat said, "Earth has no rain, Earth has no food, Earth asks for rain!"

"I'll help you," replied the Sun, "in return for a favor. After the rain falls, choose for me the greenest patch on the forest top, and build me a nest there. Then no longer will I have to journey to the horizon at the end of each day but will rest for the night in the cool and quiet of the forest."

The Bat quickly replied, "I'm only a Bat and don't know how to build nests, but the birds will happily make you one. Nothing will be easier—there are so many of them. They will do it right after the harvest, I promise—all in a day!"

And down the sky's sunlit paths the Bat flew, excited to bring the good news to the birds.

The birds readily promised to build the nest.

"The very day after the harvest," said the Sparrow.

"All in a day," said the Owl.

"A beautiful nest it'll be," said the Canary.

"With all the colors of the rainbow," said the Peacock.

So the Sun burnt down upon the earth, steam rose, Winds blew, and Clouds gathered. Then rain fell. The savannah bloomed, and streams flowed. Green and thick and tall, the forest grew until it touched the sky. Crops flourished and ripened—maize, bananas, cassava, millet, and peanuts—and the birds harvested. The morning after the harvest, the Bat reminded the birds about

▲ "After the rain falls, choose for me the greenest patch on the forest top, and build me a nest there," the sun said.

horizon *n.*: the place where the Earth and the sky appear to meet

**Predict** Do you think the birds will ever build the nest for the sun?

the nest. Suddenly the birds were in no mood for work. All they cared about was the harvest celebrations, which were to start that night and last several days.

"I have to adorn myself," said the Peacock.

"I have to practice my flute," said the Canary.

"I have to heat up my drums," said the Owl.

"I have to help prepare the feast," said the Sparrow.

"Wait until after the celebrations," they said. "We'll do it then." But their hearts were not in it, and the Bat knew they would never build the nest.

What was she to do? A promise is a promise, she believed, yet she didn't know anything about making a nest. Even if she did, how could she, all on her own, hope to make one big enough for the sun?

The Sun set, and the Moon rose. The celebrations began. The drums throbbed, the flutes wailed, and the dancers pounded the earth with their feet.

Alone with her thoughts and tired, the Bat fell fast asleep.

She awoke in a panic. The Moon had vanished, the Stars faded. Soon the Sun would rise!

Slowly, the Sun peered out over the horizon in search of the nest.

Certain the Sun was looking for her, the Bat scrambled behind a banana leaf. The Sun moved up in the sky. One of its rays glared over the leaf. With a cry of fear, the Bat fled to the forest.

But even there, she was not long at peace. There was a gust of wind, and the forest opened for a moment overhead. The Bat looked up anxiously. Peeking down at her was the Sun.

She let out a shriek and flew away.

As she flew, a cave came into view below. She dived down and quickly darted in.

There, silent and out of reach, she hid from the glare of the Sun.

She hid from the shame of a broken promise, a shame the birds did not feel.

Outside, the celebrations went on. The Owl's drums roared furiously.

throb *v.*: to beat

shriek *v.*: to cry out with a sharp, shrill sound

▼ The Sun inched down toward the horizon.

The Canary's flute pierced the air. And the Sparrow cheered the Peacock's wild dancing.

The Sun inched down toward the horizon. It lingered over the forest and cast one more glance at the treetops, hoping for a miracle. Then, disappointed, it began to set. The birds carried on unconcerned, the sounds of their festivities reaching into the cave.

But the Bat did not stir from her hiding place that night. Nor the next day. For many days and nights she huddled in the cave. Then gradually she got up enough courage to venture out— but never in daylight! Only after sunset with Earth in the embrace of night.

Days and months and years went by, but the birds didn't build the nest. The Sun never gave up wishing, though. Every day as it set, it would linger to cast one last, hopeful glance at the forest top. Then, slowly, very slowly, it would sink away below the horizon.

Year after year the Sun continued to drag up steam, so the Winds would blow, the Clouds gather, and rain fall. It continues to do so today, hoping that the birds will one day keep their promise and build a nest among the treetops.

As for the Bat, . . . she made a home in the cave, and there she lives to this day. Whenever it rains, though, she listens eagerly. From the dark silence of her perch, the sound of the downpour, ripening the crops and renewing the forest, is to her a magical song she wishes she could be out dancing to.

And as she listens, the trees outside sway and bow toward the cave. It is their thank-you salute to the hero who helped turn the forests green and thick and tall as the sky.

**Connect** How do you feel if you break a promise?

venture *v.:* to move in the face of danger
embrace *v.:* to hug

# EXPLORING YOUR READING

## Look Back
1. What favor did the Sun ask of the Bat? Why didn't the Bat keep her promise?

## Think It Over
2. What natural events are explained by this story?

3. Based on this story, how dependable do you think the Maasai people consider nature to be?

4. Why do you think that the birds did not feel as ashamed as the Bat?

## Go Beyond
5. What lesson does this story teach about how all the different parts of the world relate to each other? What lesson does it teach about how the animals relate to each other?

## Ideas for Writing: Short Story
6. Using this story as a model, write a story in which the Bat makes her peace with the Sun.

# Exploring Central and Southern Africa

**KEY**
— National boundary
⊛ National capital
Lambert Azimuthal Equal-Area Projection

CAMEROON
CENTRAL AFRICAN REPUBLIC
EQUATORIAL GUINEA
Malabo
⊛Bangui
Yaoundé
SÃO TOMÉ & PRÍNCIPE
São Tomé
Lebreville
GABON
ZAIRE
Brazzaville
CONGO
Kinshasa
CABINDA (ANGOLA)
Equator
Luanda
INDIAN OCEAN
ANGOLA
MALAWI
COMOROS
Moroni
ZAMBIA
Lilongwe
Lusaka
MOZAMBIQUE
Harare
Antananarivo
MAURITIUS
NAMIBIA
ZIMBABWE
MADAGASCAR
Réunion (Fr.)
Port Louis
Windhoek
BOTSWANA
Pretoria
Gaborone
Maputo
Mbabane
SWAZILAND
ATLANTIC OCEAN
Maseru
SOUTH AFRICA
LESOTHO
Cape Town
Mozambique Channel
Tropic of Capricorn

0     400     800 mi
0   400   800 km

# MAP ACTIVITIES

*This map shows the nations that make up Central and Southern Africa. To help you get to know this region, do the following activities.*

## Consider the geography

How many countries can you count on this map? Which country is the biggest? The smallest? Which countries are near water? Which countries are landlocked, or surrounded by other countries?

## Find the island countries

Look at the west coast of Central Africa. How many countries are completely surrounded by the Atlantic Ocean? Look at the east coast of Central and Southern Africa. How many countries are completely surrounded by the Indian Ocean?

# Zaire

## RICH BUT POOR

**Reach Into Your Background**

What resources do you think a country needs to provide a good life for its people? Make a list of these resources. Share your list with the rest of the class.

**Questions to Explore**

1. Why is mining important to Zaire's economy?
2. What economic challenges has Zaire faced since independence?

**Key Terms**
authoritarian
nationalize

**Key People and Places**
King Leopold II
Mobutu Sese Seko
Shaba

opper mining in what today is Zaire began in ancient times. The demand for copper brought Europeans to the area in the early 1900s. In 1930, a mining company found copper in a place called Kolwezi (kohl WAY zee). The company built a mine and hired miners, truck drivers, and a host of other workers. Soon a small city of workers' houses arose. Meanwhile, miners started to tunnel down into the earth to find the copper. They found it, too—right under their houses.

The Kolwezi area proved so rich in copper that, at first, miners found that they barely had to scratch the surface to find the mineral. After time, however, the miners had to dig deeper. Soon, they had dug a huge pit. Miners are still digging for copper there today. The Kolwezi mine in southern Zaire is one of the largest open-pit mines in Africa.

## Zaire's Physical Geography

Since the 1930s, Zaire has become one of the world's main sources of copper. Zaire also has supplies of many other resources, including gold, diamonds, copper, forests, water, and wildlife. Look at the map in the Country Profile and identify these resources. Zaire's minerals and other resources have played an important role in the nation's history.

▼ In Zaire, miners take copper out of the ground in layers, leaving an open pit behind.

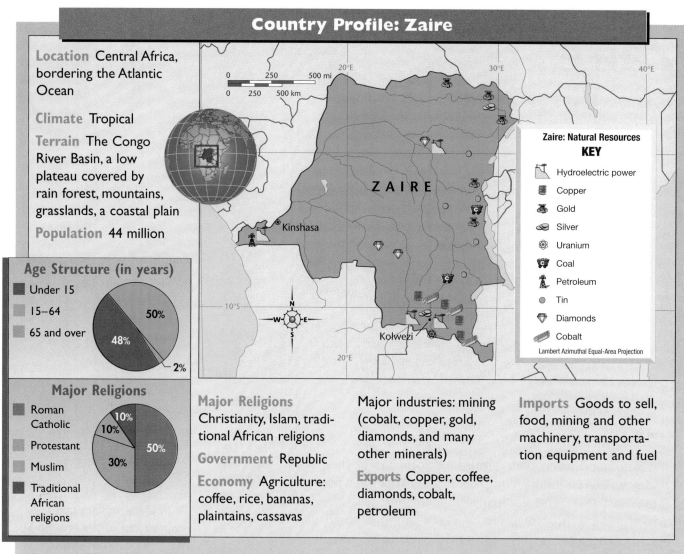

**Location** Central Africa, bordering the Atlantic Ocean

**Climate** Tropical

**Terrain** The Congo River Basin, a low plateau covered by rain forest, mountains, grasslands, a coastal plain

**Population** 44 million

**Age Structure (in years)**

- Under 15
- 15–64
- 65 and over

50%
48%
2%

**Major Religions**

- Roman Catholic
- Protestant
- Muslim
- Traditional African religions

50%
30%
10%
10%

**Zaire: Natural Resources KEY**

- Hydroelectric power
- Copper
- Gold
- Silver
- Uranium
- Coal
- Petroleum
- Tin
- Diamonds
- Cobalt

Lambert Azimuthal Equal-Area Projection

**Major Religions** Christianity, Islam, traditional African religions

**Government** Republic

**Economy** Agriculture: coffee, rice, bananas, plaintains, cassavas

Major industries: mining (cobalt, copper, gold, diamonds, and many other minerals)

**Exports** Copper, coffee, diamonds, cobalt, petroleum

**Imports** Goods to sell, food, mining and other machinery, transportation equipment and fuel

**Map and Chart Study** This map shows Zaire's natural resources. **Location** Where are Zaire's copper deposits located? **Interaction** How many hydroelectric power sites are located close to mineral deposits? Why would it be useful to have a power plant near a mine? Read the information about Zaire's economy. Which of its natural resources does Zaire export? **Critical Thinking** Compare Zaire's age structure with that of other countries profiled in this book. How is Zaire's age structure similar to that of other African countries?

**Connect** How do people make a living on the grasslands of the United States?

**Forests and Grasslands**   The Republic of Zaire is located in west Central Africa. Equal in size to the United States east of the Mississippi River, it is Africa's third largest country. Zaire has four major physical regions: The Congo Basin, the Northern Uplands, the Eastern Highlands, and the Southern Uplands.

The Congo Basin is covered by a dense rain forest. People who live in this region mostly hunt and fish for a living. Most Zaireans live in the country's other regions. The Northern Uplands, along the country's northern border, are covered with savanna, or grasslands. The Eastern Highlands have grasslands and occasional thick forests. The Southern Uplands are high, flat plains of grasslands and wooded areas. In these regions, most people make a living by subsistence farming.

**A Mineral-Rich Nation** While about two thirds of Zaire's people work as farmers, mining produces most of the country's wealth. Zaire has huge copper deposits in the southern province of Shaba (SHAHB uh). (In Swahili, *shaba* means "copper.") The country also has reserves of gold and other minerals. Zaire produces more diamonds than any other country except Australia. And Zaire has enough water power to run many hydroelectric plants. However, as is the case with many of its mineral resources, Zaire has developed only a small part of its potential water power.

## Natural Resources in Zaire's History

Resources dominate the history of Zaire. By the 1400s, the kingdoms of Kongo, Luba, and Lunda ruled Central Africa. The power of these kingdoms was based on their knowledge of ironworking. The first Europeans who arrived in the area—the Portuguese in the 1480s—were not interested in iron. They came in search of gold.

Some 400 years later, during the scramble for Africa, Belgium took control of the area, calling it the Congo Free State. King Leopold II of Belgium ruled brutally, forcing Africans to harvest wild rubber. He grew wealthy while Africans suffered and starved. Later, Belgian government officials ruled less harshly. But they still were interested only in the Congo's resources, especially its copper and diamonds.

During the 1950s, calls for independence echoed throughout Africa, including the Congo. After a time of unrest, the Congo won its independence in 1960.

**READ ACTIVELY**

**Predict** How do you think that Zaire's mineral resources have affected its history?

## Agriculture in Eastern Zaire

Although Zaire is rich in natural resources, not all Zairians make a living as miners. Many Zaireans work as farmers. They grow bananas, cassavas, corn, peanuts, and rice for their families. Others make a living growing cash crops such as cocoa, coffee, cotton, and tea. **Critical Thinking** The fields shown in this photograph are in a hilly area of Zaire. How do you think the shape of the land here creates challenges for farmers?

The Congo's first years as an independent country were difficult. Various groups fought each other for power. This worried the foreign companies that controlled many of the Congo's industries. The unrest, they feared, might hurt their businesses. In 1965, these foreign companies helped a military leader, Mobutu Sese Seko (muh BOO too SAY say SAY koh), take power. With a strong ruler in control, they thought, their businesses would thrive.

## Zaire Under Mobutu

Mobutu quickly took charge. First he set up an **authoritarian** government. In this form of government, a single leader or small group of leaders have all the power. An authoritarian government is not democratic. Also, Mobutu tried to cut all ties with the colonial past. First, he renamed the country *Zaire*. Then, Mobutu **nationalized,** or took under government control, industries that had been owned by foreign companies. At the same time, he borrowed money from foreign countries to build more industries.

Mobutu's plans to help Zaire's industries failed. Some government officials who ran companies were bad managers. Others simply stole their companies' profits. Then, in the late 1970s, the world price of copper dropped sharply. Suddenly, Zaire was earning less and less from the sale of its major export. It could not pay back the money it had borrowed. The country's economy quickly collapsed.

Mobutu responded by cutting government spending, especially on health services and schools. This hit the poor people of Zaire especially hard. When they protested Mobutu's actions, he cracked down. People who opposed his government were thrown into prison.

## Zaire Looks to the Future

Calls for reform came from inside and outside Zaire. Many times, Mobutu promised to improve the economy and to allow the people more say in government. However, he rarely took any action. Meanwhile, ordinary Zaireans grew poorer and poorer. By the

**Links ACROSS THE WORLD**

**Latin American Economies** Like Zaire, many Latin American countries used to depend on one resource. These countries have been working to diversify their economies. They are trying to earn more money by growing more types of cash crops. They are also working to build their own industries and mine their own resources without help from foreign countries.

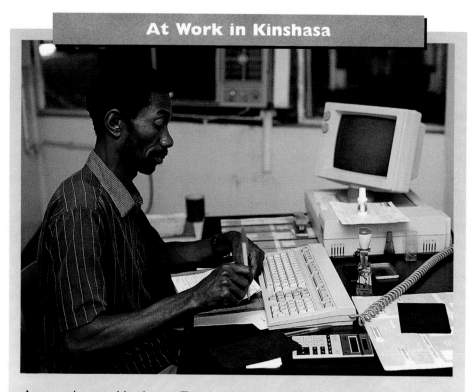

**At Work in Kinshasa**

At a truck assembly plant in Zaire's capital city, Kinshasa, an employee works on a computer in an air-conditioned office. **Critical Thinking** What kind of work might he be doing? How does this office resemble one in the United States?

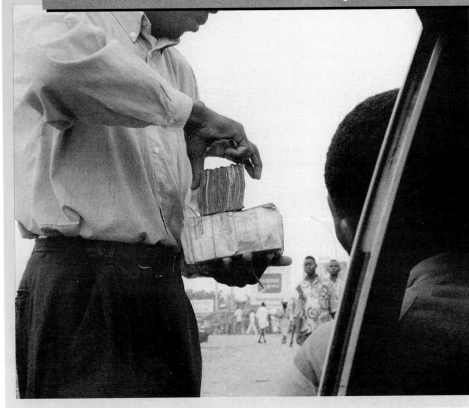

## A Breakaway Province?

In recent years, the province of Eastern Kasai (kuh SY) has thrived while the rest of the country has sunk deeper into poverty. Many people in Eastern Kasai fear that their province's wealth might be used to help the rest of the country climb out of poverty. As a result, they have called for Eastern Kasai to break away from the rest of Zaire. In this picture, residents of Eastern Kasai declare their "independence" by continuing to use Zaire's old currency, even though new currency has been issued.

1990s, the buying power of average wages was only 10 percent of what it was in the 1960s. Some middle-class Zaireans left the country rather than stay and watch their wages and living conditions steadily decline.

Those who stayed looked to the future with both hope and uncertainty. They hoped that the leaders after Mobutu would start a democratic government. And they trusted that these leaders, finally, would find a way to develop Zaire's resources for the benefit of all the people.

## SECTION 1 REVIEW

1. **Define** (a) authoritarian, (b) nationalize.

2. **Identify** (a) King Leopold II, (b) Mobutu Sese Seko, (c) Shaba.

3. (a) What are some of Zaire's natural resources? (b) What role have they played in Zaire's development as a nation?

4. (a) What programs did Mobutu Sese Seko introduce when he took power? (b) How successful were these programs?

**Critical Thinking**

5. **Drawing Conclusions** Why do you think Zaireans' wages and living conditions have declined since independence?

**Activity**

6. **Writing to Learn** Write a title and short description for a book about the history of Zaire. Design a cover for your book by deciding what images best represent Zaire's history.

# SKILLS ACTIVITY

# Organizing Your Time

"**Y**our reports are due Monday," the teacher said on Friday afternoon. To Claudia the teacher's words sounded more like this: "You will not have any fun this weekend. You will not have time to see your friends or play basketball. And if you're lucky, you will finish your report late Sunday night and come to school tired Monday morning."

"There goes the weekend," she muttered to Timothy, who sat at the next desk.

"Oh, I don't know," he responded. "I just need to fix up my final copy, and I'll be done."

"How come you're so far along?"

"Well, I started two weeks ago, when she assigned the reports." He paused. "You haven't started yet?"

"No," Claudia said. "But I guess I'd better get on it."

Has this ever happened to you? Or are you more like Timothy, who got an early start—and then a better grade and free time over the weekend for his efforts? The key is to organize your time.

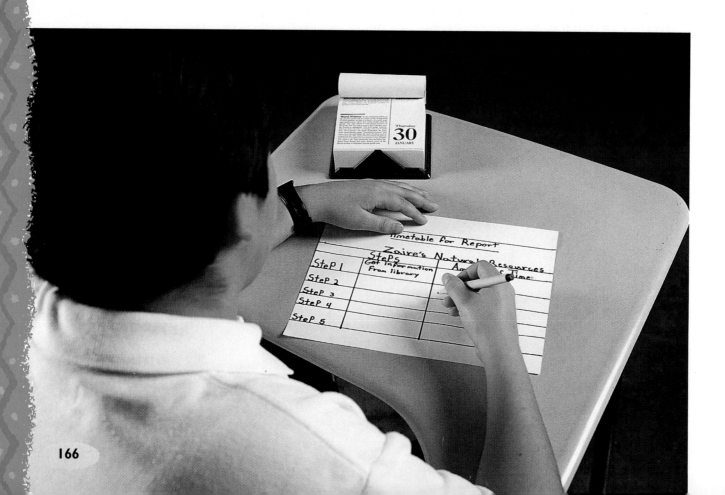

## Get Ready

Teachers know how long it takes for students to complete assignments. So they make sure to give you a reasonable amount of time. But they expect you to start assignments soon after they make them. This is the first rule of organizing your time—get started early.

But an early start does not guarantee success. You must also organize your time carefully.

### Timetable for Report on Apartheid

| | Steps | Amount of Time |
|---|---|---|
| Step 1 | | |
| Step 2 | | |
| Step 3 | | |
| Step 4 | | |
| Step 5 | | |

## Try It Out

First, set a goal. Then identify the steps you need to take to reach it. Put these steps in the form of a chart to make a plan.

**A. Set your goal.** Include it in the title of your chart. Suppose that your goal is to turn in a one-page report by Friday. The title of your chart might be "Timetable for Report on Zaire's Natural Resources."

**B. Identify the first step you will need to take to reach your goal.** What do you need to find out about Zaire's natural resources? How can you find the information?

**C. Continue toward your goal.** Write every single step in your chart. What will you need to do after you find books and magazine articles about your topic? List the steps you need to carry out to end up with your written report.

**D. Estimate the time for each step.** Look back over the steps you need to take. Think about the time you need to complete each one. Write the amount of time next to each step in the chart.

## Apply the Skill

To see how your chart can help you organize your time, complete these steps.

**1. Identify the steps.** Suppose you must write a two-page paper on the history of apartheid in South Africa. Make a chart of the steps you will take to reach this goal.

**2. Use your chart to organize your time.** You have two weeks to complete this assignment. Estimate how long each step will take. A step might take a few minutes, a few hours, or several days. Next to each step, write how long you think it will take. Remember, *the total amount of time for this assignment cannot be more than two weeks.*

**3. Transfer this information to a calendar.** Copy each step in the chart onto the proper days on the calendar. If you follow the calendar, you will reach your goal.

# South Africa
## THE END OF APARTHEID

**BEFORE YOU READ**

**Reach Into Your Background**

Have you ever experienced being left out when you should have been included? Maybe you didn't get to do something you had planned, or you weren't chosen for a team. How did you deal with the experience of being unfairly left out?

**Questions to Explore**

1. How did the people of South Africa change their government and society?

2. How has life changed for the people of South Africa in the years since the end of apartheid?

**Key Terms**
apartheid
discriminate
homeland

**Key People and Places**
F. W. de Klerk
Nelson Mandela
Cape Town

▼ Many black South African children go to schools with real classrooms now, but on nice days they enjoy studying outside.

**M**onique du Preez, a white woman, grew up in a world of white privilege. The only black people she knew were her family's servants. Du Preez admits: "Even very small children in the household would [tell the servants], 'Do this. Do that.' . . . Everything was done for us." Today, du Preez faces a world in which everything has changed.

Her school, for example, once was for whites only. Now, however, it is open to people of all races.

Life has changed for other South Africans, too. Just outside Johannesburg (joh HAN is burg), on a rural settlement called Orange Farm, Mavis Lufhugu teaches reading classes. "[People] want to better themselves," she explains. Black South Africans escaping poor rural areas and crowded cities founded Orange Farm in 1989. The original residents lived in tents. Children attended school in what used to be chicken coops and horses' stables.

Today, more than 900 Orange Farm children attend grade school in real school buildings. A team of health-care workers helps the residents stay healthy. And an adult reading program attracts eager students.

The changes experienced by du Preez and Lufhugu have been a long time coming. For many years, the Republic of South Africa was a divided country.

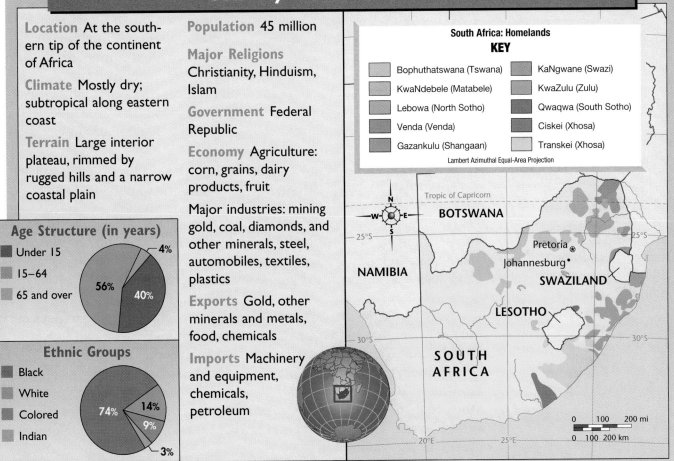

**Location** At the southern tip of the continent of Africa

**Climate** Mostly dry; subtropical along eastern coast

**Terrain** Large interior plateau, rimmed by rugged hills and a narrow coastal plain

**Population** 45 million

**Major Religions** Christianity, Hinduism, Islam

**Government** Federal Republic

**Economy** Agriculture: corn, grains, dairy products, fruit

Major industries: mining gold, coal, diamonds, and other minerals, steel, automobiles, textiles, plastics

**Exports** Gold, other minerals and metals, food, chemicals

**Imports** Machinery and equipment, chemicals, petroleum

**South Africa: Homelands**
**KEY**
- Bophuthatswana (Tswana)
- KwaNdebele (Matabele)
- Lebowa (North Sotho)
- Venda (Venda)
- Gazankulu (Shangaan)
- KaNgwane (Swazi)
- KwaZulu (Zulu)
- Qwaqwa (South Sotho)
- Ciskei (Xhosa)
- Transkei (Xhosa)

Lambert Azimuthal Equal-Area Projection

**Age Structure (in years)**
- Under 15
- 15–64
- 65 and over

4%
56%
40%

**Ethnic Groups**
- Black
- White
- Colored
- Indian

74%
14%
9%
3%

**Map and Chart Study** This map shows South Africa's former homelands. For many years, the white South African government forced thousands of blacks to move to these regions. They generally were far from cities and had few resources and poor soil. The homeland policy was part of a pattern of racial discrimination called apartheid. **Critical Thinking** Look at the graph of South Africa's ethnic groups. Which group forms the majority of the population? **Regions** Notice that most of South Africa's land is not included in the homelands. What do you think it might have been like to live in one of the homelands? **Critical Thinking** Why do you think South Africa's white government created the homelands?

# One Country, Two Worlds

South Africa lies at the southern tip of Africa. Look at the map in the Country Profile. Like the United States, South Africa has seacoasts on two oceans—the Atlantic Ocean and the Indian Ocean. The country of South Africa is larger than the states of Texas and California combined. It is one of the wealthiest African countries. Yet, until recently, white people controlled almost all its riches. Society was divided by law along racial and ethnic lines. How did such a system come to be?

**Cultures Clash** People have lived in southern Africa for millions of years. The ancestors of most of today's black South Africans arrived some 1,500 years ago during the Bantu migrations. White

**Predict** How do you think South Africa came to have laws that divided people by race?

Europeans first arrived in South Africa about 400 years ago. In 1652, Dutch settlers set up a colony at Cape Town on the southern tip of the continent. In time, these people thought of themselves as Africans rather than Europeans. They called themselves *Afrikaners* (af rih KAHN erz). And they spoke their own language, Afrikaans.

British, French, and German settlers also settled in South Africa. For years, the black South Africans who already lived there battled the white settlers. But by the late 1800s, the white settlers had forced the Africans off the best land.

The British and Afrikaners also fought each other for control of South Africa. To get away from the British, the Afrikaners founded their own states, Transvaal (tranz VAHL) and Orange Free State. Soon, however, diamonds and gold were discovered in the Transvaal. British prospectors pushed Afrikaners off their farms. The British and the Afrikaners fought for three years over the territory. Britain finally won, and declared South Africa an independent country in 1910.

**White Rule in South Africa**   The white-led government of the new country passed several laws to keep land and wealth in white hands. The Natives Land Act of 1913, for example, stated that blacks could live in only 8 percent of the country. The rest of the land belonged to whites. Blacks could work in white areas—for very low wages. But they could not own land there. Other laws passed in the 1920s separated white and black workers. And the best jobs and the highest pay were reserved for whites.

In 1948, the Afrikaners' political party, the National Party, won the election and took over the country. Afrikaner leaders added new laws to the system of white power. And they gave the system a new name—**apartheid** (uh PAHR tayt), which is an Afrikaans word meaning "separateness." Apartheid laws placed every South African into a category based on race. The laws also made it legal to discriminate on the basis of race. To **discriminate** means to treat people differently, and often unfairly, based on race, religion, or sex.

Apartheid separated South Africans into four groups—blacks, whites, coloreds, and Asians. Blacks included all

▼ Under apartheid, blacks and whites were even forced to sit separately at sports events.

Africans. Whites included people of European heritage. Coloreds were people of mixed race. The term Asians usually meant people from India. Coloreds and Asians had a few rights. Blacks had practically no rights at all.

Apartheid forced thousands of South African blacks to move to 10 poor rural areas called **homelands.** These homelands had the driest and least fertile land. There, black South Africans lived in poverty.

Apartheid affected not only where blacks could live but every aspect of their lives. It denied them citizenship rights, including the right to vote. The system kept blacks and coloreds in low-paying jobs. It put them in poor schools. It barred blacks and coloreds from white restaurants, schools, and hospitals. Apartheid also strengthened the pass laws that required all blacks to carry identification. In short, apartheid kept whites in control of the country.

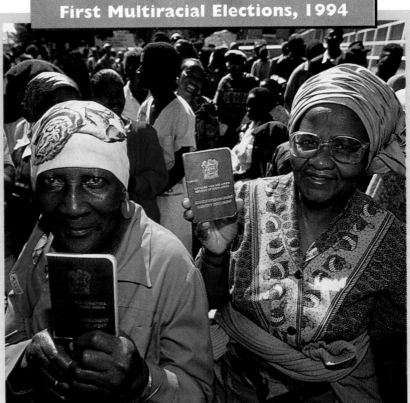

## First Multiracial Elections, 1994

Women in Johannesburg joyously displayed the identification papers that allowed them to vote in the historic election on April 26, 1994. Blacks had to wait in line for as long as eight hours to cast ballots for the first time in their lives. As a 93-year-old woman finally reached the polling booth, she said, "I am happy this day has come. I never thought it could happen here."

**The Deadly Struggle Against Apartheid** Many South Africans fought apartheid. During the 1950s and 1960s, blacks and some whites took to the streets in peaceful protest against it. The well-armed South African police met them with deadly force. Hundreds of men, women, and children were wounded or killed. Thousands more were thrown in jail. In the 1970s, black students and black workers protested against inequality. The government tried to end these protests with more force. But the demonstrations kept growing.

Countries around the world joined the movement against apartheid. Many nations stopped trading with South Africa. Its athletes were banned from the Olympic Games and other international sports events.

In 1990, these struggles began to have an effect. Faced with a weakening economy and continuing protests, South Africa's president, F. W. de Klerk, pushed through laws that tore down the apartheid system.

In April 1994, for the first time, South Africans of all colors peacefully elected a president. They chose Nelson Mandela, a black man who had spent 28 years in prison for fighting apartheid.

## CITIZEN HEROES

**To Be a Leader** The end of apartheid inspired Ivy Nonqayi to make a change. She made $80 a month tending the big house of a white town councilor, Peb Saunders. Nonqayi wanted jobs and housing for blacks, so in 1995 she took a brave step. She ran for her boss's seat—and easily ousted her. Despite her win, Nonqayi stayed on as Saunders' maid.

# New Challenges

Under Nelson Mandela's government, legal discrimination on the basis of race finally ended. Blacks and some whites welcomed the changes. But many whites who had grown up with the privileges of apartheid were not as happy.

Despite new opportunities for millions of blacks, South Africa remained a divided society. Blacks and whites usually lived in different neighborhoods. Whites still controlled most of the country's biggest businesses and newspapers. Compared to blacks, whites had better-paying jobs and owned more property.

Even though they still held a lot of power, many whites did not like the recent changes in South Africa. Some opposed government plans to help blacks get jobs. Monique du Preez, for example, wondered whether her white skin would be a drawback when she looks for a job. Other whites feared their children's education would suffer in schools attended by all races. Mandela's government had to find ways to reassure whites while making certain that blacks had an equal chance for a good life. To meet its challenges, South Africa's government will need the help of all its citizens, regardless of race.

**Connect** What do you think South Africans could learn from people who remember integration in the United States?

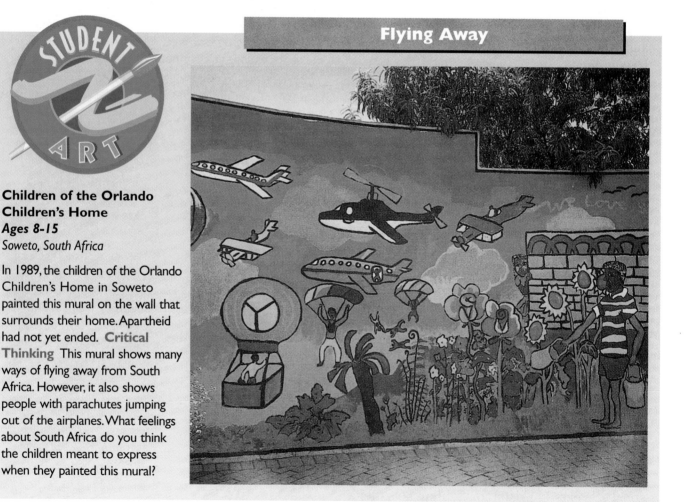

**Flying Away**

**Children of the Orlando Children's Home**
*Ages 8-15*
*Soweto, South Africa*

In 1989, the children of the Orlando Children's Home in Soweto painted this mural on the wall that surrounds their home. Apartheid had not yet ended. **Critical Thinking** This mural shows many ways of flying away from South Africa. However, it also shows people with parachutes jumping out of the airplanes. What feelings about South Africa do you think the children meant to express when they painted this mural?

# Building a New Nation

Nearly every day, television, radio, and newspapers report on the changes that have taken place in South Africa. But the new South Africa has yet to be built. Both black and white South Africans are struggling to replace white rule and apartheid with something better.

David Bailes, a white South African, left the country in the early 1970s because he hated apartheid. Since then, he has been living in the United States. Today, Bailes is thinking about returning to South Africa to live. After a recent visit to Cape Town, he said:

▼ In 1993, South Africa's president, F. W. de Klerk, and Nelson Mandela—soon to be elected the first black president of South Africa—share a triumphant moment.

"There's still a lot of inequality there. Whites still own most of the wealth, and they still have the best jobs and homes. On the surface, things don't appear much different. But you know they are—you can feel it. The laws have changed, and that's a big deal. I can hang out with my black and Indian friends in public places. South Africa is becoming a brand new country. There's still a lot of pain there, but to me, it's the most beautiful country in the world."

## SECTION 2 REVIEW

1. **Define** (a) apartheid, (b) discriminate, (c) homeland.

2. **Identify** (a) F. W. de Klerk, (b) Nelson Mandela, (c) Cape Town.

3. How did apartheid affect South Africans?

4. What changes have taken place in South Africa since the collapse of apartheid?

**Critical Thinking**

5. **Expressing Problems Clearly** What challenges must the South African government meet in order to build a new nation based on equality for all?

**Activity**

6. **Writing to Learn** Write a letter to a friend, explaining your view of the changes in South Africa.

# Review and Activities

## Reviewing Main Ideas

1. (a) Describe Zaire's four main geographic regions. (b) Which region brings in the most income?

2. How has mining affected the history of Zaire?

3. What actions did Mobutu Sese Seko take after coming to power?

4. (a) How did the system of apartheid affect South Africans in their daily lifes? (b) How did South Africans struggle against apartheid?

5. (a) How is life in today's South Africa different than it was under apartheid? (b) How are people still divided by race?

6. What are some challenges faced by the new government of South Africa?

## Reviewing Key Terms

Match the definitions in Column I with the key terms in Column II.

**Column I**

1. form of government in which a single leader or small group of leaders have all the power
2. a system of laws that legalized racial discrimination
3. rural areas in which black South Africans were forced to live
4. to treat people in a different way based on their race, religion, or sex
5. to put under government control

**Column II**

a. nationalize

b. authoritarian

c. discrimination

d. apartheid

e. homelands

## Critical Thinking

1. **Recognizing Cause and Effect** How have the actions of Mobutu Sese Seko affected Zaire's economy?

2. **Drawing Conclusions** South Africa's new government is trying to persuade its skilled white workers to remain in the country. Based on what you know about apartheid, why do you think much of South Africa's population lacks these skills?

## Graphic Organizer

Copy the flowchart onto a sheet of paper. Then, fill in the empty boxes to show the impact of resources on Zaire's history, from the first contacts with Europeans to the present.

Portuguese arrive looking for gold

# Map Activity

## Central and Southern Africa

For each place listed below, write the letter from the map that shows its location.

1. Cape Town
2. Johannesburg
3. Kinshasa
4. Zaire
5. South Africa

**Place Location**

# Writing Activity

## Writing Interview Questions

Choose either South Africa or Zaire. Write a list of five interview questions you would ask someone who is running for president. Consider the challenges the new president will face. Then exchange questions with a partner. Pretend that you are the presidential candidate. Write answers to your partner's questions.

## Internet Activity

Use a search engine to find the **Abwenzi** site. Choose the **Abwenzi** home page icon at the bottom. Explore the links and pictures to learn what penpals in Malawi and Aspen, Colorado, learned about each other. Make a class portfolio on daily life in Malawi. Include photos, recipes, writings, and information on games and dances.

# Skills Review

Turn to the Skills Activity.

Review the steps for organizing your time. Then, in your own words, explain how a flowchart can help you to organize your time.

# How Am I Doing?

Answer these questions to check your progress.

1. Can I explain the part that resources have played in Zaire's history?
2. Do I understand the impact of Mobutu Sese Seko's actions on Zaire's economy?
3. Do I understand what apartheid was and how it came to an end?
4. Can I describe how life has changed for black and white South Africans following the collapse of apartheid?

# AFRICA
## PROJECT POSSIBILITIES

*As you study the vast continent of Africa, you will be reading and thinking about these important questions.*

☛ **What are the main physical features of Africa?**

☛ **What factors have shaped Africa's cultures?**

☛ **Why have Africans been moving to cities in recent years?**

☛ **What connections do African nations have with the United States and the world?**

☛ **What factors influence the ways in which Africans make a living?**

*Show what you know by doing a project!*

GEO CLEO

## Project Menu

The chapters in this book have some answers to these questions. Now it's time for you to find your own answers by doing projects on your own or with a group. Here are some ways to make your own discoveries about Africa.

**Africa on Stage** Write a play about growing up in a country in Africa. Set the scene for your play in one of the African countries you have studied. Choose three or four characters. Next think about plot. What situation, serious or humorous, will the main character face? How will he or she react to the situation? How will the other characters affect the plot?

Write a script for your play that shows the lines each character will speak. Then present your play. Ask classmates to read aloud the parts of your characters. You may wish to videotape your live performance and show it to other classes or your family.

# From Questions to Careers

## AGRICULTURE

Farmers have always wanted to be able to produce more food. More and more, they face the newer problem of using up too much of the Earth's resources—good soil, land, or grazing material. In some places, people need to farm differently than before because of a changing climate. In Africa and all over the world, people are working on new and different ways of farming that will solve these problems.

Agricultural scientists and farmers work together to develop and try out different farming methods. It may take much time and patience to figure out whether a method works over one or several growing seasons. Engineers invent new machinery, fertilizer, and other products for farmers. Machinists and technicians help manufacture these products. Ecologists study the effects of farming on the surrounding environment.

Agricultural scientists, engineers, and ecologists all go to college. Farmers, technicians, and machinists may go to college or they may have training in specific skills for their jobs. Many farmers learn much of what they know through direct experience.

▲ This modern Nigerian farmer is using equipment suitable for his crops and his land.

**Africa in Art** The tradition of mask-making has special meaning in some African cultures. Look through books and magazines for information about different mask-making traditions in Africa. Research the kinds of masks people make, the ways of making them, and the meanings that they have. Prepare a mini-museum display with pictures or examples and detailed explanations of the masks and traditions you research.

You may want to try making a mask of your own. Use papier-mâché and your imagination.

**Africa 2000** Hold an "All Africa" conference about life in Africa in the twenty-first century. Decide on several major topics for the conference, such as economic growth, agriculture, literature, and arts. Form committees to plan the conference. For example, a speakers' committee can find speakers to discuss the topics. Speakers can be students who have done research on these topics. A scheduling committee can plan the agenda for the conference. A publicity committee can make posters to let other students know about the conference. A food committee can make and serve African foods. A press committee can write news reports. Invite other classes to attend the conference.

# Reference

## TABLE OF CONTENTS

MAP AND Handbook GLOBE

This Map and Globe Handbook is designed to help you develop some of the skills you need to be a world explorer. These can help you whether you explore from the top of an elephant in India or from a computer at school.

You can use the information in this handbook to improve your map and globe skills. But the best way to sharpen your skills is to practice. The more you practice the better you'll get.

**GEO CLEO and GEO LEO**

## Table of Contents

# Five Themes of Geography

Studying the geography of the entire world can be a huge task. You can make that task easier by using the five themes of geography: location, place, human-environment interaction, movement, and regions. The themes are tools you can use to organize information and to answer the where, why, and how of geography.

**1 Location** answers the question, "Where is it?" You can think of the location of a continent or a country as its address. You might give an absolute location such as "22 South Lake Street" or "40°N and 80°W." You might also use a relative address, telling where one place is by referring to another place. "Between school and the mall" and "eight miles east of Pleasant City" are examples of relative locations.

**2 Place** identifies the natural and human features that make one place different from every other place. You can identify a specific place by its landforms, climate, plants, animals, people, or cultures. You might even think of place as a geographic signature. Use the signature to help you understand the natural and human features that make one place different from every other place.

**1. Location**
Chicago, Illinois, occupies one location on the Earth. No other place has exactly the same absolute location.

**2. Place**
Ancient cultures in Egypt built distinctive pyramids. Use the theme of place to help you remember features that exist only in Egypt.

**3 Human-Environment Interaction** focuses on the relationship between people and the environment. As people live in an area, they often begin to make changes to it, usually to make their lives easier. For example, they might build a dam to control flooding during rainy seasons. Also, the environment can affect how people live, work, dress, travel, and communicate.

**4 Movement** answers the question "How do people, goods, and ideas move from place to place?" Remember that, often, what happens in one place can affect what happens in another. Use the theme of movement to help you trace the spread of goods, people, and ideas from one location to the next.

**5 Regions** is the last geographic theme. A region is a group of places that share common features. Geographers divide the world into many types of regions. For example, countries, states, and cities are political regions. The people in these places live under the same type of government. Other features can be used to define regions. Places that have the same climate belong to a particular climate region. Places that share the same culture belong to a cultural region. The same place can be found in more than one region. The state of Hawaii is in the political region of the United States. Because it has a tropical climate, Hawaii is also part of a tropical climate region.

## PRACTICE YOUR WORLD EXPLORER SKILLS

1. What is the absolute location of your school? What is one way to describe its relative location?

2. What might be a "geographic signature" of the town or city you live in?

3. Give an example of human-environment interaction where you live.

4. Name at least one thing that comes into your town or city and one that goes out. How is each moved? Where does it come from? Where does it go?

5. What are several regions you think your town or city belongs in?

**3. Human-Environment Interaction**
Peruvians have changed steep mountain slopes into terraces suitable for farming. Think how this environment looked before people made changes.

**4. Movement**
Arab traders brought not only goods to Kuala Lumpur, Malaysia, but also Arab building styles and the Islamic religion.

**5. Regions**
Wheat farming is an important activity in Kansas. This means that Kansas is part of a farming region.

# Understanding Movements of the Earth

Planet Earth is part of our solar system. The Earth revolves around the sun in a nearly circular path called an orbit. A revolution, or one complete orbit around the sun, takes 365 1/4 days, or a year. As the Earth revolves around the sun, it is also spinning around in space. This movement is called a rotation. The Earth rotates on its axis—an invisible line through the center of the Earth from the North Pole to the South Pole. The Earth makes one full rotation about every 24 hours. As the Earth rotates, it is daytime on the side facing the sun. It is night on the side away from the sun.

The Earth's axis is tilted at an angle. Because of this tilt, sunlight strikes different parts of the Earth at certain points in the year, creating different seasons.

## Earth's Revolution and the Seasons

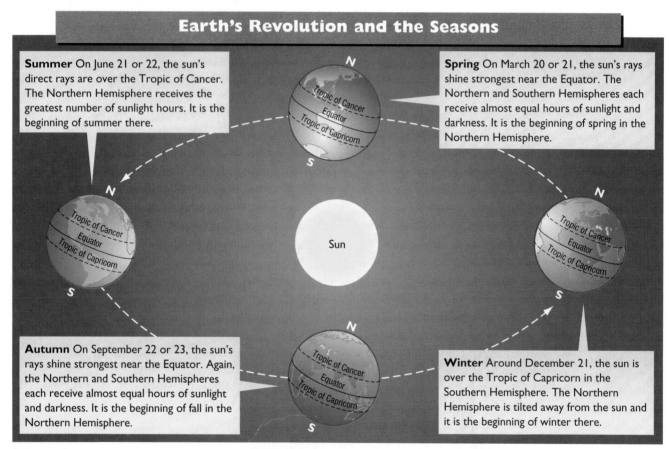

**Summer** On June 21 or 22, the sun's direct rays are over the Tropic of Cancer. The Northern Hemisphere receives the greatest number of sunlight hours. It is the beginning of summer there.

**Spring** On March 20 or 21, the sun's rays shine strongest near the Equator. The Northern and Southern Hemispheres each receive almost equal hours of sunlight and darkness. It is the beginning of spring in the Northern Hemisphere.

**Autumn** On September 22 or 23, the sun's rays shine strongest near the Equator. Again, the Northern and Southern Hemispheres each receive almost equal hours of sunlight and darkness. It is the beginning of fall in the Northern Hemisphere.

**Winter** Around December 21, the sun is over the Tropic of Capricorn in the Southern Hemisphere. The Northern Hemisphere is tilted away from the sun and it is the beginning of winter there.

▲ **Location** This diagram shows how the Earth's tilt and orbit around the sun combine to create the seasons. Remember, in the Southern Hemisphere the seasons are reversed.

1 What causes the seasons in the Northern Hemisphere to be the opposite of those in the Southern Hemisphere?

2 During which two months of the year do the Northern and Southern Hemispheres have about equal hours of daylight and darkness?

# Maps and Globes Represent the Earth

## Globes

A globe is a scale model of the Earth. It shows the actual shapes, sizes, and locations of all the Earth's landmasses and bodies of water. Features on the surface of the Earth are drawn to scale on a globe. This means a smaller unit of measure on the globe stands for a larger unit of measure on the Earth.

Because a globe is made in the true shape of the Earth, it offers these advantages for studying the Earth.

- The shape of all land and water bodies are accurate.
- Compass directions from one point to any other point are correct.
- The distance from one location to another is always accurately represented.

However, a globe presents some disadvantages for studying the Earth. Because a globe shows the entire Earth, it cannot show small areas in great detail. Also, a globe is not easily folded and carried from one place to another. For these reasons, geographers often use maps to learn about the Earth.

## Maps

A map is a drawing or representation, on a flat surface, of a region. A map can show details too small to be seen on a globe. Floor plans, mall directories, and road maps are among the maps we use most often.

While maps solve some of the problems posed by globes, they have some disadvantages of their own. Maps flatten the real round world. Mapmakers cut, stretch, push, and pull some parts of the Earth to get it all flat on paper. As a result, some locations may be distorted. That is, their size, shape, and relative location may not be accurate. For example, on most maps of the entire world, the size and shape of the Antarctic and Arctic regions are not accurate.

**PRACTICE YOUR WORLD EXPLORER SKILLS**

1. What is the main difference between a globe and a map?

2. What is one advantage of using a globe instead of a map?

### Global Gores

**◀ Location**
When mapmakers flatten the surface of the Earth, curves become straight lines. As a result, size, shape, and distance are distorted.

# Locating Places on a Map or a Globe

## The Hemispheres

Another name for a round ball like a globe is a sphere. The Equator, an imaginary line halfway between the North and South Poles, divides the globe into two hemispheres. (The prefix *hemi* means "half.") Land and water south of the Equator are in the Southern Hemisphere. Land and water north of the Equator are in the Northern Hemisphere.

Mapmakers sometimes divide the globe along an imaginary line that runs from North Pole to South Pole. This line, called the Prime Meridian, divides the globe into the Eastern and Western Hemispheres.

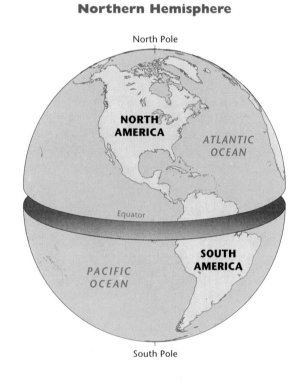

**Southern Hemisphere**

▲ The Equator divides the Northern Hemisphere from the Southern Hemisphere.

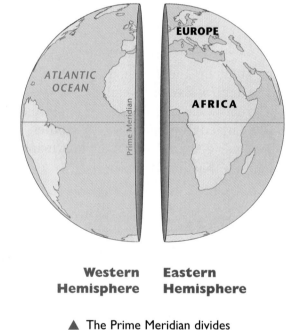

**Western Hemisphere**  **Eastern Hemisphere**

▲ The Prime Meridian divides the Eastern Hemisphere from the Western Hemisphere.

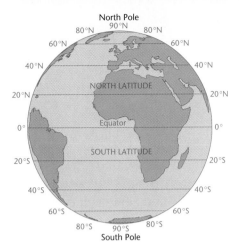

### Parallels of Latitude

The Equator, at 0° latitude, is the starting place for measuring latitude or distances north and south. Most globes do not show every parallel of latitude. They may show every 10, 20, or even 30 degrees.

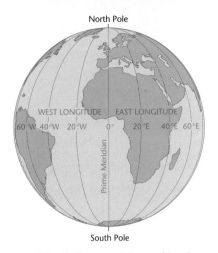

### Meridians of Longitude

The Prime Meridian, at 0° longitude, runs from pole to pole through Greenwich, England. It is the starting place for measuring longitude or distances east and west. Each meridian of longitude meets its opposite longitude at the North and South Poles.

# The Global Grid

Two sets of lines cover most globes. One set of lines runs parallel to the Equator. These lines, including the Equator, are called *parallels of latitude*. They are measured in degrees (°). One degree of latitude represents a distance of about 70 miles (112 km). The Equator has a location of 0°. The other parallels of latitude tell the direction and distance from the Equator to another location.

The second set of lines runs north and south. These lines are called *meridians of longitude*. Meridians show the degrees of longitude east or west of the Prime Meridian, which is located at 0°. A meridian of longitude tells the direction and distance from the Prime Meridian to another location. Unlike parallels, meridians are not the same distance apart everywhere on the globe.

Together the pattern of parallels of latitude and meridians of longitude is called the global grid. Using the lines of latitude and longitude, you can locate any place on Earth. For example, the location of 30° north latitude and 90° west longitude is usually written as 30°N, 90°W. Only one place on Earth has these coordinates—the city of New Orleans, in the state of Louisiana.

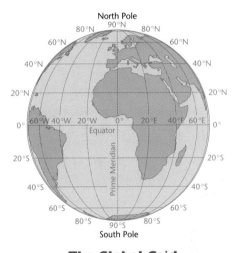

### The Global Grid

By using lines of latitude and longitude, you can give the absolute location of any place on the Earth.

**PRACTICE YOUR WORLD EXPLORER SKILLS**

1. Which continents lie completely in the Northern Hemisphere? The Western Hemisphere?

2. Is there land or water at 20°S latitude and the Prime Meridian? At the Equator and 60°W longitude?

# Map Projections

*I*magine trying to flatten out a complete orange peel. The peel would split. The shape would change. You would have to cut the peel to get it to lie flat. In much the same way, maps cannot show the correct size and shape of every landmass or body of water on the Earth's curved surface. Maps shrink some places and stretch others. This shrinking and stretching is called distortion—*a change made to a shape.*

To make up for this disadvantage, mapmakers use different map projections. Each map projection is a way of showing the round Earth on flat paper. Each type of projection has some distortion. No one projection can accurately show the correct area, shape, distance, and direction for the Earth's surface. Mapmakers use the projection that has the least distortion for the information they are studying.

## Same-Shape Maps

Some map projections can accurately show the shapes of landmasses. However, these projections often greatly distort the size of landmasses as well as the distance between them.

One of the most common same-shape maps is a Mercator projection, named for the mapmaker who invented it. The Mercator projection accurately shows shape and direction, but it distorts distance and size. In this projection, the northern and southern areas of the globe appear stretched more than areas near the Equator. Because the projection shows true directions, ships' navigators use it to chart a straight line course between two ports.

**Mercator Projection**

## Equal-Area Maps

Some map projections can show the correct size of landmasses. Maps that use these projections are called equal-area maps. In order to show the correct size of landmasses, these maps usually distort shapes. The distortion is usually greater at the edges of the map and less at the center.

## Robinson Maps

Many of the maps in this book use the Robinson projection. This is a compromise between the Mercator and equal-area projections. It gives a useful overall picture of the world. The Robinson projection keeps the size and shape relationships of most continents and oceans but does distort size of the polar regions.

## Azimuthal Maps

Another kind of projection shows true compass direction. Maps that use this projection are called azimuthal maps. Such maps are easy to recognize—they are usually circular. Azimuthal maps are often used to show the areas of the North and South Poles. However, azimuthal maps distort scale, area, and shape.

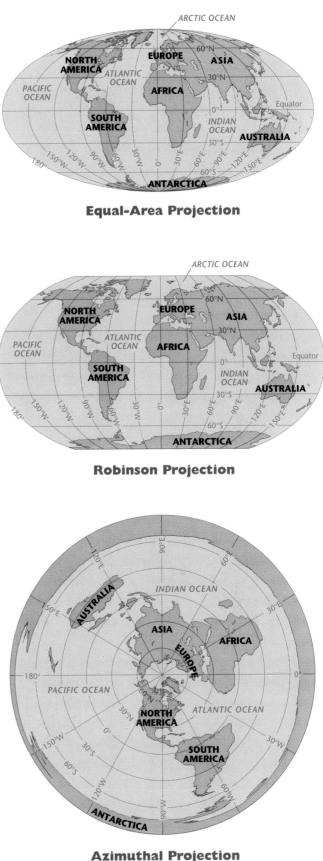

**Equal-Area Projection**

**Robinson Projection**

**Azimuthal Projection**

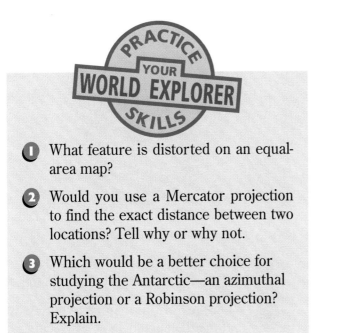

**PRACTICE YOUR WORLD EXPLORER SKILLS**

1 What feature is distorted on an equal-area map?

2 Would you use a Mercator projection to find the exact distance between two locations? Tell why or why not.

3 Which would be a better choice for studying the Antarctic—an azimuthal projection or a Robinson projection? Explain.

# Parts of a Map

apmakers provide several clues to help you understand the information on a map. As an explorer, it is your job to read and interpret these clues.

## Compass
Many maps show north at the top of the map. One way to show direction on a map is to use an arrow that points north. There may be an N shown with the arrow. Many maps give more information about direction by displaying a compass showing the directions, north, east, south, and west. The letters N, E, S, and W are placed to indicate these directions.

## Title
The title of a map is the most basic clue. It signals what kinds of information you are likely to find on the map. A map titled *West Africa: Population Density* will be most useful for locating information about where people live in West Africa.

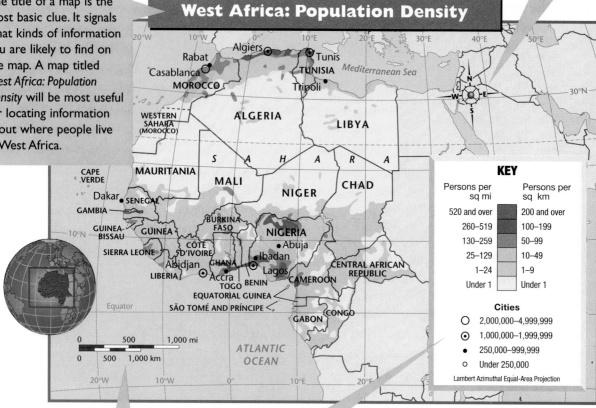

### West Africa: Population Density

**KEY**

| Persons per sq mi | | Persons per sq km |
|---|---|---|
| 520 and over | | 200 and over |
| 260–519 | | 100–199 |
| 130–259 | | 50–99 |
| 25–129 | | 10–49 |
| 1–24 | | 1–9 |
| Under 1 | | Under 1 |

**Cities**

○ 2,000,000–4,999,999
◉ 1,000,000–1,999,999
• 250,000–999,999
○ Under 250,000

Lambert Azimuthal Equal-Area Projection

## Scale
A map scale helps you find the actual distances between points shown on the map. You can measure the distance between any two points on the map, compare them to the scale, and find out the actual distance between the points. Most map scales show distances in both miles and kilometers.

## Key
Often a map has a key, or legend, that shows the symbols used on the map and what each one means. On some maps, color is used as a symbol. On those maps, the key also tells the meaning of each color.

**PRACTICE YOUR WORLD EXPLORER SKILLS**

1. What part of a map tells you what the map is about?

2. Where on the map should you look to find out the meaning of this symbol? •

3. What part of the map can you use to find the distance between two cities?

# Comparing Maps of Different Scale

ere are three maps drawn to three different scales. The first map shows Moscow's location in the northeastern portion of Russia. This map shows the greatest area—a large section of northern Europe. It has the smallest scale (1 inch = about 900 miles) and shows the fewest details. This map can tell you what direction to travel to reach Moscow from Finland.

Find the red box on Map 1. It shows the whole area covered by Map 2. Study Map 2. It gives a closer look at the city of Moscow. It shows the features around the city, the city's boundary, and the general shape of the city. This map can help you find your way from the airport to the center of town.

Now find the red box on Map 2. This box shows the area shown on Map 3. This map moves you closer into the city. Like the zoom on a computer or camera, Map 3 shows the smallest area but has the greatest detail. This map has the largest scale (1 inch = about 0.8 miles). This is the map to use to explore downtown Moscow.

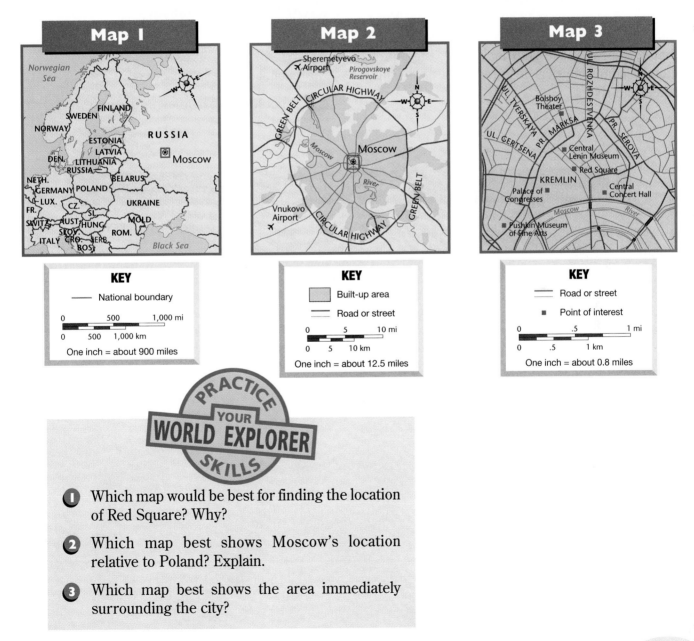

## Map 1

**KEY**

— National boundary

0 — 500 — 1,000 mi

0 — 500 — 1,000 km

One inch = about 900 miles

## Map 2

**KEY**

▢ Built-up area

— Road or street

0 — 5 — 10 mi

0 — 5 — 10 km

One inch = about 12.5 miles

## Map 3

**KEY**

···· Road or street

■ Point of interest

0 — .5 — 1 mi

0 — .5 — 1 km

One inch = about 0.8 miles

## PRACTICE YOUR WORLD EXPLORER SKILLS

1. Which map would be best for finding the location of Red Square? Why?

2. Which map best shows Moscow's location relative to Poland? Explain.

3. Which map best shows the area immediately surrounding the city?

# Political Maps

Mapmakers create maps to show all kinds of information. The kind of information presented affects the way a map looks. One type of map is called a political map. Its main purpose is to show continents, countries, and divisions within countries such as states or provinces. Usually different colors are used to show different countries or divisions within a country. The colors do not have any special meaning. They are used only to make the map easier to read.

Political maps also show where people have built towns and cities. Symbols can help you tell capital cities from other cities and towns. Even though political maps do not give information that shows what the land looks like, they often include some physical features such as oceans, lakes, and rivers.

Political maps usually have many labels. They give country names, and the names of capital and major cities. Bodies of water such as lakes, rivers, oceans, seas, gulfs, and bays are also labeled.

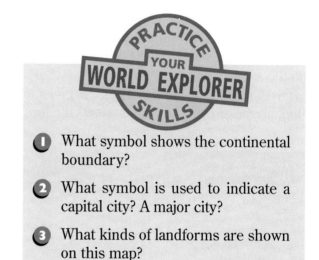

**PRACTICE YOUR WORLD EXPLORER SKILLS**

1. What symbol shows the continental boundary?

2. What symbol is used to indicate a capital city? A major city?

3. What kinds of landforms are shown on this map?

▲ The keys of political maps may include symbols. Study the key to learn what the symbols on this map mean.

# Physical Maps

Like political maps, physical maps show country labels and labels for capital cities. However, physical maps also show what the land of a region looks like by showing the major physical features such as plains, hills, plateaus, or mountains. Labels give the names of features such as mountain peaks, mountains, plateaus, and river basins.

In order to tell one landform from another, physical maps often show elevation and relief.

Elevation is the height of the land above sea level. Physical maps in this book use color to show elevation. Browns and oranges show higher lands while blues and greens show lands that are at or below sea level.

Relief shows how quickly the land rises or falls. Hills, mountains, and plateaus are shown on relief maps using shades of gray. Level or nearly level land is shown without shading. Darkly shaded areas indicate steeper lands.

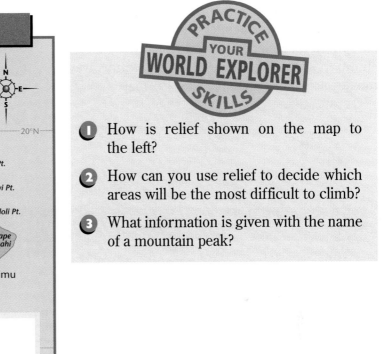

## Hawaii: Physical

PACIFIC OCEAN

155°W

Alenuihaha Channel

Upolu Point
Hawi
Makapala
Waipio Bay
Honokaa
Kawaihae
Kawaihae Bay
Waimea
Laupahoehoe
Puako
Kiholo Bay
Hakalau
Puuanahulu
Mauna Kea 13,796 ft (4,205 m) ▲
Pepeekeo Pt.
Papaikou
Hilo Bay
Leleiwi Pt.
Keahole Pt.
Kalaoa
▲ Hualalai 8,271 ft (2,521 m)
*Hawaii*
Hilo
Kailua-Kona
Keaau
Kaloli Pt.
Captain Cook
Mauna Loa 13,677 ft ▲ (4,169 m)
Mokuaweoweo Crater
Kilauea Crater
Cape Kumukahi
Hookena
HAWAII VOLCANOES NATIONAL PARK
Kaimu
Milolii
Pahala
Apua Point
Honuapo
Naalehu
Kauna Pt.
Ka Lae (South Cape)

20°N

0    10    20 mi
0    10   20 km

**KEY**
•  City

Lambert Conformal Conic Projection

▲ On a physical map, shading is sometimes used to show relief. Use the shading to locate the moutains in Hawaii.

**PRACTICE YOUR WORLD EXPLORER SKILLS**

**1** How is relief shown on the map to the left?

**2** How can you use relief to decide which areas will be the most difficult to climb?

**3** What information is given with the name of a mountain peak?

▼ Mauna Kea, an extinct volcano, is the highest peak in the state of Hawaii. Find Mauna Kea on the map.

# Special Purpose Maps

As you explore the world, you will encounter many different kinds of special purpose maps. For example, a road map is a special purpose map. The title of each special purpose map tells the purpose and content of the map. Usually a special purpose map highlights only one kind of information. Examples of special purpose maps include land use, population distribution, recreation, transportation, natural resources, or weather.

The key on a special purpose map is very important. Even though a special purpose map shows only one kind of information, it may present many different pieces of data. This data can be shown in symbols, colors, or arrows. In this way, the key acts like a dictionary for the map.

Reading a special purpose map is a skill in itself. Look at the map below. First, try to get an overall sense of what it shows. Then, study the map to identify its main ideas. For example, one main idea of this map is that much of the petroleum production in the region takes place around the Persian Gulf.

**PRACTICE YOUR WORLD EXPLORER SKILLS**

1 What part of a special purpose map tells what information is contained on the map?

2 What part of a special purpose map acts like a dictionary for the map?

## North Africa and the Middle East: Oil Production

**KEY**
- Oil fields
- Pipelines
- Major sea routes

Mercator Projection

◀ The title on a special purpose map indicates what information can be found on the map. The symbols used on the map are explained in the map's key.

# Landforms, Climate Regions, and Natural Vegetation Regions

Maps that show landforms, climate, and vegetation regions are special purpose maps. Unlike the boundary lines on a political map, the boundary lines on these maps do not separate the land into exact divisions. A tropical wet climate gradually changes to a tropical wet and dry climate. A tundra gradually changes to an ice cap. Even though the boundaries between regions may not be exact, the information on these maps can help you understand the region and the lives of people in it.

## Landforms

Understanding how people use the land requires an understanding of the shape of the land itself. The four most important landforms are mountains, hills, plateaus, and plains. Human activity in every region in the world is influenced by these landforms.

- **Mountains** are high and steep. Most are wide at the bottom and rise to a narrow peak or ridge. Most geographers classify a mountain as land that rises at least 2,000 feet (610 m) above sea level. A series of mountains is called a mountain range.

- **Hills** rise above surrounding land and have rounded tops. Hills are lower and usually less steep than mountains. The elevation of surrounding land determines whether a landform is called a mountain or a hill.

- A **plateau** is a large, mostly flat area of land that rises above the surrounding land. At least one side of a plateau has a steep slope.

- **Plains** are large areas of flat or gently rolling land. Plains have few changes in elevation. Many plains areas are located along coasts. Others are located in the interior regions of some continents.

▶ A satellite view of the Earth showing North and South America. What landforms are visible in the photograph?

# Climate Regions

Another important influence in the ways people live their lives is the climate of their region. Climate is the weather of a given location over a long period of time. Use the descriptions in the table below to help you visualize the climate regions shown on maps.

| Climate | Temperatures | Precipitation |
|---|---|---|
| **Tropical** | | |
| Tropical wet | Hot all year round | Heavy all year round |
| Tropical wet and dry | Hot all year round | Heavy when sun is overhead, dry other times |
| **Dry** | | |
| Semiarid | Hot summers, mild to cold winters | Light |
| Arid | Hot days, cold nights | Very light |
| **Mild** | | |
| Mediterranean | Hot summers, cool winters | Dry summers, wet winters |
| Humid subtropical | Hot summers, cool winters | Year round, heavier in summer than in winter |
| Marine west coast | Warm summers, cool winters | Year round, heavier in winter than in summer |
| **Continental** | | |
| Humid continental | Hot summers, cold winters | Year round, heavier in summer than in winter |
| Subarctic | Cool summers, cold winters | Light |
| **Polar** | | |
| Tundra | Cool summers, very cold winters | Light |
| Ice Cap | Cold all year round | Light |
| **Highlands** | Varies, depending on altitude and direction of prevailing winds | Varies, depending on altitude and direction of prevailing winds |

# Natural Vegetation Regions

Natural vegetation is the plant life that grows wild without the help of humans. A world vegetation map tells what the vegetation in a place would be if people had not cut down forests or cleared grasslands. The table below provides descriptions of natural vegetation regions shown on maps. Comparing climate and vegetation regions can help you see the close relationship between climate and vegetation.

| Vegetation | Description |
|---|---|
| Tropical rain forest | Tall, close-growing trees forming a canopy over smaller trees, dense growth in general |
| Deciduous forest | Trees and plants that regularly lose their leaves after each growing season |
| Mixed forest | Both leaf-losing and cone-bearing trees, no type of tree dominant |
| Coniferous forest | Cone-bearing trees, evergreen trees and plants |
| Mediterranean vegetation | Evergreen shrubs and small plants |
| Tropical savanna | Tall grasses with occasional trees and shrubs |
| Temperate grassland | Tall grasses with occasional stands of trees |
| Desert scrub | Low shrubs and bushes, hardy plants |
| Desert | Little or no vegetation |
| Tundra | Low shrubs, mosses, lichens; no trees |
| Ice Cap | No vegetation |
| Highlands | Varies, depending on altitude and direction of prevailing winds |

 How are mountains and hills similar? How are they different?

2 What is the difference between a plateau and a plain?

# Atlas

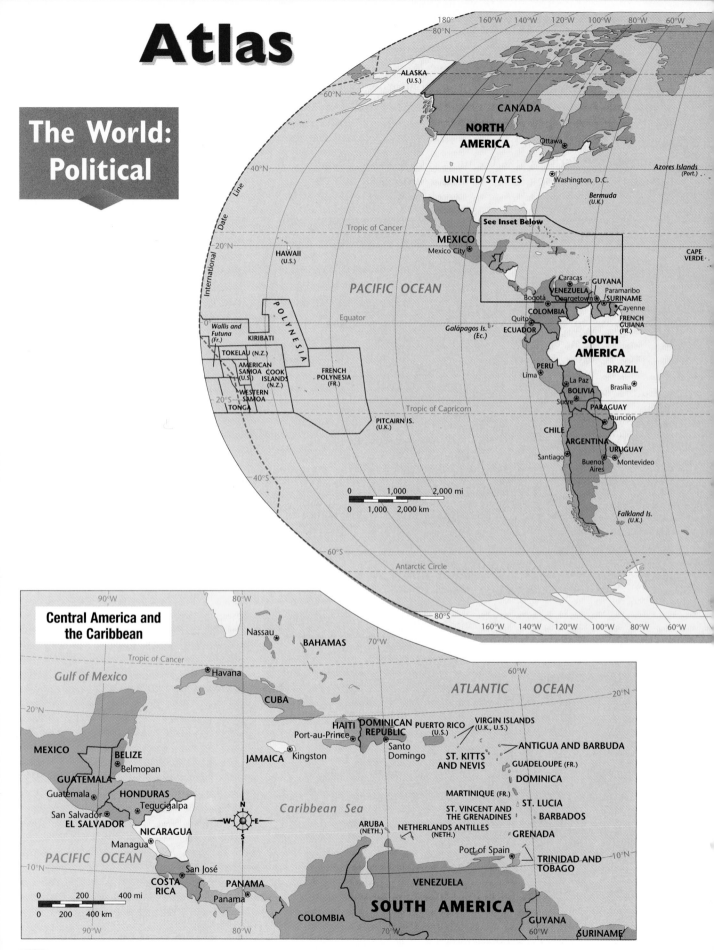

## The World: Political

**Central America and the Caribbean**

ARCTIC OCEAN

GREENLAND
(DEN.)

Arctic Circle

ICELAND
Reykjavik

RUSSIA

Moscow

EUROPE

ASIA

KAZAKSTAN

UZBEKISTAN
Bishkek

Ulan Bator

MONGOLIA

GEORGIA
ARMENIA
T'bilisi
Yerevan
Baku
TURKMENISTAN
Tashkent
Almaty
KYRGYZSTAN
TAJIKISTAN
Ashkhabad
Dushanbe

NORTH
KOREA
P'yŏngyang
Seoul
JAPAN

TURKEY
Algiers
Rabat
MOROCCO
TUNISIA
Tripoli

SYRIA
JORDAN
ISRAEL
Cairo
IRAQ
Baghdad
Amman
KUWAIT
IRAN
Tehran
Kabul
AFGHANISTAN
Islamabad

CHINA

Beijing

SOUTH
KOREA

Tokyo

PACIFIC OCEAN

Tropic of Cancer

WESTERN
SAHARA
(MOROCCO)

ALGERIA

LIBYA

EGYPT

SAUDI
ARABIA
Riyadh
BAHRAIN
QATAR
Abu Dhabi
UNITED ARAB
EMIRATES
Muscat
OMAN

PAKISTAN
New
Delhi
NEPAL
Kathmandu
BHUTAN
Dhaka

INDIA

BANGLADESH

MYANMAR
(BURMA)
LAOS
Hanoi
Vientiane
THAILAND
Bangkok
Yangon

VIETNAM

Taipei

TAIWAN

Hong Kong

Manila

PHILIPPINES

NORTHERN MARIANA
ISLANDS (U.S.)

GUAM (U.S.)

MARSHALL
ISLANDS

MICRONESIA

See Inset Below

AFRICA

See Inset Below

NIGER
CHAD
Khartoum
Asmara
SUDAN
ERITREA
Sanaa
YEMEN
DJIBOUTI
Djibouti
Addis Ababa
ETHIOPIA

Niamey
NIGERIA
Abuja
N'Djamena
CENTRAL
AFRICAN REP.
Bangui
CAMEROON
EQUATORIAL GUINEA
SÃO TOMÉ AND
PRINCIPE
Yaoundé
CONGO
GABON
Libreville
Brazzaville
Kinshasa
CABINDA
(ANGOLA)
RWANDA
BURUNDI
ZAIRE
UGANDA
Kampala
KENYA
Nairobi
SOMALIA
Mogadishu

SRI
LANKA
Colombo

Kuala Lumpur
BRUNEI
MALAYSIA
SINGAPORE

Koror
PALAU

FEDERATED STATES
OF MICRONESIA

Equator

NAURU

KIRIBATI

MELANESIA

PAPUA
NEW GUINEA

SOLOMON
ISLANDS

TUVALU

INDONESIA

Jakarta

Port Moresby

ATLANTIC
OCEAN

Luanda

TANZANIA
Dar es Salaam

COMOROS

INDIAN OCEAN

VANUATU

FIJI

ANGOLA
ZAMBIA
Lusaka
MALAWI
Lilongwe
Harare
MADAGASCAR
Antananarivo

NEW CALEDONIA
(FR.)

NAMIBIA
Windhoek
BOTSWANA
Gaborone
Pretoria
ZIMBABWE
MOZAMBIQUE
Maputo
MAURITIUS
Réunion
(Fr.)

Tropic of Capricorn

AUSTRALIA

SOUTH
AFRICA
Cape Town
SWAZILAND
LESOTHO

Prime Meridian

Canberra

NEW
ZEALAND
Wellington

60°S

Antarctic Circle

ANTARCTICA

80°S

## Europe

NORWAY
Oslo
SWEDEN
Stockholm
FINLAND
Helsinki
Tallinn
ESTONIA
Riga
LATVIA
LITHUANIA
Vilnius
Minsk
BELARUS
RUSSIA

MAURITANIA
Nouakchott

MALI

IRELAND
Dublin
UNITED
KINGDOM
North
Sea
DENMARK
Copenhagen
RUSSIA

Dakar
SENEGAL
Banjul
GAMBIA
NIGER
Niamey

The
Hague
London
NETHERLANDS
Amsterdam
Berlin
Warsaw
Kiev
BELGIUM
Brussels
GERMANY
POLAND
UKRAINE

GUINEA-
BISSAU
Bissau
BURKINA FASO
Bamako
Ouagadougou

Paris
LUXEMBOURG
Prague
CZECH REP.
SLOVAKIA
MOLDOVA
Chişinău

GUINEA
Conakry
Freetown
BENIN

FRANCE
LIECH.
Vienna
Bratislava
Bern
AUSTRIA
Budapest
SWITZERLAND
SLOVENIA
HUNGARY
ROMANIA
Bucharest

SIERRA
LEONE
Monrovia
CÔTE
D'IVOIRE
TOGO
GHANA
Porto-
Novo
NIGERIA

ANDORRA
PORTUGAL
Lisbon
Madrid
MONACO
Ljubljana
Zagreb
CROATIA
BOS.
HERZ.
SERBIA
Belgrade
GEORGIA

LIBERIA
Yamoussoukro
Accra
Lomé

SPAIN
SAN
MARINO
ITALY
Rome
Sarajevo
MONTENEGRO
Tirane
MACEDONIA
Skopje
Sofia
BULGARIA
Black Sea

ATLANTIC OCEAN

Equator

GIBRALTAR (U.K.)
ALBANIA

GREECE

Ankara

TURKEY

MOROCCO

ALGERIA
Tunis
Athens
CYPRUS
Nicosia
SYRIA
LEBANON
Beirut

0    300    600 mi
0    300    600 km

0    400    800 mi
0    400    800 km

TUNISIA
LIBYA
Mediterranean Sea
EGYPT
ISRAEL
Jerusalem
Damascus
JORDAN
Amman

# The World: Physical

ARCTIC OCEAN
GREENLAND (DEN.)
Beaufort Sea
Yukon R.
Mackenzie R.
Bering Sea
Hudson Bay
NORTH AMERICA
ROCKY MOUNTAINS
CANADIAN SHIELD
Great Plains
Missouri R.
Great Lakes
St. Lawrence R.
Aleutian Islands
Colorado R.
Rio Grande
Mississippi R.
APPALACHIAN MTS.
ATLANTIC OCEAN
SIERRA MADRE OCCIDENTAL
SIERRA MADRE ORIENTAL
Gulf of Mexico
Tropic of Cancer
Hawaiian Islands
West Indies
Caribbean Sea
PACIFIC OCEAN
Orinoco R.
GUIANA HIGHLANDS
AMAZON BASIN
Amazon R.
Equator
P O L Y N E S I A
SOUTH AMERICA
ANDES MOUNTAINS
BRAZILIAN HIGHLANDS
Tropic of Capricorn
PAMPAS
Rio de la Plata
PATAGONIA
Cape Horn
Drake Passage
Antarctic Circle
ANTARCTIC PENINSULA
180° 160°W 140°W 120°W 100°W 80°W 60°W
80°N
60°N
40°N
20°N
0°
20°S
40°S
60°S
80°S
160°W 140°W 120°W 100°W 80°W 60°W

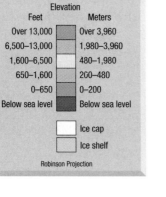

## KEY

**Elevation**

| Feet | | Meters |
|------|---|--------|
| Over 13,000 | | Over 3,960 |
| 6,500–13,000 | | 1,980–3,960 |
| 1,600–6,500 | | 480–1,980 |
| 650–1,600 | | 200–480 |
| 0–650 | | 0–200 |
| Below sea level | | Below sea level |

Ice cap

Ice shelf

Robinson Projection

## South Pole

ATLANTIC OCEAN
QUEEN MAUD LAND
INDIAN OCEAN
Permanent Ice Pack
Weddell Sea
COATS LAND
ENDERBY LAND
Antarctic Peninsula
Amery Ice Shelf
Ronne Ice Shelf
ANTARCTICA
Prime Meridian
QUEEN MAUD MTS.
TRANSANTARCTIC MTS.
South Pole
Ross Ice Shelf
Roosevelt I.
WILKES LAND
Permanent Ice Pack
Ross Sea
VICTORIA LAND
South Magnetic Pole
PACIFIC OCEAN
International Date Line
0 800 mi
0 800 km

20°W 0° 20°E 40°E 60°E 80°E 100°E 120°E 140°E 160°E 180°

80°N

ARCTIC OCEAN

Arctic Circle

SCANDINAVIAN PEN.

British Isles

North Sea

NORTHERN EUROPEAN PLAIN

URAL MTS.

Ob R.

Volga R.

WEST SIBERIAN PLAIN

Yenisei R.

SIBERIA

Lena R.

60°N

KOLYMA MTS.

KAMCHATKA PENINSULA

EUROPE

ALPS

CAUCASUS MTS.

Black Sea

ASIA

L. Baikal

Amur R.

ALTAI MTS.

GOBI DESERT

40°N

IBERIAN PEN.

BALKAN PEN.

Aral Sea

Caspian Sea

TIAN SHAN

HINDU KUSH

KUNLUN SHAN

NORTH CHINA PLAIN

Huang He

Sea of Japan

PACIFIC OCEAN

Mediterranean Sea

ATLAS MTS.

PLATEAU OF IRAN

ZAGROS MTS.

Indus R.

TIBETAN PLATEAU

HIMALAYAS

Yangzi R.

SAHARA

ARABIAN PENINSULA

Red Sea

Persian Gulf

Ganges R.

Mt. Everest 29,028 ft. (8,848 m)

Tropic of Cancer

20°N

AFRICA

Nile R.

SUDAN

Arabian Sea

DECCAN PLATEAU

Bay of Bengal

Philippine Sea

Niger R.

ETHIOPIAN PLATEAU

South China Sea

MICRONESIA

Congo R.

Equator

MELANESIA

0°

ATLANTIC OCEAN

Lake Victoria

INDIAN OCEAN

Sumatra

Borneo

Celebes

East Indies

New Guinea

Zambezi R.

Madagascar

20°S

KALAHARI

Tropic of Capricorn

AUSTRALIA

Darling R.

GREAT DIVIDING RANGE

Cape of Good Hope

N W E S

40°S

0 1,000 2,000 mi
0 1,000 2,000 km

60°S

Antarctic Circle

80°S

ANTARCTICA

20°W 0° 20°E 40°E 60°E 80°E 100°E 120°E 140°E 160°E

**North Pole**

ASIA

TAIMYR PEN.

Laptev Sea

Kara Sea

Novaya Zemlya

Barents Sea

New Siberian Islands

Severnaya Zemlya

East Siberian Sea

Permanent Ice Pack

Franz Josef Land

ARCTIC OCEAN

Svalbard (Nor.)

North Pole

International Date Line

Prime Meridian

Chukchi Sea

0 500 mi
0 500 km

North Magnetic Pole

Ellesmere Island

Baffin Bay

NORTH AMERICA

Queen Elizabeth Islands

# United States: Political

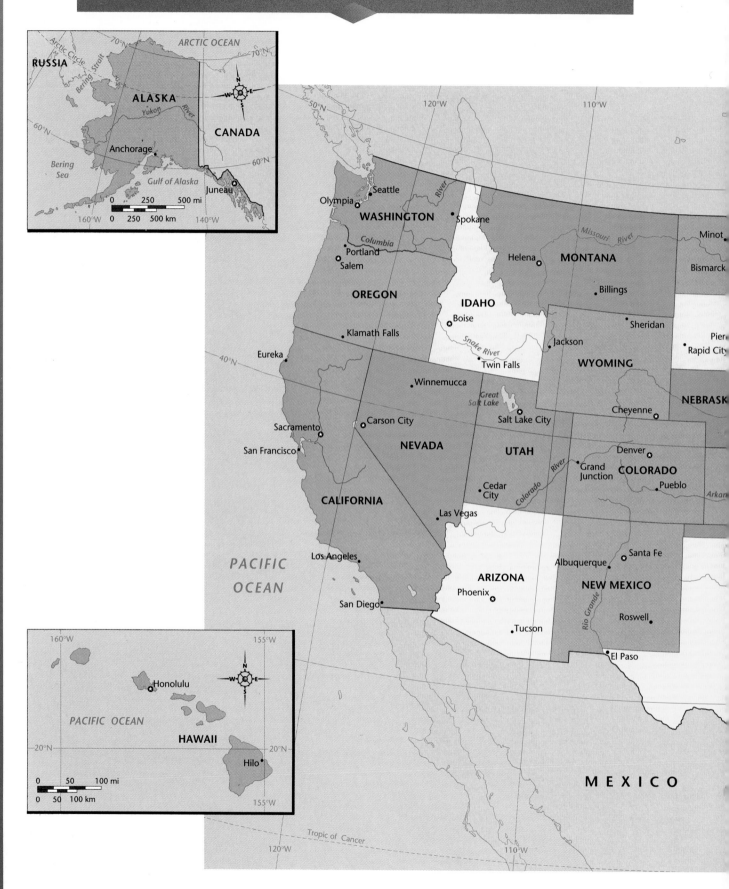

ARCTIC OCEAN

RUSSIA

ALASKA

CANADA

Bering Strait

70°N

70°N

60°N

60°N

Yukon River

Anchorage

Bering Sea

Gulf of Alaska

Juneau

| 0 | 250 | 500 mi |
| 0 | 250 | 500 km |

160°W    140°W

WASHINGTON
Seattle
Olympia
Spokane

Columbia
Portland
Salem

OREGON

Klamath Falls

Eureka

Winnemucca

Sacramento
San Francisco

Carson City

NEVADA

CALIFORNIA

PACIFIC
OCEAN

Los Angeles

San Diego

Las Vegas

ARIZONA
Phoenix

Tucson

50°N

120°W    110°W

River

IDAHO
Boise

Helena
MONTANA
Billings

Snake River
Jackson
Twin Falls

Missouri River

Minot

Bismarck

Sheridan

WYOMING

Pier
Rapid City

40°N

Great
Salt Lake
Salt Lake City

UTAH

Cedar
City

Colorado River

Grand
Junction

Cheyenne

Denver

COLORADO

Pueblo

NEBRASK

Arkan

Albuquerque

Santa Fe

NEW MEXICO

Roswell

Rio Grande

El Paso

MEXICO

160°W    155°W

Honolulu

PACIFIC OCEAN

HAWAII

20°N    20°N

Hilo

| 0 | 50 | 100 mi |
| 0 | 50 | 100 km |

155°W

Tropic of Cancer

120°W    110°W

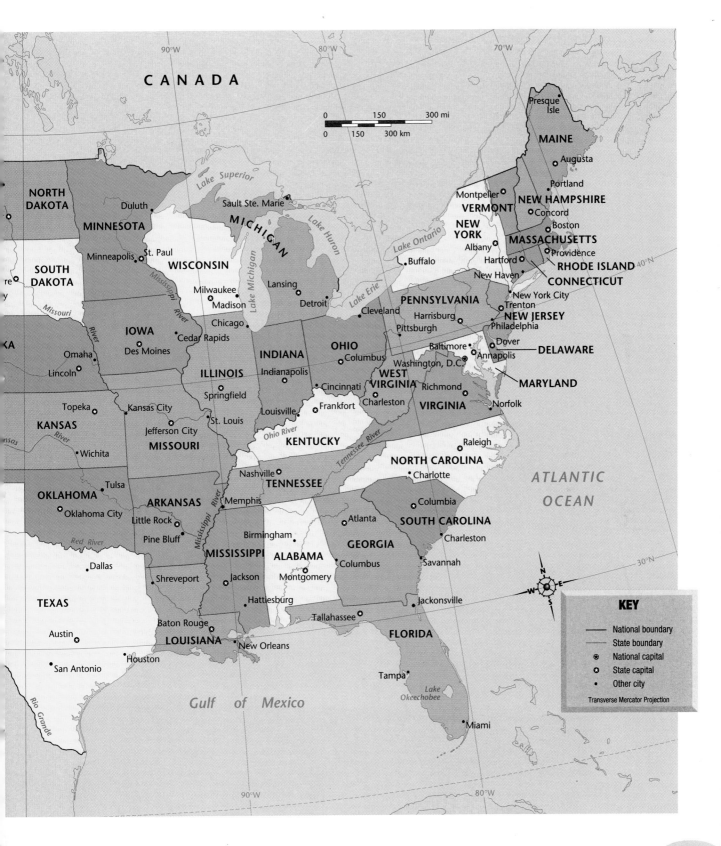

CANADA

Presque Isle

MAINE
Augusta

Portland

Montpelier
VERMONT
NEW HAMPSHIRE
Concord

Boston

NEW YORK
Albany
MASSACHUSETTS
Providence
Hartford
RHODE ISLAND
New Haven
CONNECTICUT

Buffalo

Lake Ontario

Lake Erie

PENNSYLVANIA
New York City
Harrisburg
Trenton
Cleveland
Pittsburgh
NEW JERSEY
Philadelphia

Baltimore
Dover
DELAWARE
OHIO
Columbus
Washington, D.C.
Annapolis
Indianapolis
WEST
VIRGINIA
Richmond
MARYLAND
Cincinnati
Charleston
VIRGINIA
Louisville
Frankfort
Norfolk

NORTH DAKOTA

Duluth

Sault Ste. Marie

MICHIGAN

Lake Superior

Lake Huron

MINNESOTA

Minneapolis
St. Paul

WISCONSIN

Milwaukee
Lansing
Madison
Detroit

Chicago

SOUTH DAKOTA

Missouri

Mississippi River

Lake Michigan

IOWA
Des Moines
Cedar Rapids

Omaha

ILLINOIS
INDIANA

Lincoln

Springfield

Topeka
Kansas City
St. Louis
KANSAS

Jefferson City

MISSOURI
KENTUCKY
Ohio River

Wichita

Nashville
Raleigh

TENNESSEE
Tennessee River
NORTH CAROLINA

OKLAHOMA
Tulsa
Memphis
Charlotte

ARKANSAS

Oklahoma City

Little Rock
Columbia

Red River
Pine Bluff
Birmingham
Atlanta
SOUTH CAROLINA
Charleston

MISSISSIPPI
ALABAMA
GEORGIA
Columbus
Savannah

Dallas

Shreveport
Jackson
Montgomery

Jacksonville

TEXAS
Hattiesburg

Tallahassee

Austin
Baton Rouge
LOUISIANA
FLORIDA

San Antonio
Houston
New Orleans

Tampa
Lake Okeechobee

Rio Grande

Gulf   of   Mexico

Miami

ATLANTIC
OCEAN

**KEY**

—— National boundary
—— State boundary
⊛ National capital
✪ State capital
• Other city

Transverse Mercator Projection

# North and South America: Political

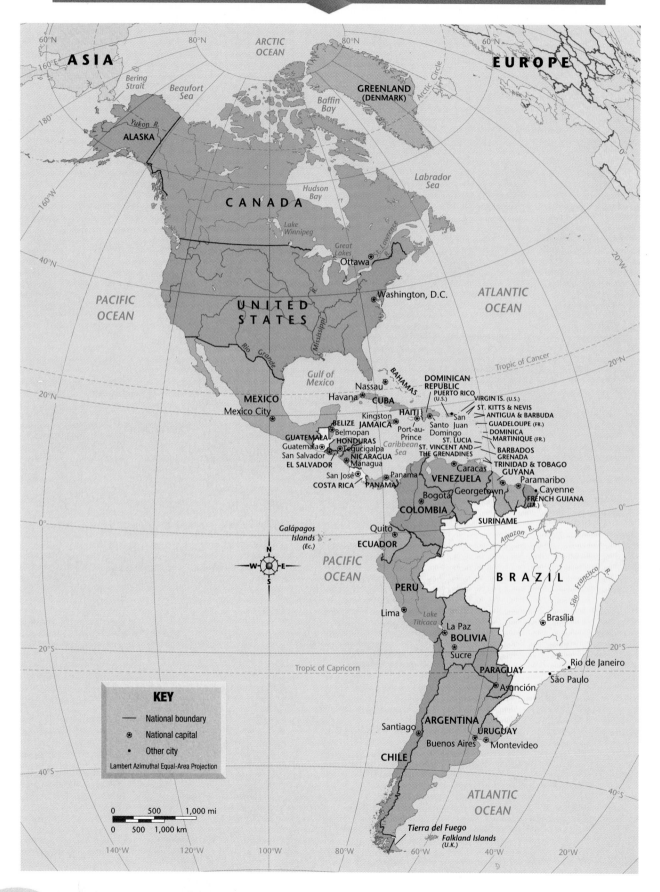

ARCTIC OCEAN

ASIA

EUROPE

Bering Strait

Beaufort Sea

Yukon R.

GREENLAND (DENMARK)

Baffin Bay

ALASKA

Arctic Circle

Labrador Sea

CANADA

Hudson Bay

Lake Winnipeg

Great Lakes

Ottawa

St. Lawrence R.

PACIFIC OCEAN

UNITED STATES

Washington, D.C.

ATLANTIC OCEAN

Rio Grande

Mississippi R.

Tropic of Cancer

Gulf of Mexico

BAHAMAS

DOMINICAN REPUBLIC

MEXICO

Nassau

Havana

CUBA

PUERTO RICO (U.S.)

VIRGIN IS. (U.S.)

Mexico City

Kingston

HAITI

San Juan

ST. KITTS & NEVIS

ANTIGUA & BARBUDA

BELIZE

JAMAICA

Santo Domingo

GUADELOUPE (FR.)

GUATEMALA

Belmopan

Port-au-Prince

DOMINICA

HONDURAS

ST. LUCIA

MARTINIQUE (FR.)

Guatemala

Tegucigalpa

Caribbean Sea

ST. VINCENT AND THE GRENADINES

BARBADOS

San Salvador

NICARAGUA

GRENADA

EL SALVADOR

Managua

TRINIDAD & TOBAGO

San José

Panama

Caracas

GUYANA

COSTA RICA

PANAMA

VENEZUELA

Paramaribo

Georgetown

Cayenne

Bogotá

FRENCH GUIANA (FR.)

COLOMBIA

SURINAME

Galápagos Islands (Ec.)

Quito

ECUADOR

Amazon R.

PACIFIC OCEAN

BRAZIL

PERU

São Francisco R.

Lima

Lake Titicaca

Brasília

La Paz

BOLIVIA

Sucre

Rio de Janeiro

Tropic of Capricorn

PARAGUAY

São Paulo

Asunción

ARGENTINA

URUGUAY

Santiago

Buenos Aires

Montevideo

CHILE

ATLANTIC OCEAN

## KEY

— National boundary

⊛ National capital

• Other city

Lambert Azimuthal Equal-Area Projection

| 0 | 500 | 1,000 mi |
| 0 | 500 | 1,000 km |

Tierra del Fuego

Falkland Islands (U.K.)

# North and South America: Physical

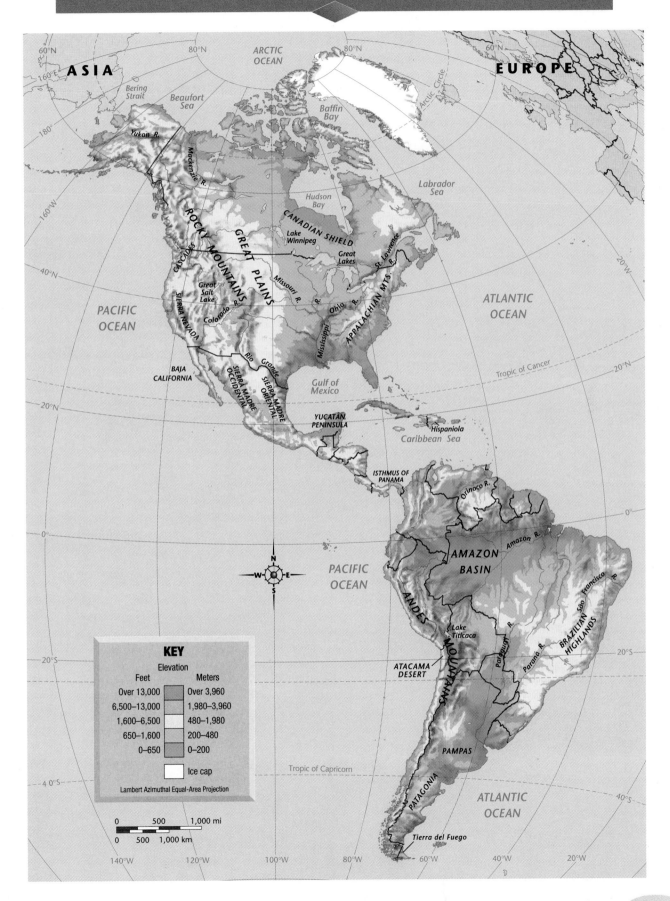

ASIA

EUROPE

ARCTIC OCEAN

60°N   80°N   80°N   60°N

Bering Strait

Beaufort Sea

Baffin Bay

Yukon R.

Mackenzie R.

Labrador Sea

Hudson Bay

CANADIAN SHIELD

ROCKY MOUNTAINS

GREAT PLAINS

CASCADES

Lake Winnipeg

Great Lakes

St. Lawrence R.

Missouri R.

Great Salt Lake

SIERRA NEVADA

Colorado R.

Ohio R.

Mississippi R.

APPALACHIAN MTS.

PACIFIC OCEAN

ATLANTIC OCEAN

BAJA CALIFORNIA

SIERRA MADRE OCCIDENTAL

SIERRA MADRE ORIENTAL

Rio Grande

Gulf of Mexico

Tropic of Cancer

YUCATÁN PENINSULA

Hispaniola

Caribbean Sea

ISTHMUS OF PANAMA

Orinoco R.

AMAZON BASIN

Amazon R.

ANDES MOUNTAINS

Lake Titicaca

São Francisco R.

BRAZILIAN HIGHLANDS

Paraguay R.

Paraná R.

ATACAMA DESERT

PACIFIC OCEAN

PAMPAS

PATAGONIA

ATLANTIC OCEAN

Tropic of Capricorn

Tierra del Fuego

**KEY**

Elevation

| Feet | Meters |
|------|--------|
| Over 13,000 | Over 3,960 |
| 6,500–13,000 | 1,980–3,960 |
| 1,600–6,500 | 480–1,980 |
| 650–1,600 | 200–480 |
| 0–650 | 0–200 |

Ice cap

Lambert Azimuthal Equal-Area Projection

0   500   1,000 mi
0   500   1,000 km

60°N   20°E

40°N   20°W

20°N

0°

20°S

40°S

160°E   180°   160°W   140°W   120°W   100°W   80°W   60°W   40°W   20°W

# Europe: Political

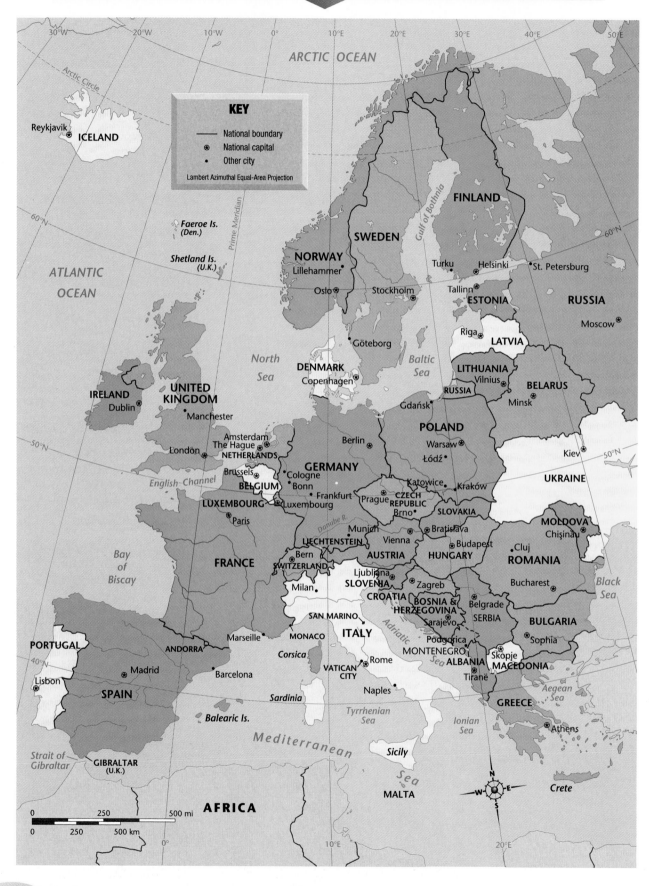

KEY

— National boundary
⊛ National capital
• Other city

Lambert Azimuthal Equal-Area Projection

ARCTIC OCEAN

ATLANTIC OCEAN

Arctic Circle

60°N

Reykjavik ⊛ ICELAND

Faeroe Is. (Den.)

Shetland Is. (U.K.)

Prime Meridian

FINLAND

Gulf of Bothnia

SWEDEN

NORWAY
Lillehammer •

Turku •  Helsinki ⊛    • St. Petersburg

Oslo ⊛   Stockholm ⊛   Tallinn ⊛ ESTONIA

RUSSIA

Göteborg •                Moscow ⊛

North Sea

DENMARK    Riga ⊛ LATVIA

Copenhagen ⊛   LITHUANIA

Baltic Sea    Vilnius ⊛   BELARUS

IRELAND
Dublin ⊛

UNITED KINGDOM
• Manchester

London ⊛

RUSSIA    Minsk ⊛

Gdańsk •

POLAND
Warsaw ⊛
Łódź •            Kiev ⊛

50°N

Amsterdam ⊛
The Hague •
NETHERLANDS

Berlin ⊛

UKRAINE

Brussels ⊛
BELGIUM    • Cologne
GERMANY    Bonn •

Frankfurt •

Katowice •   Kraków •

LUXEMBOURG
Luxembourg ⊛

Prague ⊛ CZECH REPUBLIC    SLOVAKIA
Brno •

Danube R.

• Paris

Munich •    Vienna ⊛
LIECHTENSTEIN

MOLDOVA
Chişinău ⊛

FRANCE

Bratislava ⊛

Budapest ⊛   • Cluj

Bay of Biscay

Bern ⊛
SWITZERLAND
AUSTRIA    HUNGARY    ROMANIA

Ljubljana ⊛
SLOVENIA    Zagreb ⊛    Bucharest ⊛

Black Sea

Milan •

CROATIA

Belgrade ⊛

SAN MARINO •

BOSNIA &
HERZEGOVINA    SERBIA

BULGARIA

Marseille •   MONACO    Sarajevo ⊛

PORTUGAL    ANDORRA

Corsica    ITALY    Podgorica ⊛   Sophia ⊛

VATICAN CITY    Rome ⊛   MONTENEGRO   Skopje ⊛

40°N    Madrid ⊛    • Barcelona    Sardinia    Naples •    ALBANIA   MACEDONIA
Tiranë ⊛

Adriatic Sea

Lisbon ⊛    Aegean Sea

SPAIN    Tyrrhenian Sea    GREECE

Balearic Is.    Ionian Sea

Mediterranean    Athens ⊛

Strait of Gibraltar    Sicily    Crete

GIBRALTAR (U.K.)    N

W   E

AFRICA    MALTA    S

0   250   500 mi

0   250   500 km

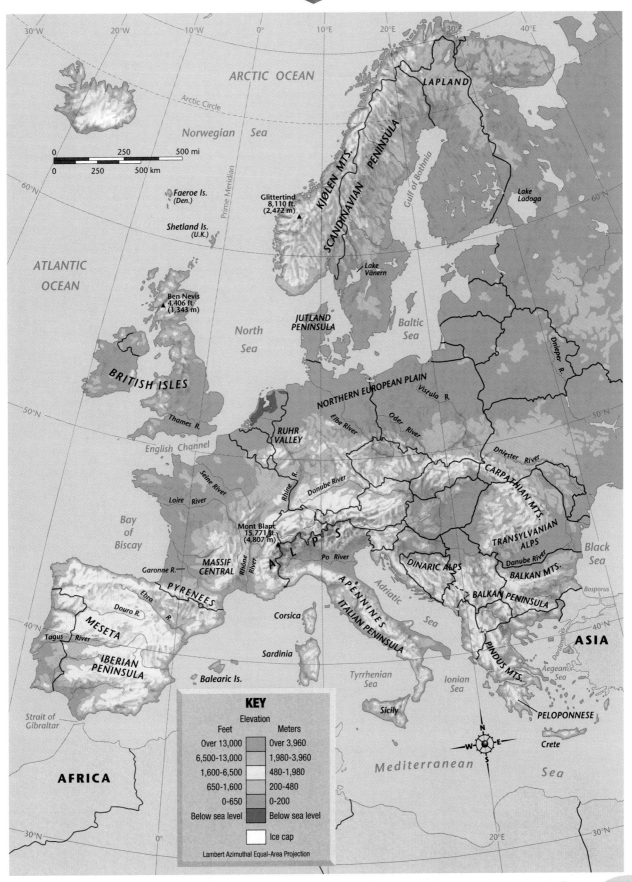

30°W  20°W  10°W  0°  10°E  20°E  30°E  40°E

ARCTIC OCEAN

LAPLAND

Arctic Circle

Norwegian Sea

500 mi

250

250  500 km

Faeroe Is.
(Den.)

Glittertind
8,110 ft.
(2,472 m)

60°N

Shetland Is.
(U.K.)

Gulf of Bothnia

Lake
Ladoga

ATLANTIC
OCEAN

Ben Nevis
4,406 ft
(1,343 m)

North
Sea

JUTLAND
PENINSULA

Lake
Vänern

Baltic
Sea

60°N

BRITISH ISLES

NORTHERN EUROPEAN PLAIN

Dnieper R.

Thames R.

50°N

RUHR
VALLEY

Elbe River

Oder River

Vistula R.

50°N

English Channel

Seine River

Rhine R.

Danube River

Dniester River

CARPATHIAN MTS.

Loire River

Bay
of
Biscay

Mont Blanc
15,771 ft.
(4,807 m)

A  L  P  S

Po River

TRANSYLVANIAN
ALPS

Black
Sea

MASSIF
CENTRAL

Rhône
River

DINARIC ALPS

Danube River

BALKAN MTS.

Garonne R.

PYRENEES

A P E N N I N E S

Adriatic

BALKAN PENINSULA

Bosporus

Ebro
R.

Douro R.

ITALIAN PENINSULA

Sea

Corsica

PINDUS MTS.

40°N

MESETA

Tagus River

Sardinia

Tyrrhenian
Sea

Ionian
Sea

Aegean
Sea

ASIA

40°N

IBERIAN
PENINSULA

Balearic Is.

PELOPONNESE

Strait of
Gibraltar

N

W  E

S

Crete

AFRICA

Sicily

Mediterranean

Sea

30°N

0°  20°E  30°N

**KEY**

Elevation

| Feet | | Meters |
|---|---|---|
| Over 13,000 | | Over 3,960 |
| 6,500-13,000 | | 1,980-3,960 |
| 1,600-6,500 | | 480-1,980 |
| 650-1,600 | | 200-480 |
| 0-650 | | 0-200 |
| Below sea level | | Below sea level |
| | Ice cap | |

Lambert Azimuthal Equal-Area Projection

# Africa: Political

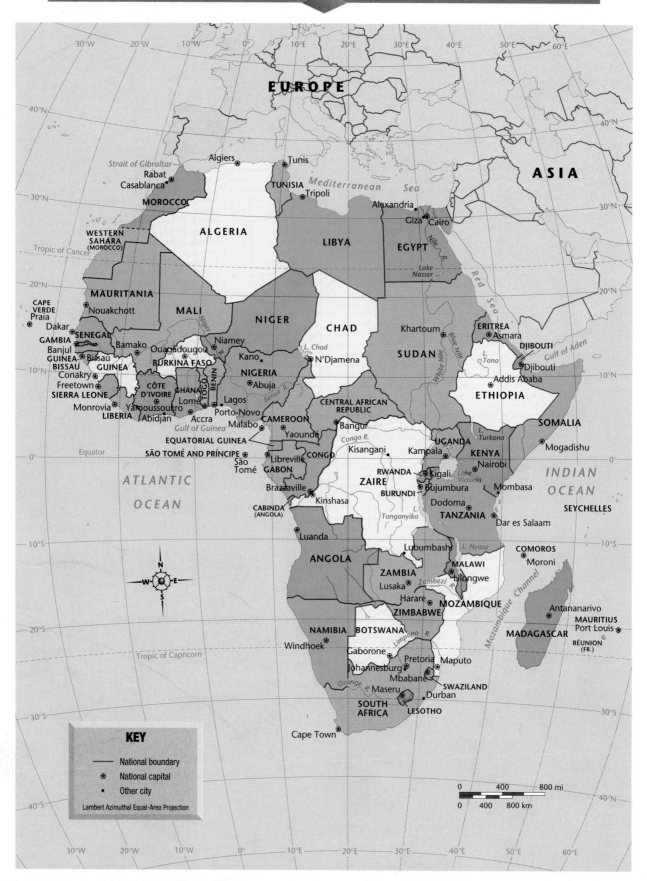

EUROPE

ASIA

Strait of Gibraltar
Algiers ⊛
Tunis ⊛
TUNISIA
Rabat ⊛
Casablanca •
MOROCCO
⊛ Tripoli
Mediterranean Sea

WESTERN SAHARA (MOROCCO)
Tropic of Cancer
ALGERIA
LIBYA
Alexandria •
Giza • ⊛ Cairo
EGYPT
Lake Nasser

MAURITANIA
Nouakchott ⊛
MALI
NIGER
CHAD
Khartoum ⊛
SUDAN
ERITREA
⊛ Asmara
DJIBOUTI
Red Sea

CAPE VERDE
Praia ⊛
Dakar •
SENEGAL
GAMBIA
Banjul ⊛
GUINEA-BISSAU
Bissau ⊛
Conakry ⊛
GUINEA
Bamako ⊛
Niamey ⊛
Ouagadougou ⊛
BURKINA FASO
Kano •
Niger R.
N'Djamena ⊛
L. Chad
L. Tana
White Nile
Blue Nile
⊛ Djibouti
Addis Ababa •
Gulf of Aden

SIERRA LEONE
Freetown ⊛
Monrovia ⊛
LIBERIA
Yamoussoukro ⊛
CÔTE D'IVOIRE
GHANA
Accra ⊛
Abidjan •
TOGO
BENIN
Lomé ⊛
Porto-Novo ⊛
Lagos •
NIGERIA
Abuja •
Benue R.
CENTRAL AFRICAN REPUBLIC
Bangui ⊛
ETHIOPIA
SOMALIA
Mogadishu •

EQUATORIAL GUINEA
Malabo ⊛
CAMEROON
Yaoundé ⊛
Gulf of Guinea
SÃO TOMÉ AND PRÍNCIPE ⊛
São Tomé •
Libreville ⊛
GABON
CONGO
Congo R.
Kisangani •
ZAIRE
UGANDA
Kampala ⊛
RWANDA
Kigali ⊛
BURUNDI
Bujumbura ⊛
Lake Victoria
KENYA
Nairobi ⊛
Mombasa •
INDIAN OCEAN
SEYCHELLES
Equator

ATLANTIC OCEAN
Brazzaville ⊛
Kinshasa ⊛
CABINDA (ANGOLA)
L. Turkana
L. Tanganyika
Dodoma •
TANZANIA
Dar es Salaam •

Luanda ⊛
ANGOLA
Lubumbashi •
L. Nyasa
ZAMBIA
Lusaka ⊛
MALAWI
Lilongwe ⊛
COMOROS
Moroni •

Zambezi R.
Harare ⊛
ZIMBABWE
MOZAMBIQUE
Mozambique Channel
Antananarivo ⊛
MAURITIUS
Port Louis •
RÉUNION (FR.)

Tropic of Capricorn
NAMIBIA
Windhoek ⊛
BOTSWANA
Gaborone ⊛
Limpopo R.
Pretoria ⊛
Maputo ⊛
MADAGASCAR

Johannesburg •
Mbabane ⊛
SWAZILAND
Orange R.
Maseru ⊛
Durban •
SOUTH AFRICA
LESOTHO
Cape Town ⊛

## KEY

— National boundary
⊛ National capital
• Other city

Lambert Azimuthal Equal-Area Projection

0    400    800 mi
0    400    800 km

# Africa: Physical

Strait of Gibraltar
ATLAS MOUNTAINS
Canary Islands
Tropic of Cancer
AHAGGAR MOUNTAINS
Cape Verde Islands
Senegal R.
FOUTA DJALLON
Niger R.
S A H A R A
S A H E L
LIBYAN DESERT
QATTARA DEPRESSION
Suez Canal
Lake Nasser
ARABIAN DESERT
Nile R.
Red Sea
Gulf of Aden
L. Chad
MANDARA MTS.
Benue R.
Gulf of Guinea
Ubangi R.
Congo R.
C O N G O
B A S I N
L. Mai-Ndombe
Kasai R.
White Nile
Blue Nile
L. Tana
ETHIOPIAN PLATEAU
SUDD
L. Albert
L. Edward
Lake Victoria
GREAT RIFT VALLEY
L. Turkana
Kilimanjaro 19,340 ft. (5,895 m)
SERENGETI PLAIN
L. Tanganyika
Zanzibar
Lake Nyasa
Comoros Islands
Mozambique Channel
Mauritius
Réunion
Zambezi R.
NAMIB DESERT
Okavango Basin
Limpopo R.
KALAHARI DESERT
Orange R.
Cape of Good Hope
Cape Agulhas

EUROPE
ASIA
Mediterranean Sea

ATLANTIC OCEAN
INDIAN OCEAN

Equator

Tropic of Capricorn

## KEY

### Elevation

| Feet | Meters |
| --- | --- |
| Over 13,000 | Over 3,960 |
| 6,500–13,000 | 1,980–3,960 |
| 1,600–6,500 | 480–1,980 |
| 650–1,600 | 200–480 |
| 0–650 | 0–200 |
| Below sea level | Below sea level |

Lambert Azimuthal Equal-Area Projection

0    400    800 mi
0    400    800 km

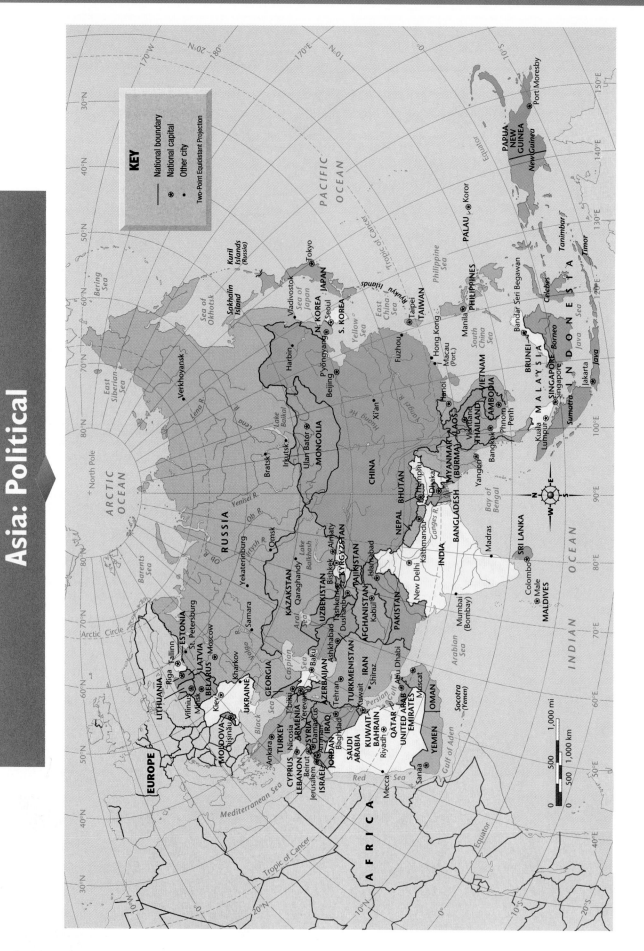

# Asia: Political

**KEY**
— National boundary
⊛ National capital
• Other city
Two-Point Equidistant Projection

EUROPE

ARCTIC OCEAN

North Pole

Arctic Circle

Barents Sea

East Siberian Sea

Bering Sea

Sea of Okhotsk

Verkhoyansk

RUSSIA

Sakhalin Island

Kuril Islands (Russia)

Bratsk

Irkutsk

Lake Baikal

Lena R.

Yenisei R.

Ob R.

Omsk

Yekaterinburg

Samara

Volga R.

Irtysh R.

Vladivostok

Sea of Japan

Tokyo

JAPAN

N. KOREA

Pyŏngyang

Seoul

S. KOREA

Yellow Sea

East China Sea

Ryukyu Islands

Taipei

TAIWAN

Hong Kong

Macau (Port.)

Fuzhou

PHILIPPINES

Manila

Philippine Sea

PACIFIC OCEAN

Tropic of Cancer

PALAU

Koror

PAPUA NEW GUINEA

Port Moresby

New Guinea

Equator

Harbin

Beijing

MONGOLIA

Ulan Bator

Xi'an

Huang He

Yangtze R.

CHINA

Hanoi

VIETNAM

LAOS

Vientiane

THAILAND

Bangkok

CAMBODIA

Phnom Penh

MYANMAR (BURMA)

Yangon

Bay of Bengal

Naypyidaw

BHUTAN

Thimphu

Dhaka

BANGLADESH

NEPAL

Kathmandu

BRUNEI

Bandar Seri Begawan

MALAYSIA

Kuala Lumpur

SINGAPORE

Singapore

Borneo

INDONESIA

Sumatra

Jakarta

Java

Java Sea

Celebes

Timor

Tanimbar

South China Sea

KAZAKSTAN

Lake Balkhash

Qaraghandy

Aral Sea

UZBEKISTAN

Tashkent

Bishkek

KYRGYZSTAN

Almaty

TAJIKISTAN

Dushanbe

Ashkhabad

TURKMENISTAN

AFGHANISTAN

Kabul

PAKISTAN

Islamabad

INDIA

New Delhi

Ganges R.

Madras

SRI LANKA

Colombo

Male

MALDIVES

Mumbai (Bombay)

Arabian Sea

INDIAN OCEAN

Socotra (Yemen)

OMAN

Muscat

UNITED ARAB EMIRATES

Abu Dhabi

Gulf of Oman

Persian Gulf

QATAR

BAHRAIN

Riyadh

KUWAIT

Kuwait

SAUDI ARABIA

IRAN

Tehran

Shiraz

IRAQ

Baghdad

Caspian Sea

AZERBAIJAN

Baku

ARMENIA

Yerevan

Tbilisi

GEORGIA

TURKEY

Ankara

CYPRUS

Nicosia

LEBANON

Beirut

Damascus

SYRIA

Amman

JORDAN

ISRAEL

Jerusalem

Mediterranean Sea

AFRICA

Red Sea

Mecca

YEMEN

Sanaa

Gulf of Aden

Tropic of Cancer

Equator

LITHUANIA

Vilnius

Riga

Tallinn

ESTONIA

LATVIA

St. Petersburg

Moscow

BELARUS

Minsk

Kharkov

Kiev

UKRAINE

MOLDOVA

Chişinău

Black Sea

500

0   500   1,000 km

0            1,000 mi

N

S

W   E

# Asia: Physical

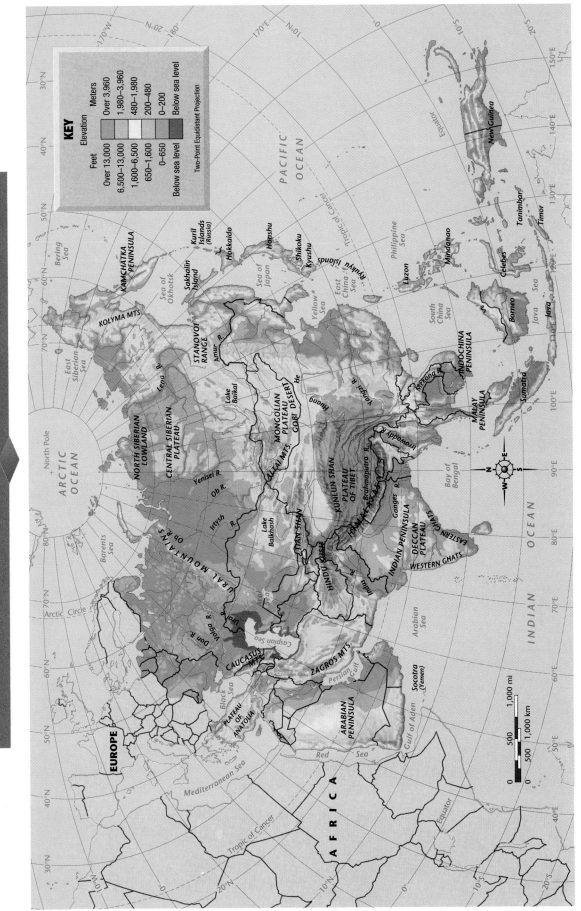

KEY

Elevation

| Feet | Meters |
|------|--------|
| Over 13,000 | Over 3,960 |
| 6,500–13,000 | 1,980–3,960 |
| 1,600–6,500 | 480–1,980 |
| 650–1,600 | 200–480 |
| 0–650 | 0–200 |
| Below sea level | Below sea level |

Two-Point Equidistant Projection

EUROPE

AFRICA

PACIFIC OCEAN

ARCTIC OCEAN

North Pole

INDIAN OCEAN

Bering Sea

Sea of Okhotsk

East Siberian Sea

Barents Sea

Sea of Japan

Yellow Sea

East China Sea

Philippine Sea

South China Sea

Java Sea

Celebes Sea

Bay of Bengal

Arabian Sea

Persian Gulf

Gulf of Aden

Red Sea

Mediterranean Sea

Black Sea

Caspian Sea

Aral Sea

Lake Baikal

Lake Balkhash

KAMCHATKA PENINSULA

KOLYMA MTS.

STANOVOY RANGE

NORTH SIBERIAN LOWLAND

CENTRAL SIBERIAN PLATEAU

URAL MOUNTAINS

MONGOLIAN PLATEAU

GOBI DESERT

ALTAI MTS.

TIAN SHAN

KUNLUN SHAN

PLATEAU OF TIBET

HIMALAYAS

HINDU KUSH

DECCAN PLATEAU

INDIAN PENINSULA

EASTERN GHATS

WESTERN GHATS

CAUCASUS MTS.

ZAGROS MTS.

PLATEAU OF ANATOLIA

ARABIAN PENINSULA

INDOCHINA PENINSULA

MALAY PENINSULA

Kuril Islands (Russia)

Sakhalin Island

Hokkaido

Honshu

Shikoku

Kyushu

Ryukyu Islands

Luzon

Mindanao

Borneo

Java

Sumatra

Celebes

Timor

Tanimbar

New Guinea

Socotra (Yemen)

Amur R.

Lena R.

Yenisei R.

Ob R.

Irtysh R.

Ural R.

Volga R.

Don R.

Huang He

Yangtzi R.

Mekong R.

Irrawaddy R.

Brahmaputra R.

Ganges R.

Indus R.

Tigris R.

Euphrates R.

North Pole

Arctic Circle

Tropic of Cancer

Equator

Tropic of Cancer

Tropic of Capricorn

Equator

80°W
170°W
170°E
10°N
0°
10°S
20°S

20°N
30°N
40°N
50°N
60°N
70°N
80°N

N

S

E

W

NE
NW
SE
SW

0   500   1,000 mi

0   500   1,000 km

# Australia, New Zealand, and the Pacific Islands: Physical–Political

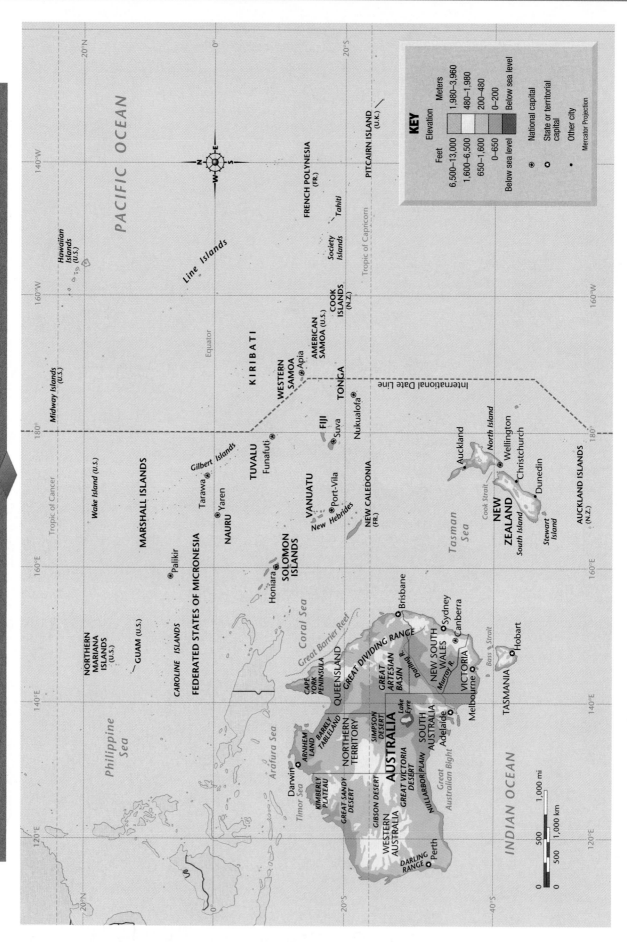

PACIFIC OCEAN

Hawaiian Islands (U.S.)

Midway Islands (U.S.)

Line Islands

French Polynesia (Fr.)

Tahiti
Society Islands

PITCAIRN ISLAND (U.K.)

Tropic of Capricorn

COOK ISLANDS (N.Z.)

AMERICAN SAMOA (U.S.)

KIRIBATI

WESTERN SAMOA
Apia

Equator

TONGA
Nukualofa

International Date Line

Wake Island (U.S.)

MARSHALL ISLANDS

Gilbert Islands

Tarawa

TUVALU
Funafuti

FIJI
Suva

VANUATU
Port-Vila

New Hebrides

NEW CALEDONIA (Fr.)

North Island
Auckland

Wellington
Christchurch
Dunedin

Cook Strait

NEW ZEALAND

South Island

Stewart Island

AUCKLAND ISLANDS (N.Z.)

Tasman Sea

Tropic of Cancer

NAURU
Yaren

SOLOMON ISLANDS
Honiara

NORTHERN MARIANA ISLANDS (U.S.)

GUAM (U.S.)

CAROLINE ISLANDS

FEDERATED STATES OF MICRONESIA

Palikir

Coral Sea

Great Barrier Reef

Brisbane
Sydney
Canberra

GREAT DIVIDING RANGE

NEW SOUTH WALES

GREAT ARTESIAN BASIN

Darling R.

Murray R.

VICTORIA
Melbourne

Bass Strait
Hobart

TASMANIA

Philippine Sea

Arafura Sea

Timor Sea

CAPE YORK PENINSULA

QUEENSLAND

ARNHEM LAND

BARKLY TABLELAND

NORTHERN TERRITORY

SIMPSON DESERT

AUSTRALIA

Lake Eyre

SOUTH AUSTRALIA
Adelaide

Darwin

KIMBERLEY PLATEAU

GREAT SANDY DESERT

GIBSON DESERT

WESTERN AUSTRALIA

GREAT VICTORIA DESERT

NULLARBOR PLAIN

Great Australian Bight

Perth
DARLING RANGE

INDIAN OCEAN

KEY

Elevation

| Feet | Meters |
|---|---|
| 6,500–13,000 | 1,980–3,960 |
| 1,600–6,500 | 480–1,980 |
| 650–1,600 | 200–480 |
| 0–650 | 0–200 |
| Below sea level | Below sea level |

⊛ National capital

✪ State or territorial capital

• Other city

Mercator Projection

1,000 mi
1,000 km

500
500

N E S W

**210**  ATLAS

# The Arctic

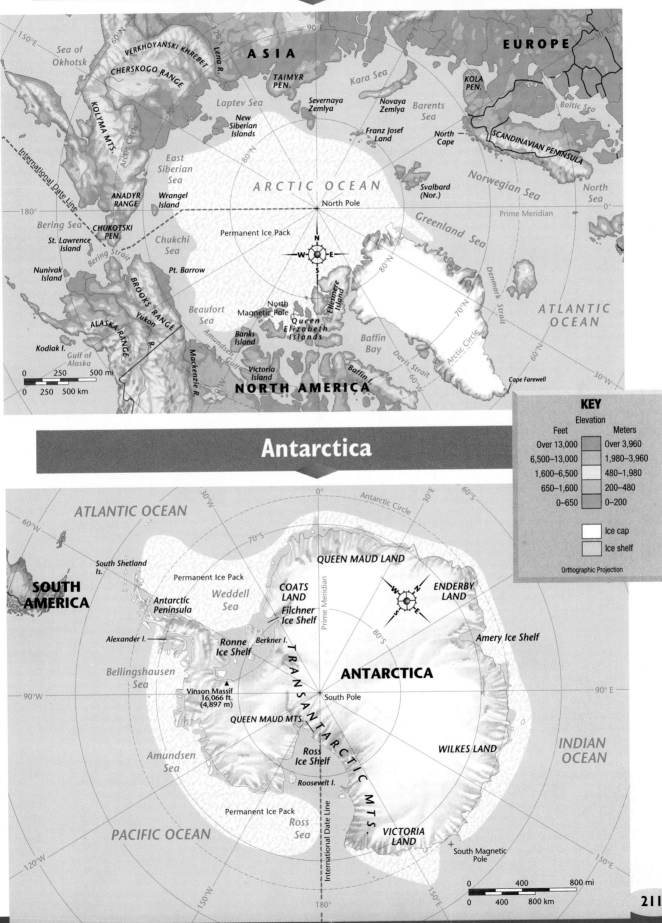

**SOUTH AMERICA**

**North America**

Sea of Okhotsk

VERKHOYANSKI KHREBET

CHERSKOGO RANGE

Lena R.

**ASIA**

TAIMYR PEN.

Kara Sea

**EUROPE**

KOLA PEN.

Baltic Sea

KOLYMA MTS.

Laptev Sea

New Siberian Islands

Severnaya Zemlya

Novaya Zemlya

Franz Josef Land

Barents Sea

North Cape

SCANDINAVIAN PENINSULA

Arctic Circle

East Siberian Sea

Svalbard (Nor.)

Norwegian Sea

North Sea

International Date Line

ANADYR RANGE

Wrangel Island

ARCTIC OCEAN

North Pole

Prime Meridian

Bering Sea

CHUKOTSKI PEN.

Chukchi Sea

Permanent Ice Pack

Greenland Sea

Denmark Strait

ATLANTIC OCEAN

St. Lawrence Island

Bering Strait

Nunivak Island

Pt. Barrow

Beaufort Sea

North Magnetic Pole

Ellesmere Island

Baffin Bay

Arctic Circle

BROOKS RANGE

Yukon R.

Queen Elizabeth Islands

Banks Island

Davis Strait

Baffin I.

Kodiak I.

ALASKA RANGE

Gulf of Alaska

Victoria Island

Mackenzie R.

Cape Farewell

0    250    500 mi

0    250    500 km

**NORTH AMERICA**

# Antarctica

**KEY**

Elevation

| Feet | | Meters |
|---|---|---|
| Over 13,000 | | Over 3,960 |
| 6,500–13,000 | | 1,980–3,960 |
| 1,600–6,500 | | 480–1,980 |
| 650–1,600 | | 200–480 |
| 0–650 | | 0–200 |

Ice cap

Ice shelf

Orthographic Projection

ATLANTIC OCEAN

Antarctic Circle

South Shetland Is.

Permanent Ice Pack

QUEEN MAUD LAND

ENDERBY LAND

**SOUTH AMERICA**

Antarctic Peninsula

Weddell Sea

COATS LAND

Filchner Ice Shelf

Prime Meridian

Amery Ice Shelf

Alexander I.

Ronne Ice Shelf

Berkner I.

Bellingshausen Sea

**ANTARCTICA**

TRANSANTARCTIC MTS.

Vinson Massif 16,066 ft. (4,897 m)

South Pole

90° E

Amundsen Sea

QUEEN MAUD MTS.

WILKES LAND

INDIAN OCEAN

Ross Ice Shelf

Roosevelt I.

PACIFIC OCEAN

Permanent Ice Pack

Ross Sea

VICTORIA LAND

International Date Line

South Magnetic Pole

0    400    800 mi

0    400    800 km

# World View

## Afghanistan

CAPITAL: Kabul
POPULATION: 21,251,821
MAJOR LANGUAGES: Pashtu, Afghan Persian, Turkic, and 30 various languages
AREA: 250,010 sq mi; 647,500 sq km
LEADING EXPORTS: fruits and nuts, handwoven carpets, and wool
CONTINENT: Asia

## Albania
CAPITAL: Tiranë
POPULATION: 3,413,904
MAJOR LANGUAGES: Albanian, Tosk dialect, and Greek
AREA: 11,101 sq mi; 28,750 sq km
LEADING EXPORTS: asphalt, metals and metallic ores, and electricity
CONTINENT: Europe

## Algeria
CAPITAL: Algiers
POPULATION: 28,539,321
MAJOR LANGUAGES: Arabic (official), French, and Berber dialects
AREA: 919,626 sq mi; 2,381,740 sq km
LEADING EXPORTS: petroleum and natural gas
CONTINENT: Africa

## Andorra
CAPITAL: Andorra La Vella
POPULATION: 65,780
MAJOR LANGUAGES: Catalan (official), French, and Castilian
AREA: 174 sq mi; 450 sq km
LEADING EXPORTS: electricity, tobacco products, and furniture
CONTINENT: Europe

## Angola
CAPITAL: Luanda
POPULATION: 10,069,501
MAJOR LANGUAGES: Portuguese (official), Bantu, and various languages
AREA: 481,370 sq mi; 1,246,700 sq km
LEADING EXPORTS: oil, diamonds, and refined petroleum products
CONTINENT: Africa

## Anguilla
CAPITAL: The Valley
POPULATION: 7,099
MAJOR LANGUAGE: English (official)
AREA: 35 sq mi; 91 sq km
LEADING EXPORTS: lobster and salt
LOCATION: Caribbean Sea

## Antigua and Barbuda

CAPITAL: Saint John's
POPULATION: 65,176
MAJOR LANGUAGES: English (official) and various dialects
AREA: 170 sq mi; 440 sq km
LEADING EXPORTS: petroleum products and manufactures
LOCATION: Caribbean Sea

## Argentina
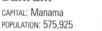
CAPITAL: Buenos Aires
POPULATION: 34,292,742
MAJOR LANGUAGES: Spanish (official), English, Italian, German, and French
AREA: 1,068,339 sq mi; 2,766,890 sq km
LEADING EXPORTS: meat, wheat, corn, oilseed, and manufactures
CONTINENT: South America

## Armenia
CAPITAL: Yerevan
POPULATION: 3,557,284
MAJOR LANGUAGES: Armenian and Russian
AREA: 11,506 sq mi; 29,800 sq km
LEADING EXPORTS: gold and jewelry, and aluminum
CONTINENT: Asia

## Australia

CAPITAL: Canberra
POPULATION: 18,322,231
MAJOR LANGUAGES: English and various languages
AREA: 2,968,010 sq mi; 7,686,850 sq km
LEADING EXPORTS: coal, gold, meat, wool, and alumina
CONTINENT: Australia

## Austria

CAPITAL: Vienna
POPULATION: 7,986,664
MAJOR LANGUAGE: German
AREA: 32,376 sq mi; 83,850 sq km
LEADING EXPORTS: machinery and equipment, and iron and steel
CONTINENT: Europe

## Azerbaijan
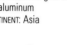
CAPITAL: Baku
POPULATION: 7,789,886
MAJOR LANGUAGES: Azeri, Russian, Armenian, and various languages
AREA: 33,438 sq mi; 86,600 sq km
LEADING EXPORTS: oil and gas, chemicals, and oil field equipment
CONTINENT: Europe and Asia

## Bahamas

CAPITAL: Nassau
POPULATION: 256,616
MAJOR LANGUAGES: English and Creole
AREA: 5,382 sq mi; 13,940 sq km
LEADING EXPORTS: pharmaceuticals, cement, rum, and crawfish
LOCATION: Caribbean Sea

## Bahrain
CAPITAL: Manama
POPULATION: 575,925
MAJOR LANGUAGES: Arabic, English, Farsi, and Urdu
AREA: 239 sq mi; 620 sq km
LEADING EXPORTS: petroleum and petroleum products
CONTINENT: Asia

## Bangladesh
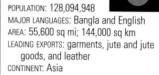
CAPITAL: Dhaka
POPULATION: 128,094,948
MAJOR LANGUAGES: Bangla and English
AREA: 55,600 sq mi; 144,000 sq km
LEADING EXPORTS: garments, jute and jute goods, and leather
CONTINENT: Asia

## Barbados
CAPITAL: Bridgetown
POPULATION: 256,395
MAJOR LANGUAGE: English
AREA: 166 sq mi; 430 sq km
LEADING EXPORTS: sugar and molasses, and rum
LOCATION: Caribbean Sea

## Belarus
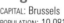
CAPITAL: Minsk
POPULATION: 10,437,418
MAJOR LANGUAGES: Byelorussian and Russian
AREA: 79,926 sq mi; 207,600 sq km
LEADING EXPORTS: machinery and transportation equipment
CONTINENT: Europe

## Belgium
CAPITAL: Brussels
POPULATION: 10,081,880
MAJOR LANGUAGES: Dutch, French, and German
AREA: 11,780 sq mi; 30,510 sq km
LEADING EXPORTS: iron and steel, and transportation equipment
CONTINENT: Europe

## Belize
CAPITAL: Belmopan
POPULATION: 214,061
MAJOR LANGUAGES: English (official), Spanish, Maya, and Garifuna
AREA: 8,865 sq mi; 22,960 sq km
LEADING EXPORTS: sugar, citrus fruits, bananas, and clothing
LOCATION: Caribbean Sea

## Benin

CAPITAL: Porto-Novo
POPULATION: 5,522,677
MAJOR LANGUAGES: Fon, Yoruba, and at least 6 various languages
AREA: 43,484 sq mi; 112,620 sq km
LEADING EXPORTS: cotton, crude oil, palm products, and cocoa
CONTINENT: Africa

## Bermuda

CAPITAL: Hamilton
POPULATION: 61,629
MAJOR LANGUAGE: English
AREA: 19.3 sq mi; 50 sq km
LEADING EXPORTS: semitropical produce and light manufactures
CONTINENT: North America

## Bhutan

CAPITAL: Thimphu
POPULATION: 1,780,638
MAJOR LANGUAGES: Dzongkha (official), Tibetan dialects, and Nepalese dialects
AREA: 18,147 sq mi; 47,000 sq km
LEADING EXPORTS: cardamon, gypsum, timber, and handicrafts
CONTINENT: Asia

## Bolivia
CAPITAL: La Paz
POPULATION: 7,896,254
MAJOR LANGUAGES: Spanish, Quechua, and Aymara
AREA: 424,179 sq mi; 1,098,580 sq km
LEADING EXPORTS: metals, natural gas, soybeans, jewelry, and wood
CONTINENT: South America

## Bosnia and Herzegovina

CAPITAL: Sarajevo
POPULATION: 3,201,823
MAJOR LANGUAGE: Serbo-Croatian
AREA: 19,782 sq mi; 51,233 sq km
LEADING EXPORTS: none
CONTINENT: Europe

## Botswana

CAPITAL: Gaborone
POPULATION: 1,392,414
MAJOR LANGUAGES: English and Setswana
AREA: 231,812 sq mi; 600,370 sq km
LEADING EXPORTS: diamonds, copper and nickel, and meat
CONTINENT: Africa

## Brazil

CAPITAL: Brasília
POPULATION: 160,737,489
MAJOR LANGUAGES: Portuguese, Spanish, English, and French
AREA: 3,286,600 sq mi; 8,511,965 sq km
LEADING EXPORTS: iron ore, soybean, bran, and orange juice
CONTINENT: South America

## British Virgin Islands

CAPITAL: Road Town
POPULATION: 13,027
MAJOR LANGUAGE: English
AREA: 58 sq mi; 150 sq km
LEADING EXPORTS: rum, fresh fish, gravel, sand, and fruits
LOCATION: Caribbean Sea

## Brunei

CAPITAL: Bandar Seri Begawan
POPULATION: 292,266
MAJOR LANGUAGES: Malay, English, and Chinese
AREA: 2,228 sq mi; 5,770 sq km
LEADING EXPORTS: crude oil and liquefied natural gas
CONTINENT: Asia

## Bulgaria

CAPITAL: Sofia
POPULATION: 8,775,198
MAJOR LANGUAGE: Bulgarian
AREA: 42,824 sq mi; 110,910 sq km
LEADING EXPORTS: machinery and agricultural products
CONTINENT: Europe

## Burkina

CAPITAL: Ouagadougou
POPULATION: 10,422,828
MAJOR LANGUAGES: French (official) and Sudanic languages
AREA: 105,873 sq mi; 274,200 sq km
LEADING EXPORTS: cotton, gold, and animal products
CONTINENT: Africa

## Burundi

CAPITAL: Bujumbura
POPULATION: 6,262,429
MAJOR LANGUAGES: Kirundi, French, and Swahili
AREA: 10,746 sq mi; 27,830 sq km
LEADING EXPORTS: coffee, tea, cotton, and hides and skins
CONTINENT: Africa

## Cambodia

CAPITAL: Phnom Penh
POPULATION: 10,561,373
MAJOR LANGUAGES: Khmer and French
AREA: 69,902 sq mi; 181,040 sq km
LEADING EXPORTS: timber, rubber, soybeans, and sesame
CONTINENT: Asia

## Cameroon

CAPITAL: Yaounde
POPULATION: 13,521,000
MAJOR LANGUAGES: 24 various languages, English, and French
AREA: 183,574 sq mi; 475,440 sq km
LEADING EXPORTS: petroleum products and lumber
CONTINENT: Africa

## Canada

CAPITAL: Ottawa
POPULATION: 28,434,545
MAJOR LANGUAGES: English and French
AREA: 3,851,940 sq mi; 9,976,140 sq km
LEADING EXPORTS: newsprint, wood pulp, timber, and crude petroleum
CONTINENT: North America

## Cape Verde

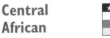

CAPITAL: Praia
POPULATION: 435,983
MAJOR LANGUAGES: Portuguese and Crioulo
AREA: 1,556 sq mi; 4,030 sq km
LEADING EXPORTS: fish, bananas, and hides and skins
CONTINENT: Africa

## Cayman Islands

CAPITAL: George Town
POPULATION: 33,192
MAJOR LANGUAGE: English
AREA: 100 sq mi; 260 sq km
LEADING EXPORTS: turtle products and manufactured goods
LOCATION: Caribbean Sea

## Central African Republic

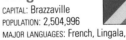

CAPITAL: Bangui
POPULATION: 3,209,759
MAJOR LANGUAGES: French, Sangho, Arabic, Hunsa, and Swahili
AREA: 240,542 sq mi; 622,980 sq km
LEADING EXPORTS: diamonds, timber, cotton, coffee, and tobacco
CONTINENT: Africa

## Chad

CAPITAL: N'Djamena
POPULATION: 5,586,505
MAJOR LANGUAGES: French, Arabic, Sara, Songo, and over 100 various languages and dialects
AREA: 495,772 sq mi; 1,284,000 sq km
LEADING EXPORTS: cotton, cattle, textiles, and fish
CONTINENT: Africa

## Chile

CAPITAL: Santiago
POPULATION: 14,161,216
MAJOR LANGUAGE: Spanish
AREA: 292,269 sq mi; 756,950 sq km
LEADING EXPORTS: copper and other metals and minerals
CONTINENT: South America

## China

CAPITAL: Beijing
POPULATION: 1,203,097,268
MAJOR LANGUAGES: Mandarin, Putonghua, Yue, Wu, Minbei, Minnan, Xiang, and Gan and Hakka dialects
AREA: 3,705,533 sq mi; 9,596,960 sq km
LEADING EXPORTS: textiles, garments, footwear, and toys
CONTINENT: Asia

## Colombia

CAPITAL: Bogota
POPULATION: 36,200,251
MAJOR LANGUAGE: Spanish
AREA: 439,751 sq mi; 1,138,910 sq km
LEADING EXPORTS: petroleum, coffee, coal, and bananas
CONTINENT: South America

## Comoros

CAPITAL: Moroni
POPULATION: 549,338
MAJOR LANGUAGES: Arabic, French, and Comoran
AREA: 838 sq mi; 2,170 sq km
LEADING EXPORTS: vanilla, ylang-ylang, cloves, and perfume oil
LOCATION: Indian Ocean

## Congo

CAPITAL: Brazzaville
POPULATION: 2,504,996
MAJOR LANGUAGES: French, Lingala, Kikongo, and other languages
AREA: 132,051 sq mi; 342,000 sq km
LEADING EXPORTS: crude oil, lumber, plywood, sugar, and cocoa
CONTINENT: Africa

## Cook Islands

CAPITAL: Avarua
POPULATION: 19,343
MAJOR LANGUAGES: English and Maori
AREA: 95 sq mi; 240 sq km
LEADING EXPORTS: copra, fresh and canned fruit, and clothing
LOCATION: Pacific Ocean

## Costa Rica

CAPITAL: San José
POPULATION: 3,419,114
MAJOR LANGUAGES: Spanish and English
AREA: 19,730 sq mi; 51,100 sq km
LEADING EXPORTS: coffee, bananas, textiles, and sugar
CONTINENT: Central America

## Côte d'Ivoire

CAPITAL: Yamoussoukro
POPULATION: 14,791,257
MAJOR LANGUAGES: French, Dioula, and 59 other dialects
AREA: 124,507 sq mi; 322,460 sq km
LEADING EXPORTS: cocoa, coffee, tropical woods, and petroleum
CONTINENT: Africa

## Croatia

CAPITAL: Zagreb
POPULATION: 4,665,821
MAJOR LANGUAGE: Serbo-Croatian
AREA: 21,830 sq mi; 56,538 sq km
LEADING EXPORTS: machinery and transportation equipment
CONTINENT: Europe

## Cuba

CAPITAL: Havana
POPULATION: 10,937,635
MAJOR LANGUAGE: Spanish
AREA: 42,805 sq mi; 110,860 sq km
LEADING EXPORTS: sugar, nickel, shellfish, and tobacco
LOCATION: Caribbean Sea

## Cyprus

CAPITAL: Nicosia
POPULATION: 736,636
MAJOR LANGUAGES: Greek, Turkish, and English
AREA: 3,572 sq mi; 9,250 sq km
LEADING EXPORTS: citrus, potatoes, grapes, wines, and cement
LOCATION: Mediterranean Sea

## Czech Republic

CAPITAL: Prague
POPULATION: 10,432,774
MAJOR LANGUAGES: Czech and Slovak
AREA: 30,388 sq mi; 78,703 sq km
LEADING EXPORTS: manufactured goods
CONTINENT: Europe

## Denmark

CAPITAL: Copenhagen
POPULATION: 5,199,437
MAJOR LANGUAGES: Danish, Faroese, Greenlandic, and German
AREA: 16,630 sq mi; 43,070 sq km
LEADING EXPORTS: meat and meat products, and dairy products
CONTINENT: Europe

## Djibouti

CAPITAL: Djibouti
POPULATION: 421,320
MAJOR LANGUAGES: French, Arabic, Somali, and Afar
AREA: 8,495 sq mi; 22,000 sq km
LEADING EXPORTS: hides and skins, and coffee (in transit)
CONTINENT: Africa

## Dominica

CAPITAL: Roseau
POPULATION: 82,608
MAJOR LANGUAGES: English and French patois
AREA: 290 sq mi; 750 sq km
LEADING EXPORTS: bananas, soap, bay oil, and vegetables
LOCATION: Caribbean Sea

## Dominican Republic

CAPITAL: Santo Domingo
POPULATION: 7,511,263
MAJOR LANGUAGE: Spanish
AREA: 18,815 sq mi; 48,730 sq km
LEADING EXPORTS: ferronickel, sugar, gold, coffee, and cocoa
LOCATION: Caribbean Sea

## Ecuador

CAPITAL: Quito
POPULATION: 10,890,950
MAJOR LANGUAGES: Spanish, Quechua, and various languages
AREA: 109,487 sq mi; 283,560 sq km
LEADING EXPORTS: petroleum, bananas, shrimp, and cocoa
CONTINENT: South America

## Egypt

CAPITAL: Cairo
POPULATION: 62,359,623
MAJOR LANGUAGES: Arabic, English, and French
AREA: 386,675 sq mi; 1,001,450 sq km
LEADING EXPORTS: crude oil and petroleum products
CONTINENT: Africa

## El Salvador

CAPITAL: San Salvador
POPULATION: 5,870,481
MAJOR LANGUAGES: Spanish and Nahua
AREA: 8,124 sq mi; 21,040 sq km
LEADING EXPORTS: coffee, sugar cane, and shrimp
CONTINENT: Central America

## Equatorial Guinea

CAPITAL: Malabo
POPULATION: 420,293
MAJOR LANGUAGES: Spanish, Pidgin English, Fang, Bubi, and Ibo
AREA: 10,831 sq mi; 28,050 sq km
LEADING EXPORTS: coffee, timber, and cocoa beans
CONTINENT: Africa

## Eritrea

CAPITAL: Asmara
POPULATION: 3,578,709
MAJOR LANGUAGES: Tigre, Kunama, Cushitic dialects, Nora Bana, and Arabic
AREA: 46,844 sq mi; 121,320 sq km
LEADING EXPORTS: salt, hides, cement, and gum arabic
CONTINENT: Africa

## Estonia

CAPITAL: Tallinn
POPULATION: 1,625,399
MAJOR LANGUAGES: Estonian, Latvian, Lithuanian, and Russian
AREA: 17,414 sq mi; 45,100 sq km
LEADING EXPORTS: textiles, food products, vehicles, and metals
CONTINENT: Europe

## Ethiopia

CAPITAL: Addis Ababa
POPULATION: 55,979,018
MAJOR LANGUAGES: Amharic, Tigrinya, Orominga, Guaraginga, Somali, Arabic, English, and various languages
AREA: 435,201 sq mi; 1,127,127 sq km
LEADING EXPORTS: coffee, leather products, and gold
CONTINENT: Africa

## Fiji

CAPITAL: Suva
POPULATION: 772,891
MAJOR LANGUAGES: English, Fijian, and Hindustani
AREA: 7,054 sq mi; 18,270 sq km
LEADING EXPORTS: sugar, clothing, gold, processed fish, and lumber
LOCATION: Pacific Ocean

## Finland

CAPITAL: Helsinki
POPULATION: 5,085,206
MAJOR LANGUAGES: Finnish, Swedish, Lapp, and Russian
AREA: 130,132 sq mi; 337,030 sq km
LEADING EXPORTS: paper and pulp, machinery, and chemicals
CONTINENT: Europe

## France

CAPITAL: Paris
POPULATION: 58,109,160
MAJOR LANGUAGES: French and regional dialects and languages
AREA: 211,217 sq mi; 547,030 sq km
LEADING EXPORTS: machinery and transportation equipment
CONTINENT: Europe

## Gabon

CAPITAL: Libreville
POPULATION: 1,185,749
MAJOR LANGUAGES: French, Fang, Myene, Bateke, Bapounou/Eschira, and Bandjabi
AREA: 103,351 sq mi; 267,670 sq km
LEADING EXPORTS: crude oil, timber, manganese, and uranium
CONTINENT: Africa

## The Gambia

CAPITAL: Banjul
POPULATION: 989,273
MAJOR LANGUAGES: English, Mandinka, Wolof, Fula, and various languages
AREA: 4,363 sq mi; 11,300 sq km
LEADING EXPORTS: peanuts and peanut products, and fish
CONTINENT: Africa

## Georgia

CAPITAL: T'bilisi
POPULATION: 5,725,972
MAJOR LANGUAGES: Armenian, Azeri, Georgian, Russian, and various languages
AREA: 26,912 sq mi; 69,700 sq km
LEADING EXPORTS: citrus fruits, tea, and wine
CONTINENT: Asia

## Germany

CAPITAL: Berlin
POPULATION: 81,337,541
MAJOR LANGUAGE: German
AREA: 137,808 sq mi; 356,910 sq km
LEADING EXPORTS: machines and machine tools, and chemicals
CONTINENT: Europe

## Ghana

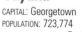

CAPITAL: Accra
POPULATION: 17,763,138
MAJOR LANGUAGES: English, Akan, Moshi-Dagomba, Ewe, Ga, and various languages
AREA: 92,104 sq mi; 238,540 sq km
LEADING EXPORTS: cocoa, gold, timber, tuna, and bauxite
CONTINENT: Africa

## Greece

CAPITAL: Athens
POPULATION: 10,647,511
MAJOR LANGUAGES: Greek, English, and French
AREA: 50,944 sq mi; 131,940 sq km
LEADING EXPORTS: manufactured goods, foodstuffs, and fuels
CONTINENT: Europe

## Grenada

CAPITAL: Saint George's
POPULATION: 94,486
MAJOR LANGUAGES: English and French patois
AREA: 131 sq mi; 340 sq km
LEADING EXPORTS: bananas, cocoa, nutmeg, and fruits and vegetables
LOCATION: Caribbean Sea

## Guatemala

CAPITAL: Guatemala
POPULATION: 10,998,602
MAJOR LANGUAGES: Spanish, Quiche, Cakchiquel, Kekchi, and various languages and dialects
AREA: 42,044 sq mi; 108,890 sq km
LEADING EXPORTS: coffee, sugar, bananas, cardamom, and beef
CONTINENT: Central America

## Guinea

CAPITAL: Conakry
POPULATION: 6,549,336
MAJOR LANGUAGES: French and various languages
AREA: 94,930 sq mi; 245,860 sq km
LEADING EXPORTS: bauxite, alumina, diamonds, gold, and coffee
CONTINENT: Africa

## Guinea Bissau

CAPITAL: Bissau
POPULATION: 1,124,537
MAJOR LANGUAGES: Portuguese, Criolo, and various languages
AREA: 13,946 sq mi; 36,210 sq km
LEADING EXPORTS: cashews, fish, peanuts, and palm kernels
CONTINENT: Africa

## Guyana

CAPITAL: Georgetown
POPULATION: 723,774
MAJOR LANGUAGES: English and various dialects
AREA: 83,003 sq mi; 214,970 sq km
LEADING EXPORTS: sugar, bauxite/alumina, rice, and shrimp
CONTINENT: South America

## Haiti

CAPITAL: Port-au-Prince
POPULATION: 6,539,983
MAJOR LANGUAGES: French and Creole
AREA: 8,784 sq mi; 22,750 sq km
LEADING EXPORTS: light manufactures and coffee
LOCATION: Caribbean Sea

## Holy See (Vatican City)

CAPITAL: Vatican City
POPULATION: 830
MAJOR LANGUAGES: Italian, Latin, and various languages
AREA: 17 sq mi; 44 sq km
LEADING EXPORTS: none
CONTINENT: Europe

## Honduras

CAPITAL: Tegucigalpa
POPULATION: 5,549,743
MAJOR LANGUAGES: Spanish and various dialects
AREA: 43,280 sq mi; 112,090 sq km
LEADING EXPORTS: bananas, coffee, shrimp, lobsters, and minerals
CONTINENT: Central America

## Hungary

CAPITAL: Budapest
POPULATION: 10,318,838
MAJOR LANGUAGES: Hungarian and various languages
AREA: 35,920 sq mi; 93,030 sq km
LEADING EXPORTS: raw materials and semi-finished goods
CONTINENT: Europe

## Iceland

CAPITAL: Reykjavik
POPULATION: 265,998
MAJOR LANGUAGE: Icelandic
AREA: 39,770 sq mi; 103,000 sq km
LEADING EXPORTS: fish and fish products, and animal products
CONTINENT: Europe

## India

CAPITAL: New Delhi
POPULATION: 936,545,814
MAJOR LANGUAGES: English, Hindi, Bengali, Telugu, Marathi, Tamil, Urdu, Gujarati, Malayam, Kannada, Oriya, Punjabi, Assamese, Kashmiri, Sindhi, Sanskrit, and Hindustani (all official)
AREA: 1,269,389 sq mi; 3,287,590 sq km
LEADING EXPORTS: clothing, and gems and jewelry
CONTINENT: Asia

## Indonesia

CAPITAL: Jakarta
POPULATION: 203,583,886
MAJOR LANGUAGES: Bahasa Indonesia, English, Dutch, Javanese, and various dialects
AREA: 741,052 sq mi; 1,919,251 sq km
LEADING EXPORTS: manufactures, fuels, and foodstuffs
CONTINENT: Asia

## Iran

CAPITAL: Tehran
POPULATION: 64,625,455
MAJOR LANGUAGES: Farsi (official) and Turkic languages
AREA: 634,562 sq mi; 1,643,452 sq km
LEADING EXPORTS: petroleum, carpets, fruit, nuts, and hides
CONTINENT: Asia

## Iraq

CAPITAL: Baghdad
POPULATION: 20,643,769
MAJOR LANGUAGES: Arabic, Kurdish, Assyrian, and Armenian
AREA: 168,760 sq mi; 437,072 sq km
LEADING EXPORTS: crude oil and refined products, and fertilizers
CONTINENT: Asia

## Ireland

CAPITAL: Dublin
POPULATION: 3,550,448
MAJOR LANGUAGES: Irish Gaelic and English
AREA: 27,136 sq mi; 70,280 sq km
LEADING EXPORTS: chemicals and data processing equipment
CONTINENT: Europe

## Israel

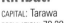

CAPITAL: Jerusalem
POPULATION: 7,566,447
MAJOR LANGUAGES: Hebrew, Arabic, and English
AREA: 10,421 sq mi; 26,990 sq km
LEADING EXPORTS: machinery and equipment, and cut diamonds
CONTINENT: Asia

## Italy

CAPITAL: Rome
POPULATION: 58,261,971
MAJOR LANGUAGES: Italian, German, French, and Slovene
AREA: 116,310 sq mi; 301,230 sq km
LEADING EXPORTS: metals, and textiles and clothing
CONTINENT: Europe

## Jamaica

CAPITAL: Kingston
POPULATION: 2,574,291
MAJOR LANGUAGES: English and Creole
AREA: 4,243 sq mi; 10,990 sq km
LEADING EXPORTS: alumina, bauxite, sugar, bananas, and rum
LOCATION: Caribbean Sea

## Japan

CAPITAL: Tokyo
POPULATION: 125,506,492
MAJOR LANGUAGE: Japanese
AREA: 145,888 sq mi; 377,835 sq km
LEADING EXPORTS: machinery, motor vehicles, and electronics
CONTINENT: Asia

## Jordan

CAPITAL: Amman
POPULATION: 4,100,709
MAJOR LANGUAGES: Arabic and English
AREA: 34,447 sq mi; 89,213 sq km
LEADING EXPORTS: phosphates, fertilizers, and potash
CONTINENT: Asia

## Kazakhstan

CAPITAL: Almaty
POPULATION: 17,376,615
MAJOR LANGUAGES: Kazakh and Russian
AREA: 1,049,191 sq mi; 2,717,300 sq km
LEADING EXPORTS: oil, and ferrous and nonferrous metals
CONTINENT: Asia

## Kenya

CAPITAL: Nairobi
POPULATION: 28,817,227
MAJOR LANGUAGES: English, Swahili, and various languages
AREA: 224,970 sq mi; 582,650 sq km
LEADING EXPORTS: tea, coffee, and petroleum products
CONTINENT: Africa

## Kiribati

CAPITAL: Tarawa
POPULATION: 79,386
MAJOR LANGUAGES: English and Gilbertese
AREA: 277 sq mi; 717 sq km
LEADING EXPORTS: copra, seaweed, and fish
LOCATION: Pacific Ocean

## Korea, North

CAPITAL: P'yongyang
POPULATION: 23,486,550
MAJOR LANGUAGE: Korean
AREA: 46,542 sq mi; 120,540 sq km
LEADING EXPORTS: minerals and metallurgical products
CONTINENT: Asia

## Korea, South

CAPITAL: Seoul
POPULATION: 45,553,882
MAJOR LANGUAGES: Korean and English
AREA: 38,025 sq mi; 98,480 sq km
LEADING EXPORTS: electronic and electrical equipment
CONTINENT: Asia

## Kuwait

CAPITAL: Kuwait
POPULATION: 1,817,397
MAJOR LANGUAGES: Arabic and English
AREA: 6,881 sq mi; 17,820 sq km
LEADING EXPORT: oil
CONTINENT: Asia

## Kyrgyzstan

CAPITAL: Bishkek
POPULATION: 4,769,877
MAJOR LANGUAGES: Kyrgyz and Russian
AREA: 76,644 sq mi; 198,500 sq km
LEADING EXPORTS: wool, chemicals, cotton, metals, and shoes
CONTINENT: Asia

## Laos

CAPITAL: Vientiane
POPULATION: 4,837,237
MAJOR LANGUAGES: Lao, French, English, and various languages
AREA: 91,432 sq mi; 236,800 sq km
LEADING EXPORTS: electricity, wood products, coffee, and tin
CONTINENT: Asia

## Latvia

CAPITAL: Riga
POPULATION: 2,762,899
MAJOR LANGUAGES: Lettish, Lithuanian, Russian, and various languages
AREA: 24,750 sq mi; 64,100 sq km
LEADING EXPORTS: oil products, timber, and ferrous metals
CONTINENT: Europe

## Lebanon

CAPITAL: Beirut
POPULATION: 3,695,921
MAJOR LANGUAGES: Arabic, French, Armenian, and English
AREA: 4,016 sq mi; 10,400 sq km
LEADING EXPORTS: agricultural products, chemicals, and textiles
CONTINENT: Asia

## Lesotho

CAPITAL: Maseru
POPULATION: 1,992,960
MAJOR LANGUAGES: Sesotho, English, Zulu, and Xhosa
AREA: 11,719 sq mi; 30,350 sq km
LEADING EXPORTS: wool, mohair, wheat, cattle, and peas
CONTINENT: Africa

## Liberia

CAPITAL: Monrovia
POPULATION: 3,073,245
MAJOR LANGUAGES: English and Niger-Congo
AREA: 43,002 sq mi; 111,370 sq km
LEADING EXPORTS: iron ore, rubber, timber, and coffee
CONTINENT: Africa

## Libya

CAPITAL: Tripoli
POPULATION: 5,248,401
MAJOR LANGUAGES: Arabic, Italian, and English
AREA: 679,385 sq mi; 1,759,540 sq km
LEADING EXPORTS: crude oil and refined petroleum products
CONTINENT: Africa

## Liechtenstein

CAPITAL: Vaduz
POPULATION: 30,654
MAJOR LANGUAGES: German and Alemannic
AREA: 62 sq mi; 160 sq km
LEADING EXPORTS: small specialty machinery and dental products
CONTINENT: Europe

## Lithuania

CAPITAL: Vilnius
POPULATION: 3,876,396
MAJOR LANGUAGES: Lithuanian, Polish, and Russian
AREA: 25,175 sq mi; 65,200 sq km
LEADING EXPORTS: electronics, petroleum products, and food
CONTINENT: Europe

## Luxembourg

CAPITAL: Luxembourg
POPULATION: 404,660
MAJOR LANGUAGES: Luxembourgisch, German, French, and English
AREA: 998 sq mi; 2,586 sq km
LEADING EXPORTS: finished steel products and chemicals
CONTINENT: Europe

## Macedonia

CAPITAL: Skopje
POPULATION: 2,159,503
MAJOR LANGUAGES: Macedonian, Albanian, Turkish, Serb, Gypsy, and various languages
AREA: 9,781 sq mi; 25,333 sq km
LEADING EXPORTS: manufactured goods and machinery
CONTINENT: Europe

## Madagascar

CAPITAL: Antananarivo
POPULATION: 13,862,325
MAJOR LANGUAGES: French and Malagasy
AREA: 226,665 sq mi; 587,040 sq km
LEADING EXPORTS: coffee, vanilla, cloves, shellfish, and sugar
CONTINENT: Africa

## Malawi

CAPITAL: Lilongwe
POPULATION: 9,808,384
MAJOR LANGUAGES: English, Chichewa, and various languages
AREA: 45,747 sq mi; 118,480 sq km
LEADING EXPORTS: tobacco, tea, sugar, coffee, and peanuts
CONTINENT: Africa

## Malaysia

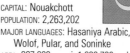

CAPITAL: Kuala Lumpur
POPULATION: 19,723,587
MAJOR LANGUAGES: Malay, English, Mandarin, Tamil, Chinese dialects, and various languages and dialects
AREA: 127,322 sq mi; 329,750 sq km
LEADING EXPORTS: electronic equipment
CONTINENT: Asia

## Maldives

CAPITAL: Male
POPULATION: 261,310
MAJOR LANGUAGES: Divehi dialect and English
AREA: 116 sq mi; 300 sq km
LEADING EXPORTS: fish and clothing
CONTINENT: Asia

## Mali

CAPITAL: Bamako
POPULATION: 9,375,132
MAJOR LANGUAGES: French, Bambara, and various languages
AREA: 478,783 sq mi; 1,240,000 sq km
LEADING EXPORTS: cotton, livestock, and gold
CONTINENT: Africa

## Malta

CAPITAL: Valletta
POPULATION: 369,609
MAJOR LANGUAGES: Maltese and English
AREA: 124 sq mi; 320 sq km
LEADING EXPORTS: machinery and transportation equipment
CONTINENT: Europe

## Marshall Islands

CAPITAL: Majuro
POPULATION: 56,157
MAJOR LANGUAGES: English, Marshallese dialects, and Japanese
AREA: 70 sq mi; 181.3 sq km
LEADING EXPORTS: coconut oil, fish, live animals, and trichus shells
LOCATION: Pacific Ocean

## Mauritania

CAPITAL: Nouakchott
POPULATION: 2,263,202
MAJOR LANGUAGES: Hasaniya Arabic, Wolof, Pular, and Soninke
AREA: 397,969 sq mi; 1,030,700 sq km
LEADING EXPORTS: iron ore, and fish and fish products
CONTINENT: Africa

## Mauritius

CAPITAL: Port Louis
POPULATION: 1,127,068
MAJOR LANGUAGES: English (official), Creole, French, Hindi, Urdu, Hakka, and Bojpoori
AREA: 718 sq mi; 1,860 sq km
LEADING EXPORTS: textiles, sugar, and light manufactures
LOCATION: Indian Ocean

## Mayotte

CAPITAL: Mamoutzou
POPULATION: 97,088
MAJOR LANGUAGES: Mahorian and French
AREA: 145 sq mi; 375 sq km
LEADING EXPORTS: ylang-ylang and vanilla
CONTINENT: Africa

## Mexico

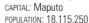

CAPITAL: Mexico City
POPULATION: 93,985,848
MAJOR LANGUAGES: Spanish and Mayan dialects
AREA: 761,632 sq mi; 1,972,550 sq km
LEADING EXPORTS: crude oil, oil products, coffee, and silver
CONTINENT: North America

## Micronesia

CAPITAL: Federated states of Kolonia (on the Island of Pohnpei)
*a new capital is being built about 10 km southwest in the Palikir Valley
POPULATION: 122,950
MAJOR LANGUAGES: English, Turkese, Pohnpeian, Yapese, and Kosrean
AREA: 271 sq mi; 702 sq km
LEADING EXPORTS: fish, copra, bananas, and black pepper
LOCATION: Pacific Ocean

## Moldova

CAPITAL: Chisinau
POPULATION: 4,489,657
MAJOR LANGUAGES: Moldovan (official), Russian, and Gagauz dialect
AREA: 13,012 sq mi; 33,700 sq km
LEADING EXPORTS: foodstuffs, wine, and tobacco
CONTINENT: Europe

## Monaco

CAPITAL: Monaco
POPULATION: 31,515
MAJOR LANGUAGES: French (official), English, Italian, and Monegasque
AREA: .73 sq mi; 1.9 sq km
LEADING EXPORTS: exports through France
CONTINENT: Europe

## Mongolia

CAPITAL: Ulaanbaatar
POPULATION: 2,493,615
MAJOR LANGUAGES: Khalkha Mongol, Turkic, Russian, and Chinese
AREA: 604,270 sq mi; 1,565,000 sq km
LEADING EXPORTS: copper, livestock, animal products, and cashmere
CONTINENT: Asia

## Morocco

CAPITAL: Rabat
POPULATION: 29,168,848
MAJOR LANGUAGES: Arabic (official), Berber dialects, and French
AREA: 172,420 sq mi; 446,550 sq km
LEADING EXPORTS: food and beverages
CONTINENT: Africa

## Mozambique

CAPITAL: Maputo
POPULATION: 18,115,250
MAJOR LANGUAGES: Portuguese and various dialects
AREA: 309,506 sq mi; 801,590 sq km
LEADING EXPORTS: shrimp, cashews, cotton, sugar, copra, and citrus
CONTINENT: Africa

## Myanmar (Burma)

CAPITAL: Rangoon
POPULATION: 45,103,809
MAJOR LANGUAGE: Burmese
AREA: 261,979 sq mi; 678,500 sq km
LEADING EXPORTS: pulses and beans, teak, rice, and hardwood
CONTINENT: Asia

## Namibia

CAPITAL: Windhoek
POPULATION: 1,651,545
MAJOR LANGUAGES: English (official), Afrikaans, German, Oshivambo, Herero, Nama, and various languages
AREA: 318,707 sq mi; 825,418 sq km
LEADING EXPORTS: diamonds, copper, gold, zinc, and lead
CONTINENT: Africa

## Nauru

CAPITAL: Government offices in Yaren District
POPULATION: 10,149
MAJOR LANGUAGES: Nauruan and English
AREA: 8 sq mi; 21 sq km
LEADING EXPORTS: phosphates
LOCATION: Pacific Ocean

## Nepal

CAPITAL: Kathmandu
POPULATION: 21,560,869
MAJOR LANGUAGES: Nepali (official) and 20 various languages divided into numerous dialects
AREA: 54,365 sq mi; 140,800 sq km
LEADING EXPORTS: carpets, clothing, and leather goods
CONTINENT: Asia

## Netherlands

CAPITAL: Amsterdam
POPULATION: 15,452,903
MAJOR LANGUAGE: Dutch
AREA: 14,414 sq mi; 37,330 sq km
LEADING EXPORTS: metal products and chemicals
CONTINENT: Europe

## New Caledonia

CAPITAL: Noumea
POPULATION: 184,552
MAJOR LANGUAGES: French and 28 Melanesian-Polynesian dialects
AREA: 7,359 sq mi; 19,060 sq km
LEADING EXPORTS: nickel metal and nickel ore
LOCATION: Pacific Ocean

## New Zealand

CAPITAL: Wellington
POPULATION: 3,407,277
MAJOR LANGUAGES: English and Maori
AREA: 103,741 sq mi; 268,680 sq km
LEADING EXPORTS: wool, lamb, mutton, beef, fish, and cheese
LOCATION: Pacific Ocean

## Nicaragua

CAPITAL: Managua
POPULATION: 4,206,353
MAJOR LANGUAGES: Spanish (official), English, and various languages
AREA: 50,000 sq mi; 129,494 sq km
LEADING EXPORTS: meat, coffee, cotton, sugar, seafood, and gold
LOCATION: Caribbean Sea

## Niger

CAPITAL: Niamey
POPULATION: 9,280,208
MAJOR LANGUAGES: French (official), Hausa, and Djerma
AREA: 489,208 sq mi; 1,267,000 sq km
LEADING EXPORTS: uranium ore and livestock products
CONTINENT: Africa

## Nigeria

CAPITAL: Abuja
POPULATION: 101,232,251
MAJOR LANGUAGES: English (official), Hausa, Yoruba, Ibo, and Fulani
AREA: 356,682 sq mi; 923,770 sq km
LEADING EXPORTS: oil, cocoa, and rubber
CONTINENT: Africa

## Niue

CAPITAL: (Free association with New Zealand)
POPULATION: 1,837
MAJOR LANGUAGES: Polynesian and English
AREA: 100 sq mi; 260 sq km
LEADING EXPORTS: canned coconut cream, copra, and honey
LOCATION: Pacific Ocean

## Norway

CAPITAL: Oslo
POPULATION: 4,330,951
MAJOR LANGUAGES: Norwegian (official), Lapp, and Finnish
AREA: 125,186 sq mi; 324,220 sq km
LEADING EXPORTS: petroleum and petroleum products
CONTINENT: Europe

## Oman

CAPITAL: Muscat
POPULATION: 2,125,089
MAJOR LANGUAGES: Arabic (official), English, Baluchi, Urdu, and Indian dialects
AREA: 82,034 sq mi; 212,460 sq km
LEADING EXPORTS: petroleum, re-exports, and fish
CONTINENT: Asia

## Pakistan

CAPITAL: Islamabad
POPULATION: 131,541,920
MAJOR LANGUAGES: Urdu (official), English (official), Punjabi, Sindhi, Pashtu, Urdu, Balochi, and other languages
AREA: 310,414 sq mi; 803,940 sq km
LEADING EXPORTS: cotton, textiles, clothing, rice, and leather
CONTINENT: Asia

## Palau

CAPITAL: Koror
POPULATION: 16,661
MAJOR LANGUAGES: English (official), Sonsorolese, Angaur, Japanese, Tobi, and Palauan
AREA: 177 sq mi; 458 sq km
LEADING EXPORTS: trochus, tuna, copra, and handicrafts
LOCATION: Pacific Ocean

## Panama

CAPITAL: Panama
POPULATION: 2,680,903
MAJOR LANGUAGES: Spanish (official) and English
AREA: 30,194 sq mi; 78,200 sq km
LEADING EXPORTS: bananas, shrimp, sugar, clothing, and coffee
CONTINENT: Central America

## Papua New Guinea

CAPITAL: Port Moresby
POPULATION: 4,294,750
MAJOR LANGUAGES: English, pidgin English, and Motu
AREA: 178,266 sq mi; 461,690 sq km
LEADING EXPORTS: gold, copper ore, oil, logs, and palm oil
LOCATION: Pacific Ocean

## Paraguay

CAPITAL: Asuncion
POPULATION: 5,358,198
MAJOR LANGUAGES: Spanish (official) and Guarani
AREA: 157,052 sq mi; 406,750 sq km
LEADING EXPORTS: cotton, soybeans, timber, and vegetable oils
CONTINENT: South America

## Peru

CAPITAL: Lima
POPULATION: 24,087,372
MAJOR LANGUAGES: Spanish (official), Quechua (official), and Aymara
AREA: 496,243 sq mi; 1,285,220 sq km
LEADING EXPORTS: copper, zinc, and fish meal
CONTINENT: South America

## Philippines

CAPITAL: Manila
POPULATION: 73,265,584
MAJOR LANGUAGES: Pilipino and English (official)
AREA: 115,834 sq mi; 300,000 sq km
LEADING EXPORTS: electronics, textiles, and coconut products
CONTINENT: Asia

## Poland

CAPITAL: Warsaw
POPULATION: 38,792,442
MAJOR LANGUAGE: Polish
AREA: 120,731 sq mi; 312,680 sq km
LEADING EXPORTS: intermediate goods
CONTINENT: Europe

## Portugal

CAPITAL: Lisbon
POPULATION: 10,562,388
MAJOR LANGUAGE: Portuguese
AREA: 35,553 sq mi; 92,080 sq km
LEADING EXPORTS: clothing and footwear, and machinery
CONTINENT: Europe

## Qatar

CAPITAL: Doha
POPULATION: 533,916
MAJOR LANGUAGES: Arabic (official) and English
AREA: 4,247 sq mi; 11,000 sq km
LEADING EXPORTS: petroleum products, steel, and fertilizers
CONTINENT: Asia

## Romania

CAPITAL: Bucharest
POPULATION: 23,198,330
MAJOR LANGUAGES: Romanian, Hungarian, and German
AREA: 91,702 sq mi; 237,500 sq km
LEADING EXPORTS: metals and metal products, and mineral products
CONTINENT: Europe

## Russia

CAPITAL: Moscow
POPULATION: 149,909,089
MAJOR LANGUAGES: Russian and various languages
AREA: 6,952,996 sq mi; 17,075,200 sq km
LEADING EXPORTS: petroleum and petroleum products
CONTINENT: Europe and Asia

## Rwanda

CAPITAL: Kigali
POPULATION: 8,605,307
MAJOR LANGUAGES: Kinyarwanda (official), French (official), and Kiswahili
AREA: 10,170 sq mi; 26,340 sq km
LEADING EXPORTS: coffee, tea, cassiterite, and wolframite
CONTINENT: Africa

## Saint Kitts and Nevis

CAPITAL: Basseterre
POPULATION: 40,992
MAJOR LANGUAGE: English
AREA: 104 sq mi; 269 sq km
LEADING EXPORTS: machinery, food, and electronics
LOCATION: Caribbean Sea

## Saint Lucia

CAPITAL: Castries
POPULATION: 156,050
MAJOR LANGUAGES: English and French patois
AREA: 239 sq mi; 620 sq km
LEADING EXPORTS: bananas, clothing, cocoa, and vegetables
LOCATION: Caribbean Sea

## Saint Vincent and the Grenadines

CAPITAL: Kingstown
POPULATION: 117,344
MAJOR LANGUAGES: English and French patois
AREA: 131 sq mi; 340 sq km
LEADING EXPORTS: bananas, and eddoes and dasheen (taro)
LOCATION: Caribbean Sea

## San Marino

CAPITAL: San Marino
POPULATION: 24,313
MAJOR LANGUAGE: Italian
AREA: 23 sq mi; 60 sq km
LEADING EXPORTS: building stone, lime, wood, and chestnuts
CONTINENT: Europe

## Sao Tome and Principe

CAPITAL: Sao Tome
POPULATION: 140,423
MAJOR LANGUAGE: Portuguese (official)
AREA: 371 sq mi; 960 sq km
LEADING EXPORTS: cocoa, copra, coffee, and palm oil
CONTINENT: Africa

## Saudi Arabia

CAPITAL: Riyadh
POPULATION: 18,729,576
MAJOR LANGUAGE: Arabic
AREA: 757,011 sq mi; 1,960,582 sq km
LEADING EXPORTS: petroleum and petroleum products
CONTINENT: Asia

## Senegal

CAPITAL: Dakar
POPULATION: 9,007,080
MAJOR LANGUAGES: French (official), Wolof, Pulaar, Diola, and Mandingo
AREA: 75,752 sq mi; 196,190 sq km
LEADING EXPORTS: fish, ground nuts, and petroleum products
CONTINENT: Africa

## Serbia and Montenegro

CAPITAL: Belgrade
POPULATION: 11,101,833
MAJOR LANGUAGES: Serbo-Croatian and Albanian
AREA: 39,436 sq mi; 102,350 sq km
LEADING EXPORTS: none
CONTINENT: Europe

## Seychelles

CAPITAL: Victoria
POPULATION: 72,709
MAJOR LANGUAGES: English (official), French (official), and Creole
AREA: 176 sq mi; 455 sq km
LEADING EXPORTS: fish, cinnamon bark, and copra
CONTINENT: Africa

## Sierra Leone

CAPITAL: Freetown
POPULATION: 4,753,120
MAJOR LANGUAGES: English (official), Mende, Temne, and Krio
AREA: 27,700 sq mi; 71,740 sq km
LEADING EXPORTS: rutile, bauxite, diamonds, coffee, and cocoa
CONTINENT: Africa

## Singapore

CAPITAL: Singapore
POPULATION: 2,890,468
MAJOR LANGUAGES: Chinese, Malay, Tamil, and English
AREA: 244 sq mi; 633 sq km
LEADING EXPORTS: computer equipment
CONTINENT: Asia

## Slovakia

CAPITAL: Bratislava
POPULATION: 5,432,383
MAJOR LANGUAGES: Slovak and Hungarian
AREA: 18,860 sq mi; 48,845 sq km
LEADING EXPORTS: machinery and transportation equipment
CONTINENT: Europe

## Slovenia

CAPITAL: Ljubljana
POPULATION: 2,051,522
MAJOR LANGUAGES: Slovenian, Serbo-Croatian, and various languages
AREA: 7,837 sq mi; 20,296 sq km
LEADING EXPORTS: machinery and transportation equipment
CONTINENT: Europe

## Solomon Islands

CAPITAL: Honiara
POPULATION: 399,206
MAJOR LANGUAGES: Melanesian pidgin and English
AREA: 10,985 sq mi; 28,450 sq km
LEADING EXPORTS: fish, timber, palm oil, cocoa, and copra
LOCATION: Pacific Ocean

## Somalia

CAPITAL: Mogadishu
POPULATION: 7,347,554
MAJOR LANGUAGES: Somali (official), Arabic, Italian, and English
AREA: 246,210 sq mi; 637,660 sq km
LEADING EXPORTS: bananas, live animals, fish, and hides
CONTINENT: Africa

## South Africa

CAPITAL: Pretoria (administrative), Cape Town (legislative), Bloemfontein (judicial)
POPULATION: 45,095,459
MAJOR LANGUAGES: Afrikaans, English, Ndebele, Pedi, Sotho, Swazi, Tsonga, Tswana, Venda, Xhosa, and Zulu (all official)
AREA: 471,027 sq mi; 1,219,912 sq km
LEADING EXPORTS: gold, other minerals and metals, and food
CONTINENT: Africa

## Spain

CAPITAL: Madrid
POPULATION: 39,404,348
MAJOR LANGUAGES: Spanish, Catalan, Galician, and Basque
AREA: 194,892 sq mi; 504,750 sq km
LEADING EXPORTS: cars and trucks, and semifinished goods
CONTINENT: Europe

## Sri Lanka

CAPITAL: Colombo
POPULATION: 18,342,660
MAJOR LANGUAGES: Sinhala (official) and Tamil
AREA: 25,333 sq mi; 65,610 sq km
LEADING EXPORTS: garments and textiles, teas, and diamonds
CONTINENT: Asia

## Sudan

CAPITAL: Khartoum
POPULATION: 30,120,420
MAJOR LANGUAGES: Arabic (official), Nubian, Ta Bedawie, Nilotic, Nilo-Hamitic, and Sudanic dialects
AREA: 967,532 sq mi; 2,505,810 sq km
LEADING EXPORTS: gum arabic, livestock/meat, and cotton
CONTINENT: Africa

## Suriname

CAPITAL: Paramaribo
POPULATION: 429,544
MAJOR LANGUAGES: Dutch (official), English, Sranang, Tongo, Hindustani, and Japanese
AREA: 63,041 sq mi; 163,270 sq km
LEADING EXPORTS: alumina, aluminum, and shrimp and fish
CONTINENT: South America

## Swaziland

CAPITAL: Mbabane
POPULATION: 966,977
MAJOR LANGUAGES: English (official) and SiSwati (official)
AREA: 6,641 sq mi; 17,360 sq km
LEADING EXPORTS: sugar, edible concentrates, and wood pulp
CONTINENT: Africa

## Sweden

CAPITAL: Stockholm
POPULATION: 8,821,759
MAJOR LANGUAGES: Swedish, Lapp, and Finnish
AREA: 173,738 sq mi; 449,964 sq km
LEADING EXPORTS: machinery, motor vehicles, and paper products
CONTINENT: Europe

## Switzerland

CAPITAL: Bern
POPULATION: 7,084,984
MAJOR LANGUAGES: German, French, Italian, Romansch, and various languages
AREA: 15,943 sq mi; 41,290 sq km
LEADING EXPORTS: machinery and equipment
CONTINENT: Europe

## Syria

CAPITAL: Damascus
POPULATION: 15,451,917
MAJOR LANGUAGES: Arabic (official), Kurdish, Armenian, Aramaic, Circassian, and French
AREA: 71,501 sq mi; 185,180 sq km
LEADING EXPORTS: petroleum, textiles, cotton, and fruits
CONTINENT: Asia

## Taiwan

CAPITAL: Taipei
POPULATION: 21,500,583
MAJOR LANGUAGES: Mandarin Chinese (official), Taiwanese, and Hakka dialects
AREA: 13,892 sq mi; 35,980 sq km
LEADING EXPORTS: electrical machinery and electronics
CONTINENT: Asia

## Tajikistan

CAPITAL: Dushanbe
POPULATION: 6,155,474
MAJOR LANGUAGES: Tajik (official) and Russian
AREA: 55,253 sq mi; 143,100 sq km
LEADING EXPORTS: cotton, aluminum, fruits, and vegetable oil
CONTINENT: Asia

## Tanzania
CAPITAL: Dar Es Salaam
POPULATION: 28,701,077
MAJOR LANGUAGES: Swahili, English, and various languages
AREA: 364,914 sq mi; 945,090 sq km
LEADING EXPORTS: coffee, cotton, tobacco, tea, and cashew nuts
CONTINENT: Africa

## Thailand
CAPITAL: Bangkok
POPULATION: 60,271,300
MAJOR LANGUAGES: Thai and English
AREA: 198,463 sq mi; 511,770 sq km
LEADING EXPORTS: machinery and manufactures
CONTINENT: Asia

## Togo
CAPITAL: Lome
POPULATION: 4,410,370
MAJOR LANGUAGES: French, Ewe and Mina, Dagomba, and Kabye
AREA: 21,927 sq mi; 56,790 sq km
LEADING EXPORTS: phosphates, cotton, cocoa, and coffee
CONTINENT: Africa

## Tonga
CAPITAL: Nukualofa
POPULATION: 105,600
MAJOR LANGUAGES: Tongan and English
AREA: 289 sq mi; 748 sq km
LEADING EXPORTS: squash, vanilla, fish, root crops, and coconut oil
LOCATION: Pacific Ocean

## Trinidad and Tobago
CAPITAL: Port-of-Spain
POPULATION: 1,271,159
MAJOR LANGUAGES: English, Hindu, French, and Spanish
AREA: 1,981 sq mi; 5,130 sq km
LEADING EXPORTS: petroleum and petroleum products
LOCATION: Caribbean Sea

## Tunisia
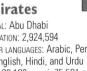
CAPITAL: Tunis
POPULATION: 8,879,845
MAJOR LANGUAGES: Arabic and French
AREA: 63,172 sq mi; 163,610 sq km
LEADING EXPORTS: hydrocarbons and agricultural products
CONTINENT: Africa

## Turkey
CAPITAL: Ankara
POPULATION: 63,405,526
MAJOR LANGUAGES: Turkish, Kurdish, and Arabic
AREA: 301,394 sq mi; 780,580 sq km
LEADING EXPORTS: manufactured products, and foodstuffs
CONTINENT: Europe and Asia

## Turkmenistan
CAPITAL: Ashgabat
POPULATION: 4,075,316
MAJOR LANGUAGES: Turkmen, Russian, Uzbek, and various languages
AREA: 188,463 sq mi; 488,100 sq km
LEADING EXPORTS: natural gas, cotton, and petroleum products
CONTINENT: Asia

## Tuvalu
CAPITAL: Fongafale, on Funafuti atoll
POPULATION: 9,991
MAJOR LANGUAGES: Tuvaluan and English
AREA: 10 sq mi; 26 sq km
LEADING EXPORT: copra
LOCATION: Pacific Ocean

## Uganda

CAPITAL: Kampala
POPULATION: 19,573,262
MAJOR LANGUAGES: English, Luganda, Swahili, Bantu languages, and Nilotic languages
AREA: 91,139 sq mi; 236,040 sq km
LEADING EXPORTS: coffee, cotton, and tea
CONTINENT: Africa

## Ukraine
CAPITAL: Kiev
POPULATION: 51,867,828
MAJOR LANGUAGES: Ukranian, Russian, Romanian, Polish, and Hungarian
AREA: 233,098 sq mi; 603,700 sq km
LEADING EXPORTS: coal, electric power, and metals
CONTINENT: Europe

## United Arab Emirates
CAPITAL: Abu Dhabi
POPULATION: 2,924,594
MAJOR LANGUAGES: Arabic, Persian, English, Hindi, and Urdu
AREA: 29,183 sq mi; 75,581 sq km
LEADING EXPORTS: crude oil, natural gas, re-exports, and dried fish
CONTINENT: Asia

## United Kingdom

CAPITAL: London
POPULATION: 58,295,119
MAJOR LANGUAGES: English, Welsh, and Scottish Gaelic
AREA: 94,529 sq mi; 244,820 sq km
LEADING EXPORTS: manufactured goods, machinery, and fuels
CONTINENT: Europe

## United States
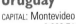
CAPITAL: Washington, D.C.
POPULATION: 263,814,032
MAJOR LANGUAGES: English and Spanish
AREA: 3,618,908 sq mi; 9,372,610 sq km
LEADING EXPORTS: capital goods and automobiles
CONTINENT: North America

## Uruguay
CAPITAL: Montevideo
POPULATION: 3,222,716
MAJOR LANGUAGES: Spanish and Brazilero
AREA: 68,041 sq mi; 176,220 sq km
LEADING EXPORT: wool and textile manufactures
CONTINENT: South America

## Uzbekistan

CAPITAL: Tashkent
POPULATION: 23,089,261
MAJOR LANGUAGES: Uzbek, Russian, Tajik, various languages
AREA: 172,748 sq mi; 447,400 sq km
LEADING EXPORTS: cotton, gold, natural gas, and minerals
CONTINENT: Asia

## Vanuatu
CAPITAL: Port-Vila
POPULATION: 173,648
MAJOR LANGUAGES: English, French, pidgin, and Bislama
AREA: 5,699 sq mi; 14,760 sq km
LEADING EXPORTS: copra, beef, cocoa, timber, and coffee
LOCATION: Pacific Ocean

## Venezuela
CAPITAL: Caracas
POPULATION: 21,004,773
MAJOR LANGUAGES: Spanish and various languages
AREA: 352,156 sq mi; 912,050 sq km
LEADING EXPORTS: petroleum, bauxite and aluminum, and steel
CONTINENT: South America

## Vietnam

CAPITAL: Hanoi
POPULATION: 74,393,324
MAJOR LANGUAGES: Vietnamese, French, Chinese, English, Khmer, and various languages
AREA: 127,248 sq mi; 329,560 sq km
LEADING EXPORTS: petroleum, rice, and agricultural products
CONTINENT: Asia

## Western Samoa

CAPITAL: Apia
POPULATION: 209,360
MAJOR LANGUAGES: Samoan and English
AREA: 1,104 sq mi; 2,860 sq km
LEADING EXPORTS: coconut oil and cream, taro, copra, and cocoa
LOCATION: Pacific Ocean

## Yemen

CAPITAL: Sanaa
POPULATION: 14,728,474
MAJOR LANGUAGE: Arabic
AREA: 203,857 sq mi; 527,970 sq km
LEADING EXPORTS: crude oil, cotton, coffee, hides, and vegetables
CONTINENT: Asia

## Zaire

CAPITAL: Kinshasa
POPULATION: 44,060,636
MAJOR LANGUAGES: French, Lingala, Swahili, Kingwana, Kikongo, and Tshiluba
AREA: 905,599 sq mi; 2,345,410 sq km
LEADING EXPORTS: copper, coffee, diamonds, cobalt, and crude oil
CONTINENT: Africa

## Zambia

CAPITAL: Lusaka
POPULATION: 9,445,723
MAJOR LANGUAGES: English (official) and about 70 various languages
AREA: 290,594 sq mi; 752,610 sq km
LEADING EXPORTS: copper, zinc, cobalt, lead, and tobacco
CONTINENT: Africa

## Zimbabwe

CAPITAL: Harare
POPULATION: 11,139,961
MAJOR LANGUAGES: English, Shona, and Sindebele
area: 150,809 sq mi; 390,580 sq km
LEADING EXPORTS: agricultural products and manufactures
CONTINENT: Africa

# Glossary of Geographic Terms

**basin**
a depression in the surface of the land; some basins are filled with water

**bay**
a part of a sea or lake that extends into the land

**butte**
a small raised area of land with steep sides

▲ butte

**canyon**
a deep, narrow valley with steep sides; often has a stream flowing through it

**cataract**
a large waterfall; any strong flood or rush of water

◄ cataract

**delta**
a triangular-shaped plain at the mouth of a river, formed when sediment is deposited by flowing water

**flood plain**
a broad plain on either side of a river, formed when sediment settles on the riverbanks

**glacier**
a huge, slow-moving mass of snow and ice

**hill**
an area that rises above surrounding land and has a rounded top; lower and usually less steep than a mountain

**island**
an area of land completely surrounded by water

**isthmus**
a narrow strip of land that connects two larger areas of land

**mesa**
a high, flat-topped landform with cliff-like sides; larger than a butte

**mountain**
an area that rises steeply at least 2,000 feet (300 m) above surrounding land; usually wide at the bottom and rising to a narrow peak or ridge

▶ glacier

◄ delta

**mountain pass**
a gap between mountains

**peninsula**
an area of land almost completely surrounded by water and connected to the mainland by an isthmus

**plain**
a large area of flat or gently rolling land

**plateau**
a large, flat area that rises above the surrounding land; at least one side has a steep slope

**river mouth**
the point where a river enters a lake or sea

**strait**
a narrow stretch of water that connects two larger bodies of water

**tributary**
a river or stream that flows into a larger river

**volcano**
an opening in the Earth's surface through which molten rock, ashes, and gasses from the Earth's interior escape

▶ volcano

# Gazetteer

## A

**Abuja** (9.12°N, 7.11°E) the federal capital of Nigeria, p. 110

**Addis Ababa** (9°N, 38.44°E) the capital city of Ethiopia, p. 139

**Aksum** an ancient city in northern Ethiopia, a powerful kingdom and trade center from about A.D. 200 to A.D. 600, p. 35

## C

**Cairo** (30°N, 31°E) the capital of Egypt and most populous city in Africa, p. 93

**Cape of Good Hope** (34°S, 18°E) a province of the Republic of South Africa; the cape at the southern end of Cape Peninsula, South Africa, p. 42

**Cape Town** (33.48°S, 18.28°E) the legislative capital of the Republic of South Africa; the capital of Cape Province, p. 170

**Central and Southern Africa** countries in the central and southern region of Africa, p. 84

**Congo River** (2°S, 17°E) a river in Central Africa that flows into the Atlantic Ocean, p. 12

## D

**Dar es Salaam** (6.48°S, 39.17°E) the capital and largest city in Tanzania, an industrial center and major port on the Indian Ocean, p. 140

## E

**East Africa** countries in the eastern region of Africa, p. 76

**Egypt** (26.58°S, 27.01°E) a country in North Africa, officially Arab Republic of Egypt, p. 33

## G

**Ghana** (8°N, 2°W) a country in West Africa, officially Republic of Ghana, p. 37

**Gorée** an island off the coast of Senegal, p. 41

**Great Rift Valley** the major branch of the East African Rift System, p. 11

## K

**Kalahari Desert** (23°S, 22.03°E) a desert region in Southern Africa, p. 19

**Kano** (12°N, 8.30°E) a city and the capital of Kano state in northern Nigeria; a historic kingdom in northern Nigeria, p. 111

**Kilwa** late tenth-century Islamic city-state located on an island off the coast of present-day Tanzania, p. 39

## L

**Lagos** (6.27°N, 3.24°E) a city and chief Atlantic port of Nigeria; a state in Nigeria, p. 110

**Lalibela** a town in Ethiopia famous for its stone churches carved in the 1100s, p. 139

## M

**Mali** (15.45°N, .15°W) an early African empire; a present-day country in West Africa, officially Republic of Mali, p. 37

**Mediterranean Sea** (36.22°N, 13.25°E) the large sea separating Europe and Africa, p. 67

**Mount Kenya** (.10°S, 37.20°E) a volcano in central Kenya, p. 148

## N

**Nairobi** (1.17°S, 36.49°E) the capital of Kenya, p. 152

**Namib Desert** (18.45°S, 12.45°E) a desert extending along the Atlantic Coast of South Africa, p. 19

**Niger** (18.02°N, 8.30°E) a country in West Africa, officially Republic of Niger, p. 53

**Niger River** (8°N, 6°E) the river in West Africa that flows from Guinea into the Gulf of Guinea, p. 13

**Nile River** (27.30°N, 31°E) the longest river in the world, flows through northeastern Africa into the Mediterranean Sea, p. 12

**North Africa** countries in the northern region of Africa, p. 63

**Nubia** an ancient region in North Africa, p. 33

## R

**Republic of South Africa** (28°S, 24.50°E) southernmost country in Africa, p. 81

## S

**Sahara** (23.44°N, 1.40°W) largest tropical desert in the world, covers almost all of North Africa, p. 9

**Sahel** (15°N, 7°E) the region in West and Central Africa that forms a changing climate zone between the dry Sahara to the north and humid savannas to the south, p. 19

**Senegal** (14.53°N, 14.58°W) a country in West Africa, officially Republic of Senegal, p. 55

**Shaba** a southern province in Zaire, p. 163

**Songhai** an empire and trading state in West Africa founded in the 1400s, p. 38

**Southern Africa** countries in the southern region of Africa, p. 82

## T

**Tombouctou** (16.46°N, 3.01°W) city in Mali near the Niger River; in the past an important center of Islamic education and a trans-Saharan caravan stop (also spelled Timbuktu), p. 38

## W

**West Africa** countries in the western region of Africa, p. 69

## Z

**Zaire** (1°S, 22.15°E) a country in Central Africa, officially Republic of Zaire, p. 84

**Zambezi River** (16°S, 29.45°E) a river in Central and Southern Africa that flows into the Indian Ocean, p. 13

**Zanzibar** (6.20°S, 39.37°E) an island in the Indian Ocean off the coast of East Africa, part of Tanzania, p. 140

**Zimbabwe** (17.50°S, 29.30°E) a country in Southern Africa, officially Republic of Zimbabwe, p. 40

# Glossary

## A

**apartheid** the South African system in which racial groups were separated and racial discrimination was legal, p. 170

**authoritarian** controlled by one person or a small group, p. 164

## B

**bazaar** a traditional open-air market with rows of shops or stalls, p. 97

**boycott** a refusal to buy or use certain products or services, p. 51

## C

**casbah** an old, crowded section of a North African city, p. 103

**cash crop** a crop that is raised for sale, p. 23

**cataract** a rock-filled rapid, p. 11

**census** a count of the people in a country, p. 113

**city-state** a city that controls much of the land around it and has its own government, p. 39

**civilization** a society with cities, a government, and social classes; a civilization also has architecture, writing, and art, p. 32

**clan** a group of lineages, p. 72

**colonize** to settle an area and take over or create a government, p. 46

**commercial farming** the large-scale production of crops for sale, often coffee, cocoa, or bananas, p. 54

**coup** the takeover of a government, often done by military force, p. 119

## cultural diffusion

**cultural diffusion** the movement of customs and ideas from one culture to another, p. 67

**cultural diversity** a wide variety of cultures, p. 69

**culture** the way of life of people who share similar customs and beliefs, p. 64

## D

**democracy** a government in which citizens have power through their elected representatives, p. 51

**desertification** the changing of fertile land into land that is too dry for crops, p. 123

**discriminate** to treat people unfairly based on race, religion, or gender, p. 170

**diversify** to add variety; a country can diversify its economy by producing more products, p. 25

**domesticate** to adapt wild plants and animals for human use, p. 32

**drought** a long period of little or no rainfall, p. 124

## E

**economy** all the things people do to make a living in a particular place, p. 24

**elevation** the height of land above sea level, p. 10

**erode** to wear away slowly, p. 124

**escarpment** a steep cliff about 100 stories high, p. 11

**ethnic group** a group that shares a language, a religion, family ties, and customs, p. 34

**extended family** a family that includes relatives other than parents and children, p. 71

## F

**fellaheen** peasants or agricultural workers in an Arab country, p. 97

**fertile** able to grow a lot of plants; productive, p. 12

**foreign debt** money owed to foreign countries, p. 144

## G

**griot** an African storyteller, p. 73

## H

**harambee** the Swahili word for "let's pull together"; the campaign in Kenya begun by President Jomo Kenyatta in 1963, after the country became independent, p. 150

**homeland** South African lands where blacks were forced to live during apartheid; driest and least fertile parts of the country, p. 171

**hunter-gatherer** person who gathers wild food and hunts animals to survive, p. 31

**hybrid** a plant that is a combination of two or more types of the same plant, p. 55

## I

**irrigate** to artificially water crops, p. 17

## K

**kinship** a family relationship, p. 71

## L

**life expectancy** how long an average person will live, p. 56

**lineage** a group of families with a common ancestor, p. 72

**literacy** the ability to read and write, p. 56

## M

**migrant worker** a person who moves from place to place to find work, p. 82

**migrate** to move from one place to another, p. 33

**monastery** a place where monks or nuns live, work, and study, p. 135

**multiethnic** containing many ethnic groups, p. 109

## N

**nationalism** a feeling of pride in one's homeland; a group's identity as members of a nation, p. 47

**nationalize** to put a once-private industry under national control, p. 164

**nomad** a person who moves around to make a living, usually by herding animals, trading, hunting, or gathering food, p. 19

**nuclear family** a family that includes parents and children, p. 71

## O

**oasis** a fertile place in a desert where there is water and vegetation, p. 17

## P

**Pan-Africanism** a movement that stressed unity among all Africans, p. 48

**pilgrimage** a religious journey; for Muslims, the journey to Mecca, p. 38

**plantation** a large farm where cash crops are grown, p. 78

**plateau** a large, mostly flat area that rises above the surrounding land, p. 10

## Q

**Quran** the holy book of the religion of Islam, p. 38

## R

**rift** a deep crack in the Earth's surface, p. 11

## S

**silt** bits of rock and dirt on river bottoms, p. 12

**souq** an open-air marketplace, p. 103

**sovereignty** political independence, p. 118

**subsistence farming** raising just enough crops to support one's family, p. 22

**surplus** more than is needed, p. 32

**Swahili** an African language that includes some Arabic words, p. 38

## T

**terrace** a platform cut into the side of a mountain, used for growing crops in steep places, p. 101

**tributary** a small stream or river that flows into a larger river, p. 13

The *italicized* page numbers refer to illustrations. The *m, c, p,* or *t* preceding the number refers to maps *(m)*, charts *(c)*, pictures *(p)*, or tables *(t)*.

# Index

# Acknowledgments

## Program Development, Design, Illustration, and Production

Proof Positive/Farrowlyne Associates, Inc.

## Cover Design

Olena Serbyn and Bruce Bond

## Cover Photo

Jon Chomitz

## Maps

GeoSystems Global Corp.

## Text

19, From *Sand and Fog: Adventures in Southern Africa,* by Jim Brandenburg. Copyright © 1994 by Jim Brandenburg. Reprinted with permission of Walker Publishing Company, Inc. 21, From *Cocoa Comes to Mampong,* by Dei Anang. Copyright © 1949. Reprinted with the permission of Methodist Book Depot. 80, From "African Statesman Still Sowing Seeds for Future," by James C. McKinley, Jr., *New York Times,* September 1, 1996. Copyright © 1996 by *The New York Times.* Reprinted by permission. 87, From *The Africans,* by David Lamb. Copyright © 1982 by David Lamb. Reprinted with the permission of Random House, Inc. 99, From "The World in Its Extreme," by William Langewiesche. Copyright © 1991 by William Langewiesche as first published in *The Atlantic Monthly,* November 1991. 117, From *Ghana in Transition,* by David E. Apter. Copyright © 1955, '63, and '72 by Princeton University Press. Used with permission. 132, "My Village" from *The Distant Talking Drum.* Text copyright © 1995 by Isaac Olaleye. Reprinted with permission of Wordsong/Boyds Mills Press, Inc. 133, "Village Weavers" from *The Distant Talking Drum.* Text copyright © 1995 by Isaac Olaleye. Reprinted with permission of Wordsong/Boyds Mills Press, Inc. 141, 143, From "Three Leaders," by Andrew Meldrum, *Africa Report,* September–October 1994. Copyright © 1994 by *Africa Report.* Reprinted by permission. 150, From *Baricho - A Village in Kenya,* by Richard Wright. Copyright © 1993 by Warwickshire World Studies Centre. Distributed by DEDU, 153, Cardigan Road, Leeds, LS6 1LJ, United Kingdom. Reprinted with permission of Warwickshire World Studies Centre. 153, From "Back to No Man's Land," by George Monbiot, *Geographical Magazine,* July 1994. Copyright © 1994 by *Geographical Magazine.* Reprinted by permission. 156, From *A Promise to the Sun* by Tololwa M. Mollel. Text Copyright © 1991 by Tololwa M. Mollel; Illustrations Copyright © 1991 by Beatriz Vidal. By permission of Little, Brown and Company.

## Photos

1 T, © John Chasson/Gamma Liaison International, 1 BL, © Jason Laure'/Laure' Communications, 1 BR, © Robert Frerck/Odyssey Productions, 5, © Mark Thayer, Boston, 7, © Kjell B. Sandved/Visuals Unlimited, 9, © Paul C. Sereno/Paul C. Sereno, 10 ©, Robert Frerck/Odyssey Productions, 10 (inset), © Wendy Stone/Odyssey Productions, 11, © G. Winters/Trip Photographic, 12, © SuperStock International, 13, © Comstock, 14, © Steve McCutcheon/Visuals Unlimited, 15, © Frans Lanting/Minden Pictures, 17, © Don W. Fawcett/Visuals Unlimited, 19, © Nicholas Parfitt/Tony Stone Images, 20, © Penny Tweedle/Tony Stone Images, 21, © Victor Englebert/Victor Englebert Photography, 21 (inset), © Cabisco/Visuals Unlimited, 22 L, © Victor Englebert/Victor Englebert Photography, 22 M, © Brian Seed/Tony Stone Images, 22 R, © Wendy Stone/Odyssey Productions, 25, © Ian Murphy/Tony Stone Images, 26–27, © David Young-Wolff/PhotoEdit, 31, © The Granger Collection, 32 L, TR, BR, © Lee Boltin/Boltin Picture Library, 33, © Courtesy of Museum of Fine Arts Boston, 35, © H. Rogers/Trip Photographic, 37, © The Granger Collection, 39 L, © SuperStock International, 39 R, © The Granger Collection, 40, © Jason Laure'/Laure' Communications, 41, © Erich Lessing/Art Resource, 42, © Robert Frerck/Odyssey Productions, 44 L, R, © The Granger Collection, 47, © Jason Laure'/Laure' Communications, 48, © L. P. Winfrey/Woodfin Camp & Associates, 49, 51, © UPI/Corbis-Bettmann, 52, © Wolfgang Kaehler/Wolfgang Kaehler Photography, 53, © W. Jacobs/Trip Photographic, 56, © Jason Laure'/Laure' Communications, 55, © M. & V. Birley/Tropix Photographic Library, 57, © Marc & Evelyn Bernheim/Woodfin Camp & Associates, 58, © Bill Aron/PhotoEdit, 62, © M. & E. Bernheim/Woodfin Camp & Associates, 63, © Glen Allison/Tony Stone Images, 64, © Robert Frerck/Woodfin Camp & Associates, 65, © Robert Azzi/Woodfin Camp & Associates, 66 L, © Bob Smith/Trip Photographic, 66 R, © Ben Nakayama/Tony Stone Images, 68, © Lorne Resnick/Tony Stone Images, 69, © Jason Laure'/Laure' Communications, 70, 71 L, © Wolfgang Kaehler/Wolfgang Kaehler Photography, 71 R, © M. & V. Birley/Tropix Photographic Library, 72, © Wolfgang Kaehler/Wolfgang Kaehler Photography, 73, © Betty Press/Woodfin Camp & Associates, 74, © M. & E. Bernheim/Woodfin Camp & Associates, 75, © Victor Englebert/Victor Englebert Photography, 76, © Robert Frerck/Odyssey Productions, 77, © P. Joynson-Hicks/Trip Photographic, 78–79, © D. Saunders/Trip Photographic, 80, © Boyd Norton/Boyd Norton, 81, 82, 83, © Jason Laure'/Laure' Communications, 84, © D. Davis/Tropix Photographic Library, 85, © Robert Caputo/Aurora & Quanta Productions, 86, © Betty Press/Woodfin Camp & Associates, 87, © Michael Newman/PhotoEdit, 90, © M. & E. Bernheim/Woodfin Camp & Associates, 91, © Adam Novick/Village Pulse, 93, © P. Mitchell/Trip Photographic, 95, © Roland & Sabrina Michaud/Woodfin Camp & Associates, 96, © Donna DeCesare/Impact Visuals, 97, © Israel Talby/Woodfin Camp & Associates, 98, © Don Smetzer/Tony Stone Images, 99, © Victor Englebert/Victor Englebert Photography, 101, © Sylvain Grandadam/Tony Stone Images, 102, © Sean Sprague/Impact Visuals, 103 L, © Wendy Stone/Odyssey Productions, 103 R, © Victor Englebert/Victor Englebert Photography, 111, © Marc & Evelyn Bernheim/Woodfin Camp & Associates, 112, © Robert Frerck/Odyssey Productions, 113 T, © Sylvan Wittwer/Visuals Unlimited, 113 B, © J. Highet/Trip Photographic, 114, © Trip/Trip Photographic, 115, © AP/Wide World Photos, 117, © Frank Fournier/Woodfin Camp & Associates, 118, © Tim Beddow/Tony Stone Images, 119, © AP/Wide World Photos, 120 L, R, © M. & V. Birley/Tropix Photographic Library, 121, © M. Jelliffe/Trip Photographic, 123, © Norman Myers/Bruce Coleman Inc., 124, © Wolfgang Kaehler/Wolfgang Kaehler Photography, 125, © Betty Press/Woodfin Camp & Associates, 126, © Michael Newman/PhotoEdit, 130, 131, © David Young-Wolff/PhotoEdit, 132, © Betty Press/Woodfin Camp & Associates, 133, © Lawrence Manning/Tony Stone Images, 135, © Robert Caputo/Aurora & Quanta Productions, 137 L, R, © The Granger Collection, 139, © R. Ashford/Tropix Photographic Library, 140, © AP/Wide World Photos, 142, © Reuters/Corbis-Bettmann, 143, © M. & V. Birley/Tropix Photographic Library, 144 L, R, © Gerald Cubitt/Gerald Cubitt Photographer, 145, © AP/Wide World Photos, 146, © James P. Rowan/Tony Stone Images, 148, © M. & E. Bernheim/Woodfin Camp & Associates, 150, © Betty Press/Woodfin Camp & Associates, 151, © Victor Englebert/Victor Englebert Photography, 152, Matutu Ride, by Ian Kamau, Kenya. Courtesy of the International Children's Art Museum, 157, © Marc Chamberlain/Tony Stone Images, 158, © Tim Davis/Tony Stone Images, 161, © Jason Laure'/Laure' Communications, 163, © M. Jelliffe/Trip Photographic, 164, © Betty Press/Woodfin Camp & Associates, 165, © Robert Grossman/New York Times Rights & Royalties, 166, © Michael Newman/PhotoEdit, 168, © B. Mnguni/Trip Photographic, 170, © Jason Laure'/Laure' Communications, 171, © Paula Bronstein/Impact Visuals, 172, © African Institute of Art, Funda Art Centre in Soweto, 173, © Reuters/Corbis-Bettman, 176, © Mark Thayer, Boston, 177, © Betty Press/Woodfin Camp & Associates, 179, © Mark Thayer, Boston, 180 T, © Steve Leonard/Tony Stone Images, 180 B, Robert Frerck/Odyssey Productions, 181 T, © Wolfgang Kaehler/Wolfgang Kaehler Photography, 181 BL, © John Elk/Tony Stone Images, 181 BR, Will & Deni McIntyre/Tony Stone Images, 191, © G. Brad Lewis/Tony Stone Images, 193, © Nigel Press/Tony Stone Images, 220 T, © A. & L. Sinibaldi/Tony Stone Images, 220 BL, © John Beatty/Tony Stone Images, 221 T, © Hans Strand/Tony Stone Images, 221 BL, © Spencer Swanger/Tom Stack & Associates, 221 BR, © Paul Chesley/Tony Stone Images.